Lady Gaga and the Sociology of Fame

Mathieu Deflem

Lady Gaga and the Sociology of Fame

The Rise of a Pop Star in an Age of Celebrity

Mathieu Deflem
University of South Carolina
Columbia, USA

ISBN 978-1-137-58467-0 (hardcover)   ISBN 978-1-137-58468-7 (eBook)
ISBN 978-1-349-95938-9 (softcover)
DOI 10.1057/978-1-137-58468-7

Library of Congress Control Number: 2016958845

© The Editor(s) (if applicable) and The Author(s) 2017, First softcover printing 2019
This work is subject to copyright. All rights are solely and exclusively licensed by the Publisher, whether the whole or part of the material is concerned, specifically the rights of translation, reprinting, reuse of illustrations, recitation, broadcasting, reproduction on microfilms or in any other physical way, and transmission or information storage and retrieval, electronic adaptation, computer software, or by similar or dissimilar methodology now known or hereafter developed.
The use of general descriptive names, registered names, trademarks, service marks, etc. in this publication does not imply, even in the absence of a specific statement, that such names are exempt from the relevant protective laws and regulations and therefore free for general use.
The publisher, the authors and the editors are safe to assume that the advice and information in this book are believed to be true and accurate at the date of publication. Neither the publisher nor the authors or the editors give a warranty, express or implied, with respect to the material contained herein or for any errors or omissions that may have been made.

Cover design by Henry Petrides

Printed on acid-free paper

This Palgrave Macmillan imprint is published by Springer Nature
The registered company is Nature America Inc.
The registered company address is: 1 New York Plaza, New York, NY 10004, U.S.A.

for Naoko

Praise for *Lady Gaga and the Sociology of Fame*

"The analysis of status is unique to sociology. Mathieu Deflem brilliantly confirms how the creation of Lady Gaga is part of a social process that creates celebrity against the backdrop of chaotic economic and moral conditions. Deflem methodically describes how fame can shape public attitudes toward controversial matters, leaving status embodied in traditional forms of professional expertise and institutional control less important than ever before."

—**Jonathan B. Imber,** Jean Glasscock Professor of Sociology, Wellesley College, USA

"There are celebrities and there are mega-celebrities and then there is Lady Gaga. The star's fame is only in small part built upon her voice and eye-popping costumes. Far more, it is her attitude: a cheerleader to all and sundry who have ever felt broken or dissed. Grasping the fullness of Gaga's appeal, Deflem's book is as appealing to her fans as it is for theorists of celebrity."

—**Deena Weinstein,** Professor of Sociology, DePaul University, USA

"In this notable book, through careful theoretical insight and an in-depth analysis of Lady Gaga's fame, Deflem illustrates a new form of pop icon defying the transient nature of the cultural industry in the postmodern age. Deflem offers valuable lessons on the importance of social conditions, which include not only the market but also factors facilitating the activism and diversity orientation of pop artists seeking to gain fame."

—**Masaya Takahashi**, Associate Professor, Saitama University, Japan

"Mathieu Deflem's study provides an intriguing and comprehensive exploration of the dynamics of Lada Gaga's rise to fame. By the end, it is clear that there is no one single factor that serves as a predictor of future fame or commercial success. Those who work in or study the music industry should give this book a read."

—**Serona Elton**, Associate Professor and Chair, Frost School of Music, University of Miami, USA

"This book delivers a stimulating sociological discussion of the mechanics behind fame and celebrity – aspects that have undoubtedly taken a stranglehold on American culture. Guiding the reader through a theory on the machinery for stardom using a unique lens focused on Lady Gaga' determined path to fame, Professor Deflem's book is an entertaining and educational read that provides a solid groundwork for further research in the areas of fame and celebrity."

—**Danwill D. Schwender**, Attorney at Law

Acknowledgments

In preparing research for and the writing this book, I am grateful to have been able to rely on a great many people who have helped me in various ways. The idea for this work originated from an undergraduate college course I taught at the University of South Carolina (USC), and I must therefore first thank the students who took the course and offered their feedback, criticisms, and research efforts for my benefit. Additional assistance and support at my present home institution of the Department of Sociology at Carolina has come from Barbara Coleman, Paul Higgins, Anne Hodasi, Alicia Hope, Shannon McDonough, Patrick Nolan, Hyomin Park, and Lala Steelman, whom I hereby thank. The major part of the writing of this book in the spring and summer of 2016 benefited from a sabbatical leave I was granted at USC.

For their support and feedback at various stages of my research and/or for reading and commenting on various chapters and sections of this book, I thank Christa Brüstle, Victor Corona, Anita Elberse, Richard J. Gray II, Joanna Harrison, Martin Kupp, Elizabeth Leverage, Kelley Madden, Yoshitaka Mori, Jörg Reckhenrich, U-Seok Seo, Hannah Silverblank, and Masaya Takahashi. For reading and helping to edit a draft version of the entire manuscript, I express very special gratitude to my friends and fellow professional sociologists Anna Rogers and Derek Silva.

Two chapters and the Epilogue of this book have been reworked and updated from earlier publications. Chapter 9 incorporates materials that were originally presented in a chapter published in an edited volume published by McFarland. Chapter 10 is in part revised and updated from a chapter that appeared in an edited volume published by transcript Verlag in Germany. The Epilogue is revised from a journal article published by Springer. I am grateful to the publishers for permission to use these materials and to the editors and reviewers of these publications for their constructive feedback.

Developing and strengthening several ideas presented in this book, I have also been able to rely on invited presentations I was happy to deliver on the fame of Lady Gaga at various academic and other settings, specifically at the Columbia Museum of Art in Columbia, South Carolina; Kunstuniversität Graz, Austria; Saitama University, Japan; Tokyo University of the Arts, Japan; University of Seoul, Republic of Korea; Haverford College, Pennsylvania; and the Library of Congress, Washington, DC. I am thankful to the organizers of these presentations and to their attendants for comments and feedback.

I am more than a just little grateful to Mireille Yanow, the now former Global Head of Sociology, Anthropology, and Criminology, Palgrave Macmillan, who first suggested the idea for me to write this book. If it was not for Mireille's special efforts, this book would simply not have happened. I also thank Kyra Saniewski, Milana Vernikova, and Mara Berkoff and everybody else at Palgrave Macmillan for their great work in getting this book published.

Finally, I thank the many fans, musicians, and friends I have been able to meet and hang out with, online and in person, alongside of my journey in the Lady Gaga music community. Their many gestures of support and kindness were more important and influential to me than they may realize. Paws up!

This book is dedicated to my girlfriend, Naoko Yoshimura, who is awesome.

May we live to see the dawn.

Contents

1 Introduction   1

2 Popular Culture and the Sociology of Fame   11

3 The Life and Times of Lady Gaga   29

4 The Business of Lady Gaga   49

5 The Laws of Lady Gaga   73

6 Gaga Media: From Internet to Radio   95

7 The Audience of Lady Gaga: Beyond the Little Monsters   121

8 Gaga Activism: The New Ethics of Pop Culture   145

9	The Sex of Lady Gaga	169
10	Art Pop: The Styles of Lady Gaga	189
11	Conclusion	211
12	Epilogue: Professor Goes Gaga—Teaching Lady Gaga and the Sociology of Fame	217
Index		235

CHAPTER 1

Introduction

This book presents a sociological study of the conditions of fame in the world of contemporary popular music. Against the background of important transformations and a general decline of the popular music industry in recent years, the book specifically develops a case-study approach to investigate the rise to fame of global pop sensation Lady Gaga. While this book is not the first to deal with the fame and career of a pop star, the reasons to undertake an analysis of the origins of the fame of Lady Gaga could not be further removed from the examinations of old that focused on famous people in the world of pop music and other forms of popular culture now dating back to relatively ancient times. In plain truth, the contemporary conditions of fame are of a different and relatively unique nature as any question on the rise to fame in the present day is centrally marked by critical transformations in popular culture, especially the popular music industry, on the one hand, and the virtually banal pervasiveness of an obsession with fame that marks our current celebrity culture, on the other. It is not without cause to remember that the comedy segment, "Hey, Remember The 80s?" on the popular TV show Saturday Night Live was already funny in the 1990s.

Questions on fame and celebrity can be approached from many disciplinary viewpoints and perspectives. This book adopts a distinctly sociological orientation that is rooted in longstanding theoretical traditions and debates in the discipline. Specifically, the study's framework is situated at the intersection of the sociology of popular culture and music, on the one hand, and the sociology of fame and celebrity, on the other, in order to offer an empirical examination of the social conditions that facilitated Lady Gaga's rise to fame from when the singer first released music in 2008 until her successful grab for global acclaim in the following years. This book's approach to offer a sociological case study is as such conventional, albeit that its application to the conditions of fame evidently pertains to relatively uncharted territory. Although there is no doubt that other disciplinary approaches and theoretical perspectives could make useful contributions to our understanding of fame as well, some often-asked questions on fame and celebrity, typically involving subjective meaning and interpretation, will in this work only be addressed inasmuch as they are relevant to the stated objective of analysis. As such, this book is exclusively concerned with providing a sociological examination of the social conditions of Lady Gaga's rise to fame.

Studying Fame

At the time of the writing of this book in the summer and fall of 2016, the media are abuzz with the centrality of celebrity in the election process for the next US president, especially as business tycoon Donald Trump emerged successfully from his sparring with other Republican candidates in terms hitherto unthinkable in politics, and both media professionals and participants in online networking sites alike are frantically competing to come up with the best interpretations and explanations of what is going on. From the viewpoint of the scholar of fame and celebrity, it is not most surprising that celebrity has come to play such a prominent role in social life, even in the political arena, but that there still is any astonishment to be detected about it. For the pervasiveness of fame in modern culture today in actuality is such that it is puzzling that not more studies, in the social sciences and elsewhere, have been devoted to its manifold dimensions and components.

Different themes and avenues are available in the contemporary study of fame (defined as the quality of being well known) and celebrity (the quality of being known for being well known). Thematically, this book focuses on the rise to fame of a star in the world of popular music. The case of Lady Gaga is not only spectacular because of its global reach but also, and especially, because it was accomplished in today's hyper-connected world whereby being noticed has, ironically, become more difficult than ever before. In terms of approach and perspective, the objectives of this book are resolutely academic, rather than popular, in seeking to offer an analysis in the sociological study of fame on the basis of a case study. This book, as such, is decidedly not a contribution to the fame and celebrity culture itself, but rather a reflection thereon from an observer point of view.

Fame and celebrity can and, as I will show in Chap. 2, have been studied from a variety of disciplinary perspectives oriented at answering a multitude of questions. The core sociological objective of the present study is to examine the social conditions of the origins of Lady Gaga's fame. Simply put, this book seeks to provide a sociologically justified answer to the question, how did Lady Gaga become famous? Of course, the totality of the answer to the question of Lady Gaga's fame cannot be offered as it would also have to include non-sociological factors, ranging from Lady Gaga's artistic abilities as a musician and performer to her personal disposition and psychological makeup, not to mention that there will have been factors at work of fortuitous circumstance that are beyond analysis. Besides acknowledging the obvious fact that the singer is both talented and driven, therefore, it must be understood that this book focuses only on those factors in the social world that can account for Lady Gaga's rise to global fame. The social conditions this study will specifically examine include: the role of the economics of the business and marketing of Lady Gaga; the legal issues involved in her career; the media through which the singer's audience has been reached; the singer's multiple publics of fans and others who give her attention; the activism Lady Gaga has engaged in and the political, ethical, and religious issues that are involved; a variety of issues concerning sex, gender, and sexuality; and the multiple artistic styles Lady Gaga has been engaged in and how her artistry has been received. Some of the central aspects of the biography and early, pre-fame career of Lady Gaga will also be discussed, but only to provide a necessary background on which to build an analysis of the societal conditions of Lady Gaga's rise to fame from a scholarly perspective that is grounded in the theoretical traditions of sociology. Thus, this is not so much a book about Lady Gaga as about the contemporary culture of fame as exemplified by the career of Lady Gaga.

There are by now a large number of books written about Lady Gaga. Yet, the vast majority of these works are of a popular nature, ranging from picture books to biographies. Needless to say, these publications are an expression of Lady Gaga's fame and popularity and are often of dubious quality. Among the biographies, some books are of value in presenting a more or less accurate account of Lady Gaga's career (e.g., Callahan 2010; Herbert 2010; Lester 2010). In the academic world, studies on various aspects of Lady Gaga have developed right along with the singer's increasing fame. By November 2010, sociologist Victor Corona (2010) already spoke of a new field of "Gaga studies." No doubt that formulation was not only premature at the time but also as misguided as the so-called Madonna studies that had popped up about two decades prior (Miklitsch 1998), for there is little unity among the writings that exist on either pop phenomenon. Instead, scattered over many disciplines and widely differing in level of quality as well as objectives, several academic publications currently exist about Lady Gaga and several issues of her fame and/or music. Besides a fairly large number of articles and essays published in academic journals (cited throughout this book), some seven academic books have to date appeared dealing with various aspects of the career and music of Lady Gaga. They include two edited volumes (Gray 2012; Iddon and Marshall 2014) and five authored books that focus on, or were at least written in relation to, various issues concerning Lady Gaga, including Jack Halberstam's (2012) metaphorical use of the persona of Lady Gaga to discuss new currents in feminism; marketing studies by Anita Elberse (2013) and Jackie Huba's (2013) writing on the business model applied to the career of Lady Gaga; a rather superficial discussion by Amber Davisson (2013) of Lady Gaga's career from the viewpoint of media studies; and a book in Italian by Massimiliano Stramaglia (2015) on the education of Lady Gaga on her path toward becoming a global pop sensation. Further, in many other academic writings, especially textbooks, as well as in presentations at academic conferences, Lady Gaga is often featured for purposes of illustration and application by means of image and text, such as on the cover of the second edition of Graeme Turner's (2014) *Understanding Celebrity*, a book that otherwise mentions Lady Gaga only twice.

As the world of popular music proceeds quickly, this book must already apply a (recent) historical focus, now that the status of Lady Gaga as a global pop star has been sufficiently attained and recognized. From the time when Lady Gaga's initial stardom developed, especially since the spring of 2009, when she scored her first hits, until the summer of 2011, when she released the massively successful album *Born This Way*, her career has already experienced some of the characteristics that mark the fragile stability of fame. Especially noteworthy in this respect is the relative up-and-down nature of success, which, in the case of Lady Gaga's career, included certain rumored problems in terms of a drop in popularity following the 2013 release of the album *ARTPOP* and a resurgence in success upon the singer's collaboration with Tony Bennett, including a critically praised jazz concert tour in 2015, two acclaimed musical performances at the 2015 and 2016 Oscars, and her equally well-received rendition of the National Anthem at the Super Bowl in 2016. Nonetheless, the outcome of ongoing developments in terms of the more or less lasting nature of Lady Gaga's status as a global pop icon in the long run can at the present time not be answered without resorting to speculation. For that reason, also, the present study will rest on a solid empirical grounding and center its focus on the dynamics of Lady Gaga's rise to fame.

This book originates from a series of inquiries that I launched in the summer of 2010 when I decided to develop a new undergraduate course at the University of South Carolina under the title, "Lady Gaga and the Sociology of the Fame." I have taught the course five times since the spring of 2011 and along the way conducted research on various aspects of Lady Gaga's fame, which led to several oral presentations and shorter publications, some of which have been integrated into this book. As I clarify further in the Epilogue of this book, the very announcement of my sociology course on Lady Gaga made it become a global news sensation before even one class was taught. As such, my study of Lady Gaga's fame had become part of its very subject matter, much to my own astonishment and the chagrin of many a celebrity studies scholar. Yet, the modicum of fame I attained as the so-called Lady Gaga professor alone cannot justify the present study. Instead, my research and teaching are founded on the notion that the career of Lady Gaga presents a unique opportunity to undertake a sociological study of the patterns and dynamics of pop stardom in an age when fame and celebrity are all the rage.

No special explanation is needed why the study of fame has moved to the center of attention in recent years. The current state of fame and celebrity as sociologically relevant topics of inquiry minimally involves a choice over two extremes in selecting an appropriate topic of investigation. First, scholarly attention could go to examining the manifestations of a celebrity status that is almost wholly exhausted with reference to fame itself ("being famous for being famous"). The prototypical examples in contemporary (American) society range from Paris Hilton over Kim Kardashian to Kylie Jenner. Second, attention could conversely also go to the attainment of fame that is achieved in relation to, and largely depends on, notable accomplishments in some field of activity. While the former case is surely interesting and puzzling, it is the persistence of the latter form that presents an interesting challenge in the study of fame precisely against the background of a celebrity culture that is routinely criticized for being shallow beyond all proportion.

The case of the fame of Lady Gaga is not so much peculiar because of its magnitude, for the fame of successful pop stars typically reaches across wide audiences. For whatever else it is and can be, popular music is by definition popular. Yet, what is especially fascinating about Lady Gaga's rise to fame is that it has taken place against the background of a commercial music industry that is distinctly transforming and declining, at times even said to be disintegrating. The critical question, then, is to examine how it was possible for Lady Gaga to have attained fame precisely at a time when popular music stardom seemed to be a thing of the past and when the consuming public appeared wholly absorbed with a fascination toward shallow celebrity.

A Look Ahead

While the topic of this book also has a popular appeal, this study is distinctly conceived as a scholarly inquiry, specifically a sociological analysis that is rooted in the best theoretical traditions of the discipline. The book will therefore begin with situating the study of Lady Gaga's rise to fame in the framework of the sociology of popular culture and music, on the one hand, and the scholarship on fame and celebrity, on the other. A brief overview will be offered of the life and times of Lady Gaga, with special attention to her personal biography and her music, in order to clarify the basic contours of what is it that we speak of when the focus is on the career of Lady Gaga. The remaining chapters will then form the heart of this book to empirically analyze the social conditions of the origins of Lady Gaga's fame.

The sociological framework adopted in this study will be clarified in Chap. 2. It will present a brief overview of the sociology of popular culture, specifically popular music and the case of pop and rock music, and review the field of the sociology of fame and celebrity. The main goal of this chapter will be to situate the sociological approach of this book and to introduce a relevant theoretical framework for the analysis of fame in the world of popular music. I will specifically develop a constructionist perspective of popular culture and fame as a meaningful social relationship.

Before the analysis in the various empirical chapters will bring out the value of the introduced perspective, it will be useful to briefly introduce the life and work of Lady Gaga in the third chapter. Chapters 4 through 10 form the center of this book, each explaining one particular social condition relevant to the rise of Lady Gaga's fame. The examinations in these chapters rely on a multitude of data retrieved from various media (in print and online), biographical sources, scholarly and popular studies, and ethnographic data. The ethnographic materials include unstructured interviews, informal conversations, and observational data, which have been compiled over the course of my participation in the Lady Gaga fan community since January 2009. While my fan involvement has, of course, been primarily oriented at an appreciation of the music and is, as such, not relevant to the present study, it has also enabled me to gather much useful information through observations and communications with a range of people involved with Lady Gaga's career. Over the course of my involvement in the Lady Gaga community, I have interacted with hundreds of fans, dozens of Lady Gaga's business associates, friends, musicians, and other artists working for the singer, met the star herself on several occasions, and attended several dozen live shows in various cities across the United States and abroad. Additionally relied upon as empirical data sources are various documents, many of them available online, such as news reports, published interviews, opinion pieces, and legal cases. The over-abundance of materials publically available on Lady Gaga (especially on the internet) is a clear expression of her fame and will necessitate, quite unlike most sociological research, a selective approach to the available mass of data. All internet links cited in this book were last accessed in June 2016. Following the requirements of publisher Palgrave Macmillan, all bibliographical sources as well as online available data are listed in separate References sections following each individual chapter.

Briefly reviewing the empirical chapters central to this book, the first condition of Lady Gaga's fame to be studied in some level of detail revolves around economic matters of business and marketing. While this book adopts a perspective that is not reductionist in economic or other respects, it would be foolish not to acknowledge that musicians, like all other artists and performers, need to rely on an infrastructure and organization to connect that which they conceive of as aesthetically valuable with that which is thought to be commercially viable. Although this economic business aspect is sometimes wrongly identified as the singular or most important aspect of Lady Gaga's and other pop stars' attained level of fame and success, there is no doubt that a well-function business and marketing machinery has been at work to bring the performer to a global audience. Among other issues, attention in this chapter will be paid to the presentation of Lady Gaga as a multi-talented artist, her team of collaborators, and the use of company sponsorships and so-called commercial "tie-ins."

Closely related to the successful economics of Lady Gaga are a variety of legal issues involved with fame in popular music. It is a distinctive mark of modern times that normative integration is accomplished through highly formalized legal means, even when something as deceptively frivolous as pop music is concerned. When it comes to legalities, indeed, consequential laws pertaining to such matters as contract, copyright, and trademark are pertinent to a career in music. Not surprisingly, in view of the scope of her commercial success, Lady Gaga has been involved in several lawsuits and legal cases since her rise to fame, the most important aspects of which Chap. 5 will review.

In order to reach their audience successfully, artists in popular music need to rely on a variety of media, situated in a landscape that has been increasingly affected by important technological changes. A manager of Lady Gaga once referred to the performer as a "digital baby," a qualification that describes the manner in which the singer rose to fame from an initial discovery on MySpace to her currently dominating presence in the social network media, especially on Facebook and Twitter. But it is not true, as Chap. 6 will show, that the internet alone was relied on to advance Lady Gaga's career. This chapter will detail how the performer's fame has been enabled by exploiting multiple communication media simultaneously.

Fame is established in interaction with an audience. Considering the breadth of Lady Gaga's fame, the role of her many devoted fans, the so-called Little Monsters, is of special interest. Discussing Lady Gaga's fan base, I will show in Chap. 7, it was precisely because there was a vacuum in the world of pop and rock music centered around stars that the rise Lady Gaga as the new pop sensation was a most fortuitous event. Moreover, Lady Gaga's live shows offer a special place of physical interaction, both for each fan in relation to his/her favorite artist and among the fans with one another. The dedication of Lady Gaga to offer a true spectacle additionally adds to her fame because it has reached beyond her most devoted fans to a much wider audience of spectators, the most important dimensions and implications of which will be analyzed in this chapter.

Extending from the relationship Lady Gaga has come to enjoy with her audience, Chap. 8 is devoted to analyzing the singer's involvement in activism, especially concerning gay rights and matters that she conceives of as being especially relevant to youth, both issues referring intimately to the primary constituents of her fan base. Lady Gaga has in this context often spoken out about social issues that relate to ethical values and political issues traditionally alien to the world of pop music. The same holds true for religion, another ethical issue Lady Gaga has been vocal about. This chapter will examine these issues and show how they have not gone without public notice and debate, thereby additionally contributing to her fame.

Next, Chap. 9 will deal with themes of sex, gender, and sexuality in the career of Lady Gaga. In 2006, Stefani Germanotta transformed herself from an indie-rock musician to a techno-pop performance artist named Lady Gaga. This transformation was at least in part motivated by the expectation that success for a female artist was more likely to be attained in the world of pop. Yet, as Lady Gaga did not want to be seen as just another blonde pop singer, she also sought to change how a female pop artist can present herself, especially with respect to standards of beauty and sexuality. This chapter will analyze these gender-related aspects, ranging from the display of sexuality in Lady Gaga's work to her characteristics as a female performer, including her sexual orientation, the sexism she encountered, and her presentation as a feminist.

In an aesthetic sense, Lady Gaga is primarily known as a pop singer. However, as Chap. 10 will explain, Lady Gaga's pop is also meant to be of a special kind as it seeks to branch out into and embrace the styles and attitudes of other forms of music as well, especially rock. Furthermore, the singer has more recently also explored vocal jazz music and classical show tunes. This chapter reviews how the resulting blend of pop, rock, and jazz is expressed in the art of Lady Gaga and her presentation and, additionally, how the singer's mixture of various styles has affected her public reception, contributing to her fame and popularity.

Following a Conclusion to this study to discuss the nature and direction of Lady Gaga's fame and popularity, the book's final section is presented as an Epilogue to take the study presented in the previous chapters back to its roots by discussing the peculiar situation when my related sociology course on the fame of Lady Gaga became a global news story. While not oriented at analyzing the conditions of Lady Gaga's rise to fame, this chapter will clarify the peculiar background to this study and will additionally show readers some of the special complexities of studying fame in an age obsessed with celebrity. As the course on Lady Gaga's fame becoming a manifestation of its very own subject matter was a rather unique and at times even entertaining episode in the process toward completing this study, the reader who is primarily interested in the subject matter of this book rather than its academic orientation may wish to first consult the Epilogue to get a flavor of the sociological approach and theme of this work. The theoretical exposition in Chap. 2 may also be more illuminating to the layperson upon reading the other chapters. For, indeed, while this book is written as an academic work oriented at students and academics in sociology and other fields of inquiry with an interest in fame and pop culture, it is also hoped to have an appeal to a broader audience of readers interested in Lady Gaga, whether her fame or her music. Both academicians and members of the general public, I hope, can through this study learn some of contributions the sociology of fame has to offer. The ambition to show the special value of sociology to the analysis of fame, culture, and other aspects of society counts, in any case, is also among the objectives of this book.

References

Callahan, Maureen. 2010. *The Rise and Rise of Lady Gaga*. New York: Hyperion.
Corona, Victor P. 2010. Gaga studies. *PopMatters, November* 24: 2010 .http://www.popmatters.com/pm/post/133577-gaga-studies
Davisson, Amber L. 2013. *Lady Gaga and the Remaking of Celebrity Culture*. Jefferson, NC: McFarland.
Elberse, Anita. 2013. *Blockbusters: Hit-making, Risk-taking, and the Big Business of Entertainment*. New York: Henry Holt and Company.
Gray, Richard J. (ed). 2012. *The Performance Identities of Lady Gaga: Critical Essays*. Jefferson, NC: McFarland.
Halberstam, J. Jack. 2012. *Gaga Feminism*. Boston: Beacon Press.
Herbert, Emily. 2010. *Lady Gaga: Behind the Fame*. New York: The Overlook Press. (Published in the United Kingdom as *Lady Gaga: Queen of Pop*, London: John Blake).
Huba, Jackie. 2013. *Monster Loyalty: How Lady Gaga Turns Followers into Fanatics*. New York: Portfolio/Penguin.
Iddon, Martin, and Melanie L. Marshall (ed). 2014. *Lady Gaga and Popular Music: Performing Gender, Fashion, and Culture*. London: Routledge.
Lester, Paul. 2010. *Lady Gaga: Looking for Fame. The Life of a Pop Princess*. London: Omnibus Press.
Miklitsch, Robert. 1998. *From Hegel to Madonna: Towards a General Economy of 'Commodity Fetishism.'* Albany: State University of New York Press.
Stramaglia, Massimiliano. 2015. *Jem e Lady Gaga: The Origin of Fame*. Milan Italy: FrancoAngeli.
Turner, Graeme. 2014. *Understanding Celebrity*, 2nd edn. London: Sage.

CHAPTER 2

Popular Culture and the Sociology of Fame

The sociology of fame and celebrity has in recent years increased in popularity and indeed itself acquired a modicum of fame among a growing number of scholars. To analyze the topic and explore the theoretical perspective adopted in this book, the rise to fame of Lady Gaga can be situated in the context of the sociology of popular culture in a twofold manner considering the theme of study pertains to the (cultural) issue of fame of a musician in the world of pop music. I therefore begin by situating this book's subject matter in terms of the sociology of culture and popular culture and next turn to the sociology of (popular) music before reviewing relevant insights of the sociology of fame and celebrity. Against reductionist perspectives of fame, I will defend a constructionist perspective that conceives of fame as an aspect of culture that concerns a meaningful, value-driven relationship that exists between an audience and the person or persons to whom fame is attributed.

CULTURE AND POPULAR CULTURE

At its most basic foundation, this book rests on a notion of sociology as the scientific study of society. This formulation might not be especially provocative but is nonetheless fundamental and far from trivial to be stated explicitly as the status of sociology as a discipline has long moved debates among sociologists, both in classical and modern times, along a number of variables, ranging from questions on theory and methodol ogy to shifting notions of sociology as a profession. This book adopts a modernist view of sociology as being interested in developing models that best account for variation in social reality. More specifically, society is conceived of from a systems perspective that allows for the analysis of its multiple constituent parts. No further assumptions need to be made about how the relationships between the development of these parts are analytically conceived, although it can be said that a general functional-structural orientation, rather than a specific functionalist theory, underlays this investigation. This study is therefore exclusively meant to serve analytical purposes oriented at explanation and has neither practical nor evaluative objectives, although its findings could inform relevant debates in such forms of normative discourse. The sociological framework of this book also implies that the study of fame in the world of popular music is undertaken from the externalist viewpoint of an observer, not that of a participant, and is oriented at an examination of social conditions, not the themes of scholarship that form part of the specialized province of other, non-sociological disciplines.

Sociologically, both music and fame are cultural issues. Culture is thereby defined as the whole of ideas and values in a society in terms of both (ideal) conceptions and (material) practices. Culture is mediated in symbolic forms, that is, in a manner that is meaningful within a given context, by means of language, words, signs, symbols, musical sounds, and the likes, which are expressed in certain material manifestations and products (e.g., writings, paintings, records, videos). Values are conceived as conceptions of desirable ways of acting and are differentiated from norms as sanctionable standards of conduct (Deflem 2008:198). Values guide actions within groups and among social actors that share them, whereas norms are intended to regulate conduct across groups and between actors on the basis of authority. Values and norms are studied in terms of both ideas and the practices that are associated therewith. Values at the level of culture and norms at the level of social organization, additionally, are sociologically demarcated from politics and economy on the basis of the conventional understanding of society as consisting of at least four differentiated institutional spheres or subsystems, to use the terminology associated with Talcott Parsons and the classical scholarship it is based on (Parsons 1971, 1977). This brief conceptual excursion will be useful, as shown in the coming chapters, to situate fame in the world of popular music in terms of the place of fame in society and its relation to the various constituent parts thereof. It is sociologically important to investigate the course, conditions, and consequences of fame in terms of its variable relationships to normative expectations, political and economic structures and processes, as well as other cultural dimensions, such as shifts in values surrounding music and the practices and institutions associated therewith.

The study of culture has a long-standing history in sociology, dating back to the seminal efforts of Max Weber and Emile Durkheim, whereby the latter classic's contributions to the study of individualism and religion were especially influential. However, at least two restrictions marked initial efforts in the sociology of culture (Griswold 2013). First, theory and research was traditionally too exclusively focused on the ideal dimension of culture to focus on "what is said" rather than also examining the practices, roles, positions, and institutions of "what is done" at the cultural level. The approach referred to as praxeology that is associated with the famous French sociologist Pierre Bourdieu (1977) counts perhaps as the sharpest expression of the sociological turn to focus on the study of cultural practices. Second, of special interest in the present context, culture is sociologically understood to refer to the structures and processes associated with human endeavors related to knowledge, ethics, and aesthetics that are institutionalized in science, justice, and art, respectively (Habermas 1981).

A society's culture refers to both the dominant forms of such ideas and practices as well as the plurality of its (subcultural) variations and deviations. Within the field of culture, sociological attention has traditionally gone to well established and dominant cultural forms that are legitimated within certain authority structures and hierarchies. In other words, culture has traditionally been understood among sociologists in a restricted fashion as that part of culture that was approved or found worthy among social elites (to whom sociologists traditionally also belonged) at the exclusion of popular culture.

The turn toward the study of popular culture in sociology was initially indeed slow in coming (Meyersohn 1977). To be sure, there were some classical scholars who devoted more than passing attention to popular culture, such as, for example, Thorsten Veblen in his famous 1899 study on leisure (1899). Most sociological reflections on popular culture in the classical and early-modern era of sociology, however, were marked by a negative and condemning orientation toward popular culture as irrational kitsch. The very word popular as referring to a sizeable mass of people partaking in such forms of culture was thought to imply a lack of quality or seriousness and hence thought to be unworthy of academic reflection. Whatever merit that was attributed to popular culture, moreover, was judged in terms of non-cultural, typically economic considerations. In other words, popular culture was not just held to be popular but also profitable and deliberately produced as a commodity. This perspective was articulated most forcefully in the 1940s by Frankfurt School sociologists Max Horkheimer and Theodor Adorno in their damning study of the so-called capitalist "culture industry" (Horkheimer and Adorno 1944). Additionally, political and other power-related motives often accompany such a market-oriented perspective. Within such a framework, then, the ambition was to develop a political economy of popular culture or, in other words, to reduce (popular) culture in terms of money and power.

The at once dismissive and reductionist views of popular culture in sociology have in more recent years been abandoned by perspectives that take culture more seriously. With respect to popular culture, in particular, this intellectual turn occurred after important demographic changes took place in the sociological profession. From the late-1960s onwards, a new breed of sociologists emerged that reversed the negative orientation toward popular culture and began to develop serious perspectives of the more playful and popular aspects of culture. The so-called counter-culture generation of sociology reversed the negativity against, but initially not yet the reductionism of the study of popular culture. Strikingly, for instance, Toby Miller (2011) writes that popular culture "*clearly* relates to markets" (p. 450, my emphasis). Studies on the basis of such a reductionist notion do not dismiss expressions of popular culture, but instead focus on its marketing, especially toward youth, and its presumed political implications. The central weakness of such perspectives is that they do not really offer a study of popular culture but rather are studies of other, non-cultural social forces that are related to popular culture. What is needed, then, and what this book hopes to contribute to is a sociology of popular culture as culture. The constructionist perspective in the sociology of music offers such an approach, which will also be useful for the sociology of fame.

Music and Popular Music

As themes of investigation in sociology, music and popular music entertain a status that is similar to their parent categories of culture and popular culture, respectively. Like culture, music has been a long-standing topic of sociological concern, albeit that there are distinct patterns of ebb and flow discernable specific to the history of the sociology of music (Blaukopf

1992; Dowd 2007; Frith et al. 2001; Shepherd and Devine 2015). In the classical age, music received the occasional sociological attention, such as in the work of Frederick Douglass (1845), who wrote about slave music as providing a window into the culture of otherwise voiceless people, and Herbert Spencer, whose 1857 study, "On the Origin and Function of Music," developed an evolutionist theory of the relation between (vocal) music and intellectual speech (Grew 1928), a perspective later criticized by Georg Simmel (Etzkorn 1964). Most famous in the classical canon is the work of Max Weber in his (unfinished) writing, "The Rational and Sociological Foundations of Music," in which he dealt with the special character of Western music (as based on theories concerning tone, tempo, scales, etc.) in terms of a wider process of rationalization (Turley 2001).

In the turn toward modern sociology, there have also been some notable scholars engaged in sociological work on music, although most sociology of culture was not concerned with music. The best illustration perhaps of the character of early modern sociology of music is found in the work of Theodor Adorno, who wrote about music from the 1930s onward (1976). What is striking about Adorno's treatment of music is not only its reductionist perspective, which fits a broader Marxist orientation, but also its dismissal of so-called light or commercial music. In 1936, for instance, Adorno wrote about jazz music in terms of the creation of a culture industry which produced a standardized form of music (differentiated from "serious" music that would not submit itself to market laws). In the 1960s, Adorno applied this reductionist approach to the burgeoning scene of rock or popular (protest) music, which he condemned as "entertainment music" that was inevitably tied up with consumption despite its stated political themes.

It was not until the coming of age of the sociological generation educated from the 1960s onwards that a new wave of sociologists would emerge that took popular forms of music more seriously. No doubt, this development was in large part due to a younger generation of sociologists also being participants in the new musical communities, whether or both as musicians and as fans. As a result, there is today a wide plurality of topics researched in the sociology of music, ranging from the content and structure of music to it production and reception (Dowd 2007). Importantly, along the course of these most recent developments, a new sociology of music has emerged that distinctly conceives of music as culture on the basis of a constructionist perspective.

The constructionist theory of music is not only important to elucidate the relevant conception of the world in which the case of Lady Gaga as a musical performer is situated, but will also inform a related sociological notion of fame. On the basis of the seminal work of Peter Martin (1996), a constructionist perspective of music clarifies the distinctly sociological take on music as distinguished from the contributions of other perspectives in the social sciences and humanities (Bennett 2008; Kotarba and Vannini 2009). Congruent with now classic insights in the sociology of knowledge (Berger and Luckmann 1967), a constructionist framework conceives of music as a culturally constructed art form that is made and remade through symbolic forms of communication. Sociologically, it is fundamental to observe that music is understood socially, that is, within a cultural context in which social actors are socialized in more or less voluntaristic or coercive ways. To some extent, music can be appreciated by choice of an individual or group of actors, but it will also depend of authoritative institutions that can effectively define taste at the social level. The existing hierarchical structure of music, as of art and culture in general, between good and bad music, between pop, rock, and classical music, and other such categorizations, is a manifestation of the various processes at work in musical socialization.

A constructionist viewpoint can best be explained in relation to the contrasting perspectives of empiricist and rationalist theories of music (Martin 1996). An empiricist perspective, most commonly associated with musicology, focuses on music as organized sound, to use the expression popularized by the French-born modern composer Edgar Varèse, and attributes the meanings transmitted through music to certain (objective) qualities of sound. A rationalist theory, typical for a psychology of music, will hold that musical meanings reside in the relatively unique (subjective) experiences of the individual listener. By contrast, a social-rationalist perspective is distinctly sociological in focusing on musical meanings as being constructed within a social context at the (inter-subjective) level of social interaction.

A social-rationalist perspective must be at the heart of any veritable sociology of music that seeks to analyze musical styles, such as pop, rock, and jazz, as well as the whole of ideas and practices associated therewith in any social setting. Sociologists do not study music as such, but music in society. The question of what is considered good music (as opposed to bad music) and, more fundamentally, what is considered music (and not another art form or cultural expression), is from a sociological viewpoint always conceived of as a social question. While a sociological perspective can remain agnostic about questions concerning the objective qualities of music as sound, a rationalist perspective focuses on the fact that people bestow meaning onto musical expressions. Yet, unlike an individualist rationalism, the social rationalism of a constructionist perspective conceives of meaning-making as a social process situated in concrete societies located in time and space. Typical for Western rationalized societies, by example, music is conceived of as an art form that is associated with the production of sound. This cultural conception is not evident as indicated by the fact that the term music is derived from the Greek *mousa* for muse, the goddess of literature and art. Thus, the very understanding of music today as a specific autonomous cultural sphere is a sign of the differentiation of culture in modern, highly rationalized societies (Martin 1996).

The constructionist understanding of music applies to all participants involved in music and thus extends well beyond the world of composers and musicians. Sociologically it is important that social actors involved in the various aspects of the production and reception of music are themselves always socially situated and hence compose, perform, and listen to music as social beings within a given social context of meaning. The intersubjective nature of music constrains the range of musical meanings, but also enables music to be explored in the first place. This relational quality of music in this work will be especially relevant for the discussions in Chaps. 6 and 7 on the role of the media and the audience of Lady Gaga as a musician of fame, yet it broadly relates to the various aspects of the subject matter of this book as fame, too, is conceived of as a cultural phenomenon to which the constructionist perspective can be applied.

Fame and Celebrity

The subject area of fame and celebrity has, like popular culture and music, for a long time been neglected in sociology and related disciplines until it moved more to the foreground in more recent years (Ferris 2007). This historical lack of attention is not as evidently connected to social development as one might initially think because research has shown that fame has a long history (Braudy 1997). Nonetheless, the growing popularity of the study of fame and celebrity to some extent reflects changes in society, especially the development of a highly visible and much debated contemporary celebrity culture that has benefited so greatly from the increasing transparency of modern society. The reality television phenomenon and the global interconnectivity that marks the evolving internet age are but two striking manifestations of this development. Yet, popularity and social significance alone cannot justify a sociological analysis, no matter the salience or novelty of its subject matter, as any sociology must always be firmly rooted with respect to theory and conceptualization within specified disciplinary boundaries. From the perspective of the present study, it is in this respect fortuitous that the topic of fame can sociologically also be approached, like the world of music in which it is studied in this book, as an aspect of culture.

Although traditionally neglected in sociology and related disciplines, there are important intellectual origins to the contemporary study of fame and celebrity (Ferris 2007; Ferris and Harris 2010; Press and Williams 2005). Among the social sciences, sociology can rely on the work of none other than Max Weber (1922) to theoretically explore fame as a cultural phenomenon, specifically conceived of in terms of the distribution of status (Kurzman et al. 2007). Differentiated from the economic and political categories of, respectively, class and party, Weber's concept of status refers to a stratification of honor, relating to lifestyle, privilege and personal qualities associated with charisma. Yet, although Weber's work is constitutive of a multitude of frameworks and specialty areas that have developed in modern sociology, especially in the realm of cultural sociology, Weber's tripartite conceptualization of class, status, and party has largely been used to benefit analyses of economy and polity, rather than culture. This turn toward political economy in sociological discourse was based on Weber's argument that culture was in decline at the dawn of the twentieth century.

In the postclassical era of sociology, the study of fame was largely the victim of the wider neglect of popular culture that also affected the study of popular music. Thus, there were in the early days of modern sociology some smaller studies on fame conducted without the development of a new specialty devoted to the sociology of fame. Examples include Joseph Schneider's (1936) study of fame on the basis of an examination of the material success attained by certain men of "genius," and Orrin Klapp's (1954) and William Goode's (1978) discussions of heroes in terms of their Durkheimian functions of norm affirmation and social control.

As another notable parallel with the sociology of popular music, the studies that took fame more seriously in the modern period of sociology typically developed reductionist perspectives that treated fame and celebrity in function, not of culture itself, but another institutional sphere in society, especially economy and polity. Most notably, the influential radical sociologist C. Wright Mills devoted an entire chapter of his famous and influential book, *The Power Elite* (1956:71–92), to the culture of fame and celebrity that had emerged in the years following World War II. Entitled "The Celebrities," the chapter is striking for its focused treatment of celebrity culture in the context of a wide-ranging study of the character of American society. Yet, it is likewise telling that Mills at once conceptualized celebrity culture to denounce it. Implicitly building on Weber's sociology of culture, Mills appropriately defined celebrity in terms of public honor and thus conceived of fame as an aspect of culture. He also introduced interesting ideas that are relevant to the study of fame today, such as the notion of the "professional celebrity" who was drawn from the world of sports, movies, and the political, corporate, and military elites (Mills 1956:74). Mills also astutely drew attention to the role of the rise of new mass communication systems in the transformation of celebrity. Yet, revealing his neo-Marxist orientation, Mills also argued that "prestige is the shadow of money and power" and had been "created from above" to distract the masses from the problematic implications of the workings of the power elites (pp. 83, 71).

Reductionist perspectives of fame (as of culture and popular culture in general) have longtime plagued much of modern sociology. Today, too, some contemporary scholars continue to focus on fame and celebrity in the distinctly economic terms of their manufacturing and consumption (Turner 2014) on the basis of a conception of the world of popular culture as industry (Rojek 2001; Orth 2004). As Jeffrey Alexander (2010) has argued, such perspectives treat celebrity "reductively" as an institution of capitalism to engage in criticism rather than social science (p. 333). Yet, despite the occasionally stubborn persistence of a concept of fame as commodity and pathology, a new sociology has also begun to emerge that investigates fame and celebrity as a separate theme of inquiry in the realm of popular culture (Ferris and Harris 2010). Since the turn to the twenty-first century, the sociological study of fame and celebrity has continued to evolve and is presently widely recognized as a reasonably diverse and worthy specialty of research. In the context of this book, it is interesting to note that the sociology of fame has from its inception devoted attention to popular music. David Marshall's (1997) influential book, in particular, included an in-depth analysis of the rise to fame of the American boy band New Kids On The Block (pp. 165–184). Other studies on fame have likewise devoted attention to rock and pop stars, such as British singing group The Spice Girls (Turner 2014) and grunge hero Kurt Cobain (Giles

2000, 2013). Also striking is that Joshua Gamson (2001) at the dawn of the current century already devoted attention to the role of the internet in creating a new kind of celebrity, specifically discussing the then curious case of Cindy Margolis, who was once referred to (mostly by herself) as the most downloaded woman on the internet.

As the sociological study of fame and celebrity marched on, Kerry Ferris could by 2007 already devote an entire paper to the history and systematics of "the" sociology of celebrity (Ferris 2007), an area Ferris herself has elaborately contributed to from a symbolic interactionist framework (Ferris 2001; Ferris and Harris 2010). Perhaps the most striking example of the acquired legitimacy of the sociology of fame and celebrity as a new area of inquiry is that relevant research has appeared in top journals in the field (e.g., van de Rijt et al. 2013) and that highly respected sociologists, such as Robert Van Krieken (2012) and Jeffrey Alexander (2010), have also studied dimensions of fame and celebrity. Further stimulating the scholarly study of fame as a legitimate field of inquiry has been the publication of anthologies (e.g., Holmes and Redmond 2006; Marshall and Redmond 2016; Redmond and Holmes 2012) and book-length studies on fame and celebrity across disciplinary boundaries (e.g., Giles 2000; Redmond 2014; Rojek 2001, 2012; Turner 2014).

To accomplish a theoretical move away from reductionist perspectives toward a conception of culture as the distinct framework from which to approach fame and celebrity sociologically, the constructionist perspective of culture introduced above can be relied upon. A brief clarification on terminology will first be in order. The word fame is etymologically rooted in Greek and Roman mythology in which the goddess *Pheme* (Greek) or *Fama* (Latin) refers to a deity associated with gossip and scandalous rumors. The attribution of fame to a person or group of people thus implied a quality of ill repute, of being spoken about through public gossip, a negative connotation that today is associated with infamy as one modality of a more neutrally understood fame. The word celebrity dates back to the late-fourteenth-century French term *celebrité*, itself derived from the Latin *celebritas* and related words, denoting the quality of being celebrated and originally adopted in the English language to refer to fame.

As mentioned before, fame and celebrity today are typically distinguished as referring to, respectively, the quality of being well-known and being known (or celebrated) for being well-known. Dating back to a formulation developed by Daniel Boorstin (1962), the distinction between fame and celebrity is nowadays widely accepted, though it should be added that it is not always identically expressed across societies because of linguistic differences. In French, for instance, *célébrité* refers to either fame or celebrity or both, while the German *Ruhm* and the Dutch *roem* are typically accepted as the translations of fame, with their respective derivatives *Berühmtheit* and *beroemdheid* referring to celebrity. In the Anglophone world, the relevant specialty field is today typically broadly referred to as the sociology of fame and celebrity. The present book, as mentioned, is a study of the social conditions of fame against the background of an advanced celebrity culture. The distinction and relation between fame and celebrity will be specified when needed, but otherwise this study pertains primarily to fame and conceives of celebrity as a specific modality of a more broadly understood concept of fame.

Extending from the constructionist perspective of music as culture, fame, and celebrity are sociologically conceptualized as cultural constructs that entail a specific social relationship among actors. Like culture and music, fame and celebrity are therefore not conceived from the viewpoint of an essentialist understanding referring to certain objective qualities, but which, adopting a rationalist approach, are conceived of relationally in terms of the meaningful categories that are attributed to those to whom fame or celebrity applies. Simply stated, fame and celebrity can sociologically only be said to pertain to a person or group of persons when those qualities are assigned to them by others. Avoiding the individualism of a psychology of fame (Giles 2000), this rationalism is understood socially at the level of groups and societies. As with any aspect of culture, fame, and celebrity are conceived of as issues involving meaning-giving processes on the part of multiple actors, as manifested in both ideas and practices. From this sociological perspective, it is therefore not surprising to observe that fame and celebrity are historically closely related to the expansion of the mass communication media as the primary vehicle of an expression of ideas at the societal level (Mills 1956:71).

The non-reductionist constructionist perspective adopted in this book should not lead to the misunderstanding that fame (and celebrity) can sociologically be studied without reference to their relationship to other institutional areas. In fact, nothing could be less sociological than a study of fame that is not always a study of fame in society. The appearance of a new field of study under the heading of so-called celebrity studies, therefore, has to be treated with a measure of caution as it could be understood to imply an abandoning of the distinct frameworks and related achievements of sociology, psychology, history, and any other discipline devoted to the scholarly study of fame. For no ill-conceived notion of interdisciplinary rather than multi-disciplinary studies can alter the fact that the subject matter of sociology is always society. And no poststructuralist or postmodern pose devolving from analysis into play can substitute for the power of analysis in the empirical study of the conditions of fame. Fame and celebrity studies scholars may know much about fame, conceptually or otherwise, but only a sociological outlook can lead to appropriately formulate a theory and explanatory framework of fame *in* society and make a scientific contribution by means of its disciplinary focus.

While fame is not the quality or property of a person or group, certain personal or group qualities can reasonably be expected to influence how and if the attention that creates fame will be achieved. As noted, originally fame was negatively conceived as ill repute, whereas in our celebrity culture of today, fame is almost invariably received in highly positive terms. Today's modern culture is such that fame is considered to be valuable and worthy to be attained not only by those who have achieved success in some respect, but also by all. Given the widespread nature of this cultural construct as well as the opposition it sometimes evokes, it is theoretically not useful to limit the sociological concept of fame to a pathology (nor its opposite). A political economy approach, for instance, typically attributed highly negative connotations to fame and celebrity. C. Wright Mills (1956), by example, writes about professional celebrities as "personalities of national glamour" whose prestige is "social nonsense" that functions to pacify society (pp. 71, 88). Today such negative visions of fame are typically presented in popular discourse, precisely as an antidote to the obsession that marks the current celebrity culture (Caulfield 2015).

Against the perspective of fame as a social pathology, I defend the argument that fame (and celebrity), like popular culture in general, can sociologically not be conceived of as good or bad without resorting to shaky interpretive exercises whereby the sociologist remains stuck in a participant perspective. Instead, fame, from a scholarly informed viewpoint, can only be studied as being perceived in evaluative terms by particular social actors located in concrete social settings and their constituent parts. It is important, in other words, not to conflate the sociological concept of fame (and celebrity) with the social constructs that exist thereon in a society at any given time. Most famous perhaps among such constructs in the recent history of fame is the slogan associated with American pop artist Andy Warhol that everybody will be famous for 15 minutes in the future. Derived from a phrase that originally appeared in the catalog to a Warhol exhibition of 1968, this construct of 15 minutes of fame has endured until today although its empirical validity in the contemporary age must be called into question. In the present era of the celebrity age that is marked by an unprecedented transparency of society at a global level, it is increasingly understood, in fact, that it would be more provocative to speak of an unattainable ideal of 15 minutes of obscurity. Fame today is (almost) unavoidable. At the same time, of course, there are considerable variations in scope and duration among the more and less famous.

The Social Conditions of Fame

Even though, as mentioned before, fame (and celebrity) can be expected to have an objective dimension in being connected to a personal quality or accomplishment of some sort, the empirical focus of this book is distinctly sociological in examining the social conditions of fame. Applied to the case of the rise to fame of pop star Lady Gaga, the study of these conditions can theoretically be clarified in terms of a cultural perspective that is rooted in, and extended from Max Weber's concept of status. For indeed, while Weber associated status with charisma at a personal level in terms of certain special qualities a person possesses (talent), the Weberian approach also enables a sociological analysis of fame, as an aspect of culture, in terms of a multi-dimensional model of society. Against reductionist perspectives of political economy, indeed, Weber's notion of elective affinity can be relied upon to avoid any preconceived notions on the precise dynamics and conditions of fame in advance of an empirical analysis. A sociological theory of fame based on Weber takes full advantage of the analytical power of a multi-dimensional model of society to investigate the processes and structures of fame in its course and outcome. Such a framework can still reveal the useful gains of an analytically understood model of society (whether it be theoretically inspired by Parsons 1977 or Habermas 1981) and the merits of a related functional-structural analysis (Merton 1968). The latter perspective in fact relates directly to the study of fame in its well-known discovery of the Matthew Effect, which shows that success in science is a function of the (inter-subjectively) recognized status of the scientist irrespective of the (objective) quality or merit of the scientific contribution itself (Merton 1996).

The sociological study of the conditions of fame can benefit from the perspective on status Max Weber (1922) developed in an otherwise relatively limited manner. For indeed, not only did Weber pay no explicit attention to fame or celebrity in his work, his writings on status were relatively scattered and underdeveloped. Informing the perspective fame as a category of culture that I introduced above, however, Weber's concept of status can be applied to fame and celebrity as a process of status group formation. Of special significance to the present study, such a Weberian conceptualization can lead to differentiate four aspects of fame (or celebrity status) useful for an analysis of its social conditions (Kurzman et al. 2007). One, fame is associated with interpersonal privilege for the famous person (or celebrity) to interact with other famous personalities as well as with members of the wider public. Two, famous people enjoy a normative privilege whereby they function as role models and can take on worthy causes far beyond the expertise for which they are primarily known. Three, perhaps the most obvious quality of many forms of contemporary fame is that it is associated with the economic privilege of lucrative financial rewards. And four, famous people can rely on special legal privileges to safeguard the benefits of their honored status. This model of the privileges of fame is reflected in the various conditions of fame this book will explore in the case of Lady Gaga. Although the totality of the model was also partly arrived at inductively, the analysis in this work will devote attention to interpersonal privilege (Chaps. 6 and 7 on media and audience), normative privilege (Chaps. 8 and 9 on activism and gender), economic privilege (Chap. 4 on business), and legal privilege (Chap. 5 on law), with additional chapters on the biography and styles of Lady Gaga (Chaps. 3 and 11).

What the identification of privilege associated with contemporary fame and its applicability to the case of Lady Gaga shows is that Weber's proclamation on the demise of status can no longer be defended. As such, the sociological study of fame from a constructionist perspective can be understood as an effort to think with Weber against Weber inasmuch as Weber's conception of status as culture and his multi-dimensional perspective are still invaluable even when his theory on the relevance of status in society is no longer valid. It would be foolish, in fact, to assume that what Weber wrote a century ago about the empirical conditions of (his) society would still apply today. Given the current climate of an obsession with fame as a near total inversion of this aspect of the Weberian (and Marxian) position, a contemporary perspective can situate today's culture of fame and celebrity in a broader historical process. Then the argument can be made that whereas the nineteenth-century expansion of industrialization marked an era of the centrality of the market, and whereas the twentieth-century experiences of two world wars and the struggle over political rights and democracy shaped an era of politics, the current dawn of the twenty-first century can be characterized as an age of culture, as manifested by such phenomena as the appearance of new social movements, religious conflict, multi-culturalism, and the rise of a celebrity age, including the less than trivial world of popular culture and pop music.

Conclusion

Fitting this book's theme of the origins of fame of global pop sensation Lady Gaga, the framework of this study is situated at the intersection of the sociology of popular culture and music, on the one hand, and the sociology of fame and celebrity, on the other. Culture is understood to refer to the ideas and ideals of a society that are mediated in symbolic form and materialized in various products of human activity. Culture is conceived of as meaningful systems of thought and judgment at the level of society at large or within certain subsections thereof (subcultures). As one element of the aesthetic dimension of culture (art), music is sociologically understood to refer to the whole of cultural ideas, roles, and institutions that are associated with the organization of sound. Judgments on what counts as (good) music are constructed within specified social settings on the basis of a meaning-making process that involved a social interaction among all relevant participants involved, including both musicians and listeners.

The sociological study of fame and celebrity can directly benefit from the constructionist perspective of popular culture and music. Abandoning the study of fame as pathology and commodity, fame concerns the quality of an interaction between the person to whom fame is attributed, on the one hand, and the multiple audiences who participate in such attributions, on the other. As such, fame is essentially social as no person can be famous, by definition, without interacting with others. Fame is accomplished by the attention that is bestowed on a person or group of people, whether this attention involves a positive or negative judgment. Conceptually, fame is understood broadly as being well-known, while celebrity and other related terms (renown, repute, stardom, notoriety) designate more particular modalities of fame.

Many empirical questions can be asked about fame from a number of different disciplinary perspectives. Among the questions that a sociological study of fame is uniquely suited to address, this book will focus on analyzing the social conditions of Lady Gaga's rise to fame. It can be said in advance that no precise conclusions will be able to be reached about the relative weight of each of the analyzed conditions. Yet, evidence will be presented to substantiate the relevance of each considered condition and strengthen the argument that they matter in the rise of Lady Gaga's fame. This study seeks to make sense of the case of Lady Gaga and also suggests factors that are relevant to other, more or less similar cases of contemporary fame in popular culture, although the findings on the conditions of Lady Gaga's rise to fame cannot readily be assumed to apply to a broader universe of cases.

Based on the constructionist framework, the question on the social conditions of Lady Gaga's fame relates to the perceptions and visions of fame that are generally and specifically articulated in the society in which that rise to fame has taken place. The growth of the contemporary celebrity culture and the general decline of the popular music industry constitute two important elements in this social context. It is additionally peculiar, as I will explain in the next chapter, that the case of Lady Gaga is of particular interest because the singer has also explicitly discussed the allure and trappings of fame in her career.

REFERENCES

Adorno, Theodor W. 1976. *Introduction to the Sociology of Music*. New York: Continuum.

Alexander, Jeffrey C. 2010. The Celebrity-Icon. *Cultural Sociology* 4(3): 323–336.

Bennett, Andy. 2008. Towards a Cultural Sociology of Popular Music. *Journal of Sociology* 44(4): 419–432.

Berger, Peter L., and Thomas Luckmann. 1967. *The Social Construction of Reality*. New York: Anchor.

Blaukopf, Kurt. 1992. *Musical Life in a Changing Society: Aspects of Music Sociology*. Portland: Amadeus Press.

Boorstin, Daniel J. 1962. *The Image, or What Happened to the American Dream*. New York: Atheneum.

Bourdieu, Pierre. 1977. *Outline of a Theory of Practice*. Cambridge, UK: Cambridge University Press.

Braudy, Leo. 1997. *The Frenzy of Renown: Fame and Its History*. New York: Vintage Books.

Caulfield, Timothy. 2015. The Celebrity Illusion. *The Chronicle of Higher Education*, April 13, 2015. http://chronicle.com/article/The-Celebrity-Illusion/229197/

Deflem, Mathieu. 2008. *Sociology of Law*. Cambridge, UK: Cambridge University Press.

Douglass, Frederick. 1845. *Narrative of the Life of Frederick Douglass, an American Slave*. Oxford, UK: Oxford University Press.
Dowd, Timothy. 2007. The Sociology of Music. In *21st Century Sociology: A Reference Handbook, Volume 2*, eds. Clifton D. Bryant and Dennis L. Peck, 249–260. Thousand Oaks, CA: Sage.
Etzkorn, K. Peter. 1964. Georg Simmel and the Sociology of Music. *Social Forces* 43(1): 101–107.
Ferris, Kerry O. 2001. Through a Glass Darkly: The Dynamics of Fan-Celebrity Encounters. *Symbolic Interaction* 24(1): 25–47.
———. 2007. The Sociology of Celebrity. *Sociology Compass* 1(1): 371–384.
Ferris, Kerry O., and Scott R. Harris. 2010. *Stargazing: Celebrity, Fame and Social Interaction*. New York: Routledge.
Frith, Simon, Will Straw, and John Street (ed). 2001. *The Cambridge Companion to Pop and Rock*. Cambridge, UK: Cambridge University Press.
Gamson, Joshua. 2001. The Web of Celebrity. *The American Prospect*, December 19, 2001. http://prospect.org/article/web-celebrity
Giles, David C. 2000. *Illusions of Immortality: A Psychology of Fame and Celebrity*. Basingstoke: Macmillan.
———. 2013. The Extended Self Strikes Back: Morrissey Fans' Reaction to Public Rejection by Their Idol. *Popular Communication* 11(2): 116–129.
Goode, William J. 1978. *The Celebration of Heroes: Prestige as a Control System*. Berkeley, CA: University of California Press.
Grew, Eva Mary. 1928. Herbert Spencer and Music. *The Musical Quarterly* 14(1): 127–142.
Griswold, Wendy. 2013. *Cultures and Societies in a Changing World*, 4th edn. Thousand Oaks, CA: Sage.
Habermas, Jürgen. 1981. *The Theory of Communicative Action, Volume 1: Reason and the Rationalization of Society*. Boston: Beacon Press.
Holmes, Su, and Sean Redmond (ed). 2006. *Framing Celebrity: New Directions in Celebrity Culture*. London: Routledge.
Horkheimer, Max, and Theodor W. Adorno. 1972 (1944). *Dialectic of Enlightenment*. New York: Herder and Herder.
Klapp, Orrin E. 1954. Heroes, Villains and Fools, as Agents of Social Control. *American Sociological Review* 19(1): 56–62.
Kotarba, J.A., and P. Vannini. 2009. *Understanding Society Through Popular Music*. New York: Routledge.
Kurzman, Charles, Chelise Anderson, Clinton Key, Youn Ok Lee, Mairead Moloney, Alexis Silver, and Maria W. Van Ryn. 2007. Celebrity Status. *Sociological Theory* 25: 347–367.
Marshall, P. David. 1997. *Celebrity and Power: Fame in Contemporary Culture*. Minneapolis, MN: University of Minnesota Press.
Marshall, P. David, and Sean Redmond (ed). 2016. *A Companion to Celebrity*. Chichester, UK: Wiley Blackwell.

Martin, Peter J. 1996. *Sounds and Society: Themes in the Sociology of Music*. Manchester, UK: Manchester University Press.
Merton, Robert K. 1968. *Social Theory and Social Structure*, Enlarged edn. New York: The Free Press.
———. 1996. *On Social Structure and Science*, ed. Piotr Sztompka. Chicago: University of Chicago Press.
Meyersohn, Rolf. 1977. *The Sociology of Popular Culture: Looking Backwards and Forwards*. Paper presented at Annual Meeting of the American Sociological Association, Chicago. http://eric.ed.gov/?id=ED148664
Miller, Toby. 2011. Popular Culture. In *The Concise Encyclopedia of Sociology*, eds. G. Ritzer and J.M. Ryan, 449–450. Malden, MA: Wiley-Blackwell.
Mills, C. Wright. 1956. *The Power Elite*. New York: Oxford University Press.
Orth, Maureen. 2004. *The Importance of Being Famous: Behind the Scenes of the Celebrity-Industrial Complex*. New York: Henry Holt and Company.
Parsons, Talcott. 1971. *The System of Modern Societies*. Englewood Cliffs, NJ: Prentice Hall.
———. 1977. *Social Systems and the Evolution of Action Theory*. New York: The Free Press.
Press, Andrea L., and Bruce A. Williams. 2005. Fame and Everyday Life. In *The Blackwell Companion to the Sociology of Culture*, eds. Mark D. Jacobs and Nancy Weiss Hanrahan. Malden, MA: Blackwell.
Redmond, Sean. 2014. *Celebrity and the Media*. Basingstoke, UK: Palgrave Macmillan.
Redmond, Sean, and Su Holmes (ed). 2012. *Stardom and Celebrity: A Reader*. London: Sage.
Rojek, Chris. 2001. *Celebrity*. London: Reaktion Books.
———. 2012. *Fame Attack: The Inflation of Celebrity and Its Consequences*. New York: Bloomsbury Academic.
Schneider, Joseph. 1936. Fame and Social Origin. *Social Forces* 14(3): 354–361.
Shepherd, John, and Kyle Devine (ed). 2015. *The Routledge Reader on the Sociology of Music*. London: Routledge.
Turley, Alan C. 2001. Max Weber and the Sociology of Music. *Sociological Forum* 16(4): 633–653.
Turner, Graeme. 2014. *Understanding Celebrity*, 2nd edn. London: Sage.
van de Rijt, Arnout, Eran Shor, Charles Ward, and Steven Siena. 2013. Only 15 Minutes? The Social Stratification of Fame in Printed Media. *American Sociological Review* 78(2): 266–289.
van Krieken, Robert. 2012. *Celebrity Society*. London: Routledge.
Veblen, Thorstein. 1992 (1899). *Theory of the Leisure Class*. New Brunswick, NJ: Transaction Publishers.
Weber, Max. 1958 (1922). Class, Status, Party. In *From Max Weber*, eds. and trans. H.H. Gerth and C. Wright Mills, 180–195. New York: Oxford University Press.

CHAPTER 3

The Life and Times of Lady Gaga

The focus of this book is on the social conditions of Lady Gaga's fame—not her music, nor even the public persona of the person today known as Lady Gaga. In that sense, as mentioned, this book is not about Lady Gaga, but about her fame. Of course, in order to undertake this analysis in any meaningful way, a brief exposition of the singer's biography and that of her work are in order to provide a basic and necessary background from which to proceed. For despite Lady Gaga's worldwide fame, many aspects of her life and career are not widely known among the public at large. In fact, the very nature Lady Gaga's fame will have brought about that certain things about her career—typically all that which is somehow thought of as spectacular, exciting, and image related—are generally very well known in more or less accurate ways, while other, more mundane or routine information has not received as much public attention. Caught in too much glitter, the basic biography of Lady Gaga will be obscured. The singer's fame, in any case, will surely not be exhausted by reference to all those who have read her Wikipedia entry.

Again indicating the fame of the singer, there are many published sources available on Lady Gaga's life and career, including information based on first-hand accounts and interviews with the star herself, especially concerning the period in her career "before the fame." This chapter will rely on some of the better biographical books that have been published (Callahan 2010a; Herbert 2010; Lester 2010; Sullivan 2013) as well as selected news and internet sources, especially those containing inter views with the star and some of her collaborators (Barton 2009; Callahan 2010b; Deflem 2011; Grigoriadis 2010; Robinson 2010), in addition to basic information available from the Lady Gaga songs and albums pages on Wikipedia (Wikipedia "Lady Gaga Discography"). An especially useful internet source is the Gagapedia website on Wikia, a specialized entertainment fan and information site (Gagapedia website). It is a striking aspect of Lady Gaga's fame that some of her most devoted fans have managed the Gagapedia pages to provide for some of the most detailed and accurate information available. Relying on these biographical books, articles, and internet sources alleviates the need to quote from all too numerous sources concerning each and every little aspect of Lady Gaga's career. Suffice it to say that all information provided in the coming sections concerning Lady Gaga's life and work has been reasonably judged to be accurate and precise by cross-checking information across multiple available sources.

Stefani Germanotta

On March 28, 1986, the person known today as Lady Gaga was born at Lenox Hill Hospital in New York City as Stefani Joanne Angelina Germanotta. Her parents are Joseph Germanotta, who originally hails from New Jersey, and Cynthia Bissett, who is originally from Glen Dale, a small town in the Ohio Valley region of West Virginia. Stefani's sister, Natali, is six years junior to her. Both college-educated parents are of Italian descent and have a strong sense of family and tradition they passed on from their parents onto their children. Joe Germanotta's father Joseph Anthony Germanotta, born Giuseppe, died at age 88 in 2010. Stefani's maternal grandfather also passed away after her career was already well established, when Paul Douglas Bissett, Sr., died in 2013 at age 86.

Stefani's parents made their living in the world of internet technology and telecommunications. Mother Cynthia worked for Verizon, while father Joe owned the company GuestWiFi, which was set up in 2002 as one of the first businesses to establish wireless internet services for hotels in New York early on during the development of the technology (Spot On 2015). Throughout Stefani's childhood, both of her parents worked from home. In the early 1990s, the family moved to a two-bedroom condominium in the Pythian Temple building on West 70th Street in the Upper West Side of New York City, where parents Joe and Cynthia presently still reside. In 2010, GuestWiFi merged with Spot On Networks, and the Germanottas became partners in the restaurant "Vince and Eddie's," located just two blocks from their home apartment in New York City. The business has since been renovated and reopened as Joanne Trattoria and is co-owned and run by Joe and Cynthia. The restaurant serves Italian food in the style of the dishes the Germanotta family knew from home.

An inherited strong sense of family is directly and indirectly reflected in various aspects of both Stefani's life and Lady Gaga's later career. The singer, called "Stef" by her family and close friends and nicknamed "Loopy" by her father, is named after her father's sister Joanne and her grandmother Angeline. Joanne died from lupus on December 18, 1974, at the young age of 19. In her career, Lady Gaga has made several references to Joanne, such as by including a poem for her in the booklet of her first album, *The Fame*, and naming her 2016 album, *Joanne*, after her. During the Monster Ball world tour of 2010–2011, the singer could also be heard to narrate the so-called Manifesto of Little Monsters, which she ends with mentioning the date of her aunt's passing. The same date is also tattooed on the singer's arm in between a quote from the Austrian poet Rainer Maria Rilke. As another indication of the strength of family, in 2009, Lady Gaga wrote the song "Speechless" in dedication of her father, who had just undergone surgery for a heart condition. The singer also had "Dad" tattooed on her shoulder, a videotaping of the tattooing itself of which could be seen projected on screen at the end of the Monster Ball theater tour in the fall and winter of 2009–2010. Either or both of Lady Gaga's parents as well as her sister Natali, who in 2014 graduated from the Parsons School of Design at The New School in New York, can often be seen attending the singer's live concerts.

Raised in the Catholic faith, Stefani (and her sister Natali) attended the Convent of the Sacred Heart, an all-female school in New York's Upper East Side. The expensive private school (presently charging around $30,000–$40,000 a year from Junior Kindergarten through 12th grade) attracts children of a social class so exclusive that Stefani, despite her parents' very successful professional careers and resulting wealth, is said to not always have quite fit in, stuck somewhere "in the middle" (Grigoriadis 2010). While the school has some relatively poor students on scholarship, it also counts the likes of Caroline Kennedy, Gloria Vanderbilt, and Nicky and Paris Hilton among its notable alumni.

Lady Gaga's musical education dates back to early in her life. Stefani began playing piano by ear at age four and enjoyed a classical musical training to further her playing skills. The young musician played on an upright piano in her parent's home, which was later replaced by a so-called baby grand model (a smaller version of a concert piano) as her skills had further developed and a music career was more realistically in sight. As a young child, Stefani wrote her first original rudimentary notation of a song she called, "Dollar Bills," on Mickey Mouse music paper. The notation was inspired by the sound of a cash register that can be heard on the famous Pink Floyd song "Money," one of the records from father Joe's classic rock collection. Though not a musician by professional standards, Joe Germanotta used to play in a Bruce Springsteen cover band and is a fan of classical rock bands such as The Beatles, The Rolling Stones, Pink Floyd, and Led Zeppelin. Her father's love of rock was also passed on to Stefani, who at age 13 wrote her first complete musical composition, the rock-oriented ballad "To Love Again."

During her adolescent years, Stefani continued her piano training and additionally expanded her musical and artistic talents by taking acting classes and vocal lessons. Although she was accepted into The Julliard School, a prestigious performing arts conservatory in New York, Stefani instead developed her artistic abilities alongside of her academic work at Sacred Heart. Starting at age 11, she began taking weekly acting classes. By a stroke of luck, from age 14 onwards, Stefani could concentrate on honing voice as her second instrument besides piano when she met vocal coach Don Lawrence. Stefani met the famed instructor after a nephew of his named Evan had overheard her sing the Backstreet Boys hit "I Want It That Way" in a boutique and suggested she contact him (Daily Motion 2008). The voice trainer had by then already acquired considerable prestige, having worked with the likes of Mick Jagger, Bono from the Irish rock band U2, and Christina Aguilera. Lawrence has been involved in Lady Gaga's singing career until this day.

Not much is known of the artistic exploits of Stefani during her teenage years, itself indicating she did not envision a career as a "teen idol" but elected to wait until her craft was more developed. She would occasionally perform at so-called open-mic nights in various clubs in New York City. Because she was under-aged, the singer was typically accompanied by her parents, who would need to convince club owners to have her perform because of her extraordinary talent. The young musician had to be actively encouraged to take the stage as she was, as both an early mentor and her father would later say, "painfully shy" in these early years (Dyball 2010). There is only one indication that a singing career at a younger age was briefly entertained because her artist website Stefanimusic, which she would go on to maintain more actively in 2006, was also in operation for about a year between 2001 and 2002 when the singer was just 15 (Stefanimusic website).

Among other artistic ventures in these early years, Stefani had a bit part in an episode of the popular television series The Sopranos that aired in April 2001. Also, an early rock band with Stefani's participation called Mackin Pulsifer is credited in the liner notes of Lady Gaga's first album *The Fame*, and may have been a cover band from around the time of her high school days. At Sacred Heart, Stefani was a member of the high school choir and performed in at least two school plays, starring in the roles of Miss Adelaide in the musical "Guys and Dolls" and as Philia in "A Funny Thing Happened on the Way to the Forum." In her high school yearbook, she is referenced as usually seen singing, with her piano as her most prized possession, and dreaming of one day headlining at Madison Square Garden.

More clearly setting her sights on a professional career in the arts, in the fall of 2004 Stefani Germanotta moved to a dorm on 11th Street and entered the musical theater program at the Tisch School of the Arts of New York University (NYU). On February 3, 2005, she performed at the NYU talent show UltraViolet Live, where she finished third on the basis of her piano-accompanied singing performances of the ballad "Captivated" and the up-tempo pop-rocker "Electric Kiss." Not without some interest to the present study, the performer today known as Lady Gaga took an undergraduate introductory sociology course while at NYU.

Arguably the most momentous turn in the young performer's career came on March 28, 2005, the day of her 19th birthday when Stefani informed her parents that she had decided to leave NYU in favor of an independently pursued music career. Her parents reluctantly accepted their daughter's decision on the proviso that she needed to establish financial independence and had one year to further her goals professionally by means of a recording contract. Stefani moved to an apartment on 176 Stanton Street in New York's Lower East Side district and took on jobs as a waitress at the Cornelia Street Café and elsewhere. She also made money go-go dancing at bars like the Slipper Room and performed her music more regularly at small clubs, such as The Bitter End, The Lion's Den, and The Knitting Factory. As a performer, the singer initially still went by her birth name and advertised herself as a singer/songwriter/pianist, occasionally performing under the heading "Stefani Live" and, from October 1, 2005 onwards, with her own group, the four-piece Stefani Germanotta Band. On October 10, 2005, the singer performed under her own name in a nationally televised performance of her ballad "No Floods" at New York's Columbus Day Parade.

Stefani's music in these years was mostly indie-rock in style, consisting of original songs, such as "Hollywood," "Wish You Were Here," and "No Floods" (an often mentioned favorite among contemporary Lady Gaga fans), and covers, such as Led Zeppelin's reggae rocker "D'yer Mak'er." The singer also recorded some of her work in demo form with producer Joe Vulpis. Now major collectors' items among Lady Gaga fans, the five-track demo discs *Words* and *Red and Blue* were self-released as unofficial CDs and were sold by her at shows in January and March 2006. None of the music from these early years has ever been officially released, but the demo recordings and even some live performances from the 2005–2006 period are now readily available as downloads or on YouTube.

Lady Gaga

On March 23, 2006, just shy of one year after her decision to leave college and her father's ultimatum, Stefani took part in the 57th New Writers Showcase organized by Bob Leone at The Cutting Room in New York. The singer's unofficial manager since earlier that month, Leone was the National Projects Director of the Songwriters Hall of Fame and had organized the concert to give music industry exposure to nine up-and-coming female singer-songwriters. Stefani's performance of "Hollywood" proved to be eventful when another singer at the show, Wendy Starland, saw her perform and decided to call her manager Rob Fusari. Having scored considerable commercial success with the Destiny's Child hit "Bootylicious" in 2000, Fusari was a New Jersey–based producer who had told Starland he was looking for a singer who could perform in the style of an imagined female lead singer modeled after the alternative rock band The Strokes. Upon seeing Stefani's performance, Starland called Fusari and told him she had found the singer he was looking for. Stefani was invited to Fusari's studio in Parsippany, New Jersey, where she arrived by bus awaited by Fusari and guitarist Tom Kafafian, for whom Fusari had just produced an album. At Fusari's studio, Stefani introduced her music by performing "Hollywood," leading Fusari, who was initially not impressed with the singer because of her look, to be instantly convinced of her special talent. A production deal was arranged with the singer, which, after some short period of rather intense and strenuous negotiation, was signed between

Fusari and Team Love Child, a company that was set up with Stefani's father Joe to represent her in her music career.

Stefani and Fusari's musical collaboration continued on in the following months and produced a considerable number of original songs. The music gradually came to be stylized as pop and dance tracks rather than the indie-pop and rock Germanotta had practiced until that time. The implications of this stylistic transformation and the gradual merger of a pop and rock attitude will be considerable for the future development of the singer's career (as discussed in Chap. 10). At least as important is the fact that producer Fusari coined the nickname "Gaga" for the singer because he thought she was as dramatic a performer as the late Freddie Mercury, the singer of the British rock band Queen, which scored a hit in 1984 with the song "Radio Ga Ga." Stefani would soon adopt the term and eventually turn it into the moniker "Lady Gaga."

The first public performance of the singer as Lady Gaga took place on October 6, 2006, at The Cutting Room in New York as part of the first event organized by On Stage Italian American Artists, an organization presently called Ti Piace that is devoted to promoting Italian American culture and art. On the internet, the singer's music was at this time promoted via webpages on PureVolume and MySpace. Assisted by Gaga's new personal manager, Laurent Besencon of New Heights Entertainment (who at that time was also Fusari's manager), the transition to pop and dance music seemed to rather quickly pay off. Fusari introduced Gaga to Joshua Sarubin of Island Def Jam, the record company led by famed music executive Antonio "L.A." Reid, who signed the singer to a recording contract on September 6, 2006. Having written more than 30 songs with producer Fusari, the singer was slated for an album release, titled *Retro-Sexual*, in the summer of 2007. However, as quickly as she had been signed to Def Jam, just a few months later Lady Gaga suddenly found herself dropped from her contract. As she would later sing in her songs "Paper Gangsta" of *The Fame* (2008) and "Marry the Night" from *Born This Way* (2011), the episode left her with resentment and depression, including a rumored hospitalization that is also visualized in the video to "Marry the Night." The singer's use of cocaine, to which she has admitted on several occasions, also roughly dates back to this period.

The early months of 2007 were a period of rejuvenation for Lady Gaga's career. From an artistic point of view, Gaga had begun to immerse herself more with the world of rock, metal, and performance art she discovered via her friends in the Lower East Side. Especially noteworthy is her chance meeting with Lüc Carl at restaurant San Loco. Her romantic interest off and on for several years to come (and her muse for most of her early love songs), Carl worked as a bartender at St. Jerome's on 155 Rivington Street, a club frequented by rock 'n' roll hipsters and other young New Yorkers with musical tastes, lifestyles, and backgrounds rather far removed from Stefani Germanotta's fanciful upbringing on the Upper West Side. At St. Jerome's (now called Jeromes), also, Gaga met Lady Starlight (born Colleen Martin), a performance artist and heavy metal DJ, with whom she would go on to perform regularly in low-budget burlesque shows under the heading of "Lady Gaga and the Starlight Revue" and "The New York Street Revival and Trash Dance." Instead of playing the piano dressed in grungy clothes as she did during her Stefani days, Lady Gaga now performs with an electronic keyboard dressed in glitter bikinis, accompanied by Lady Starlight spinning beats, and the two of them dancing to heavy metal songs. Attending one of these shows, the singer's parents were left in shock, even leading to a period of non-communication with her father, an issue she would later reference in the song "Beautiful, Dirty, Rich" of her debut album *The Fame*, wherein she sings "Daddy I'm so sorry, I'm so s-s-sorry yeah." In order to get a recording career established, manager Besencon introduced Lady Gaga to producer RedOne, the Moroccan-born Nadir Khayat, with whom she would go on to collaborate numerous times, initially in the form of the song "Boys, Boys, Boys" recorded in 2007 and eventually on several of her early smash hits, most notably "Just Dance," "Poker Face," and "Bad Romance."

Among the now more famous appearances in 2007, Lady Gaga performed a 30-minute set accompanied by Lady Starlight on a side-stage at the Lollapalooza festival in Chicago in August. At the show, Lady Gaga appears in her naturally dark hair and is reportedly mistaken for Amy Winehouse, contributing the singer to color her hair blonde later that year. The Lollapalooza appearance (which failed to garner notice from industry insiders) had been paid for by Vincent Herbert, a talent scout or A&R (artists and repertoire) representative for Interscope Records. In the spring of 2007, Herbert had been introduced to Gaga's music via her MySpace webpage, following a phone call from Fusari. Having mentored Lady Gaga ever since, Herbert also introduced the singer to Troy Carter, who became Gaga's personal manager and would go on to manage her career through her rise to fame up until the release of *ARTPOP* in 2013 (after which former assistant personal manager Bobby Campbell took over). The singer also met with Jimmy Iovine, then the head of Streamline parent company Interscope Records, with whom the singer would sign a recording contract in the summer of 2007. Other notable contacts that are established at this time include producer Martin Kierszenbaum of Cherrytree Records (with whom Lady Gaga recorded the song "The Fame") and singer Akon of KonLive Distribution (who wrote the rap section sung by Colby O'Donis in "Just Dance"). Lady Gaga was initially signed as a songwriter (composing pop songs for the likes of the Pussycat Dolls and Britney Spears) as well as a recording artist. In 2007, she also agreed on a publishing deal with Sony/ATV, the publishing company once owned by Michael Jackson, which oversees the singer's publishing rights until this day.

The Fame

On January 1, 2008, after an all-nighter with some of her best friends of the Lower East Side, Lady Gaga flew from New York to Los Angeles to begin finalizing her first album. She met with producer RedOne, which within hours resulted in the song that would later become her first hit, "Just Dance," the song's opening line ("I've had a little bit too much") telling of the state of her arrival in Hollywood after partying in New York. Over the next months, Lady Gaga records several more songs for her debut album in addition to those already recorded with producers Fusari, RedOne, and Kierszenbaum.

In March 2008, Lady Gaga began on what would become a ten-month promotional tour for her upcoming single and album releases. Later that month, she performed a short medley of her songs at an event organized by fashion company Armani Exchange in Miami, which was the subject of one of the singer's first posts on Twitter (Lady Gaga Twitter post). On March 31, a video was recorded for "Just Dance," Lady Gaga's first single, which was officially released on April 8. In the coming months, Gaga surrounded herself with a growing entourage of artistic collaborators, the so-called Haus of Gaga, consisting of choreographers, stylists, DJs, and dancers, and begins on an intensive promotional tour for her single and other songs of her debut album *The Fame*. The album is released internationally on different dates, as Lady Gaga attained gradual success in various countries across the world. The album was first issued in Canada in August 2008 and in the United States in October 2008. Canada was among the first countries where the "Just Dance" lead single became a hit, reaching the top of the charts as early as August 2008. In the United States, "Just

Dance" entered specialized dance charts in the summer of 2008 and the Billboard Hot 100 on August 16 that year. But the single did not become a hit until January 2009, when it became the up-until-then most downloaded song and topped the Hot 100 chart, some nine months after its release. In other countries around the world, "Just Dance" subsequently became a smash hit that propelled the singer's initial rise to fame.

During the spring and summer of 2009, Lady Gaga's commercial success expanded quickly, with several additional hit songs, such as "Poker Face," "LoveGame," and "Paparazzi." Initially released as a single as early as September 2008, "Poker Face" built on the success of "Just Dance" and turned into Lady Gaga's second worldwide hit, becoming the world's best-selling single of 2009. As explained in more detail in Chap. 6, during the summer of 2009 on, Lady Gaga was gradually sweeping the media, often appearing on television and radio and steadily being discussed and debated on increasingly more numerous occasions in the news media and on a variety of internet sites. By the time of the release of the single "Bad Romance" in October 2009 and the expanded reissue of her first album *The Fame Monster* the following month, Lady Gaga's level of success was already taken to the next level, to wit increasing records sales and growing concert attendance. A new worldwide concert tour, the Monster Ball, was organized on the basis of the singer's growing global popularity and would involve no less than 203 shows between November 2009 and May 2011.

In view of the global fame that has come with Lady Gaga's success, the story of her career since 2011 will be more generally known. In February 2011, Lady Gaga released the first single of her album *Born This Way*, which itself followed in May of that year. Both the single and album are giant worldwide hits. Although less success was bestowed on later single releases of the album released in the fall of 2011, especially the fan favorite "Marry the Night," it was followed by a another commercially successful concert tour, The Born This Way Ball, that was held from April 2012 until February 2013. A measure of tragedy caused the end of the tour when most all shows planned in the United States had to be canceled because Lady Gaga needed to undergo surgery to her hip, which had been damaged during the demanding show performances.

After a successful surgery to her hip in the spring of 2013, Lady Gaga largely disappeared from the spotlight for several months, electing to work more privately without much publicity on her coming records. After the summer, the singer returned with the single, "Applause," which was released in August 2013, and its album *ARTPOP*, that followed in November. Both the new single and album performed well commercially, but a certain fatigue with Lady Gaga seemed to have set in as well as news stories and online comments began to appear that contemplated a decline of her popularity. The following tour, called the artRAVE: The ARTPOP Ball, ran from May through November 2014 in countries across the globe, but grossed considerably less than her preceding arena tours.

At the time of this writing, the career of Lady Gaga had taken its last important artistic and commercial turn in the form of a detour into the world of jazz. In September 2014, the album *Cheek To Cheek* was released in a collaborative effort with legendary singer Tony Bennett, with whom Lady Gaga also went on to perform live in a series of jazz concerts in 2015. By the spring of 2016, the career of Lady Gaga looked to be ready to move to the next level. On a personal level, the singer's life appeared to have found a new sense of stability, especially following her engagement, on Valentine's Day of 2015, to actor Taylor Kinney, with whom she was romantically linked since shortly after they met on the set for the video of "Yoü and I" in July 2011. On the musical level, Lady Gaga recorded songs for a new pop album since she was performing with Tony Bennett. The album, called *Joanne*, which fans and Lady Gaga herself provisionally referred to as "LG5" as it is the fifth major release by the singer, mostly features songs produced by Mark Ronson, who gained notoriety producing the likes of Amy Winehouse, Adele, and Bruno Mars (Williott 2016). Along with a planned follow-up jazz album with Tony Bennett, the success of Lady Gaga's latest music releases will surely be an important moment in what should be the first step in the second part of her career. In any case, while Lady Gaga's commercial and critical success has already experienced some fluctuations since the singer's initial rise in popularity, her fame can surely be said to have been established.

Lady Gaga on (the) Fame

It follows from the basic sociological insight that fame is relational in nature, as suggested in Chap. 2, that an analysis of the social conditions of fame must involve consideration of the mechanisms and circumstances under which the attention that creates fame can develop. Special focus in this book will therefore go to the audience of Lady Gaga and the media through they have connected (Chaps. 6 and 7). However, as fame exists inter-subjectively, it also has two additional dimensions: the objectivity of fame that can be measured by certain observable standards, such as the amount of financial success and the legal activities that are generated (Chaps. 4 and 5), and the subjectivity of fame that exists on the part of the person to whom fame is ascribed. This subjective dimension need not necessarily be coined in psychological terms, but can also be sociologically expressed in terms of a relationship between self and other(s), such as it is theoretically grounded in the very foundations of a constructionist approach (Mead 1934). A sociological analysis of fame, therefore, would not be complete if it were not to consider the role of the self in the creation of fame as one dimension of its "lived experience" (Ferris 2010:392).

In the case of Lady Gaga, it is fortuitous that the singer has engaged with a public presentation of self, to use the well-known terminology of Erving Goffman (1959), that is directly and deliberately involved with issues of fame (see also Deflem 2012). Throughout her career and, especially, in the earlier part thereof, when her fame was being established on a gradually global scale, Lady Gaga has voiced to practice the idea of "the art of fame" which she pursued in a very explicit manner (in CBS News 2011). This subjective construct of fame is expressed in various ways, as communicated through her artistic work and in interviews, and involves a number of different components which, indicating the reflexivity of social knowledge, also relate closely to the concepts of fame and celebrity as they are sociologically understood. As discussed in the following pages, Lady Gaga has specifically recognized the social context of her work and entertained a relevant conceptualization of fame and what she calls "the" fame. She has also expressed a conception of her work as the result of a fame that is authentic and actively pursued (by her) and, relatedly, she has discussed the impact and reception (by others) of the fame she has acquired, both positive and negative.

The social context of Lady Gaga's self-understanding of fame is framed within the time period of the release of her first recorded music. The singer's 2008 debut album *The Fame* has a relation to fame that is not altogether as obvious as might be gathered from its title for not all, nor even most, songs on *The Fame* deal with fame. Apart from minimal references to fame and celebrity culture in "Starstruck" and "Paparazzi" (both of which are metaphorically titled love songs), only "Paper Gangsta" and "The Fame" address aspects of fame, specifically the drive for its pursuit and a lifestyle mimicking the rich and famous. The less obvious, but nonetheless strongest link to fame and celebrity of the songs on *The Fame* is the signature piece "Beautiful, Dirty, Rich," a song about her fellow high school students, who, Lady Gaga explained, "didn't do anything but were famous" (in Crossfield 2008). It is this attitude and the manner in which it is reflected in the drama of her work that Lady Gaga would carry further to garner the attention on which she could build her musical career.

Related more clearly to Lady Gaga's perceptions of fame than some of her individual songs is the fact that the concept of the whole of her debut album is deliberately formulated in terms of the growing celebrity culture at the time of its writing. As such, the singer's work responds directly to the most shallow aspects of celebrity whereby it seems that anybody can be famous for any or absolutely no reason at all as long as they can convince others they are worthy of attention. Seeing the celebrity culture whereby "these young blonde women were getting arrested and they had their mug shots taken," as she once explained, Lady Gaga understood that "there's really an art to fame," which she sought to cultivate because, she added in reference to herself and her friends in the Lower East Side, "we don't have any money; we're not famous; there's no paparazzi chasing us, but when we walk down the street, people wonder who we are" (OfficialOnDaGrineTV YouTube video). Yet, the celebrity element that is infused into the very origins of Lady Gaga's career is presented ironically in relation to a distinct accomplishment to "hustle and grind" and "live and breathe" her art (ibid.). This artistic pursuit, the singer says, is about "carrying yourself in a way that exudes confidence and passion for music or art or fishing, or whatever the hell it is that you're passionate about, and projecting yourself in a way that people say, 'Who the fuck is that?'" (in Barton 2009). As revealed in the spring of 2014 when she closed out New York's Roseland Ballroom with seven sold-out shows, at least one time in August 2008 the strategy was successful, when Lady Gaga was walking down the street and approached by a photographer who requested a picture before he asked her who she was. "I'm Lady Gaga," she responded, "A singer/songwriter. You're going to know me one day" (in Dockterman 2014).

Lady Gaga's endeavor to create fame in celebrity culture invokes the well-known conceptual distinction between celebrity and fame that I also introduced in this book. The construction that Lady Gaga herself has articulated in this respect is a distinction between what she refers to as "fame" and "the fame." The singer hereby differentiates between fame as a publicly recognized form of fame typically associated with celebrity and fame's darker side, while she understands "the" fame a more positive and subjectively experienced quality that is not necessarily associated with actually being well known but with feeling and hoping one is and might be. "I think there's different kinds of fame," Lady Gaga once said, "I think there's 'fame', which is plastic and you can buy it on the street, and paparazzi and money and being rich, and then there's 'the fame', which is when no one knows who you are but everybody wants to know who you are" (in Barton 2009). This conception of an inner sense of "the" fame, the singer further maintains, "is in your heart … to comfort you, to bring you self-confidence and worth whenever you need it" (in Silva 2010). Building on this notion, Lady Gaga expresses the idea that the fame can be shared among her and all those who join her as her fans and, more generally, her audience. "*The Fame* is about how anyone can feel famous," as she once posted on her website, "it's a sharable fame. I want to invite you all to the party" (in Lester 2010:104, 105). Unlike Madonna who once famously proclaimed on a 1983 show of the popular television program American Bandstand that she wanted to rule the world, Lady Gaga wants all of us to rule the world, encouraging us all, "Rule the world! What's life worth living if you don't rule it?" (Grigoriadis 2010).

With respect to that part of Lady Gaga's fame that relies on her artistic accomplishments, it is most striking, maybe more so than with many other aspiring pop stars of her generation, that the singer aspired to fame as an active pursuit based on artistic merit as well as subjective disposition. This deliberate pursuit of her own fame and success Lady Gaga expressed since well before she was realistically on her way to attain fame. The attitude dates back to her days as a high school student when she was already referred to as "very dedicated, very studious, very disciplined" (Lester 2010:15). Most famously perhaps, as she pursued her musical career her drive to be famous led to her break from her on-off boyfriend Lüc Carl against whom she would proclaim, "One day, you're not going to go into a deli without hearing me" (in Grigoriadis 2010). During her days in the Lower East Side, the singer once gave her friend and original DJ Brendan Jay Sullivan a handwritten note that, more clearly than any other indication of the strength of Lady Gaga's conviction, read: "There is a musical government, who decides what we all get to hear and listen to. And I want to be one of those people" (in mrbrendanjay Instagram post).

Exemplifying the directed manner of her artistic pursuits, Lady Gaga pursues fame as distinctly based on her many and diverse artistic accomplishments, including her music, videos, fashion, and live performances. As she mixes musical sounds with particular ways of performing, she thereby understands that art, precisely to be authentic, always needs to be communicated to an audience and that cultivating an image cannot and should not be divorced from this aspiration. Whether she can (objectively) justify this ambition or not is not as relevant, in the present context, than is the singer's (subjective) claim of authenticity. Lady Gaga will therefore emphasize that she writes and co-produces all of her songs, that she plays piano and sings (and claims to never lip-sync), and that she is generally involved in each and every aspect of her work, including music, fashion, and presentation. She conceives of this ambition as a sense of control that she judges to be necessary for her career. "Because that's your fame," she proclaims, "That's where your fame lives ... It's in my ability to know what I make is great. I know it is: I know it's great" (in Moody 2009). It is in this context, also, that Lady Gaga has proclaimed her admiration for Rainer Maria Rilke. The poet wrote a letter, published posthumously in 1929 in *Letters to a Young Poet*, wherein he tells an aspiring writer to ask himself if he would die if he were forbidden to write (OfficialOnDaGrineTV YouTube video). "Must I write?" is the question. In 2009, Lady Gaga had a short excerpt of Rilke's book in its German original tattooed on her arm.

In relation to this understanding of her own accomplishments, Lady Gaga proclaims to pursue her work as part of her life. As such, she also sees no difference between herself as a person and the persona of Lady Gaga. In this day and age when the distinction between private and public is blurred in so many ways, Lady Gaga aspires to be Lady Gaga full-time. Again, irrespective of whether the singer's stated ideal is attainable and regardless of its consequences, she sees it as her mission to embrace the fame as a student of its sociology. On the television program 60 Minutes that aired on the day of the Grammys in February 2011, Lady Gaga indeed explicitly addressed the sociology of fame in response to a question by Anderson Cooper regarding my course at University of Southern California (USC) which was discussed widely in the media at the time the interview was conducted (see Epilogue). The singer affirmed that her pursuit of the fame was an essential part of her work. "I'm a true academic when it comes to music and when it comes to my style, my fashion," she said, "When you asked me about the sociology of fame and what artists do wrong, what artists do wrong is they lie, and I don't lie" (CBS News 2011).

Yet, as Lady Gaga became successful and garnered worldwide attention, she would soon also acknowledge that she was more exposed to fame in the sense in which she understands it, as distinct from "the" fame, more negatively. In September 2009, the negativity of fame was addressed in a live performance of her song "Paparazzi" at the Video Music Awards (VMA) in New York City's Radio Music Hall. Although the song is not about paparazzi chasing the star (but about herself pursing love interest Lüc Carl), the performance was inspired by the death of Princess Diana to show the singer walking on a medical cane, blood coming out of her heart, and ultimately dying as a portrayal of the price of fame.

On her album *The Fame Monster*, released in November 2009, Lady Gaga addressed different aspects of the negativity of fame directly. Instead of songs about partying, drugs, and playful sex, the newly recorded tracks on *The Fame Monster* deal with a series of fears that had come with Lady Gaga's increased success, such as the fear of sex, love, and death. The changed direction from the themes of her debut album indicates that Lady Gaga's fame theme was applied under circumstances that had already changed rather drastically, as the singer was now, indeed, famous. Less than a year into her success, Lady Gaga already expressed a fear of fame itself, of "never being able to enjoy myself," suggesting "I love my work so much, I find it really hard to go out and have a good time" (in Vena 2009). Dealing with the dangers that come with fame, Lady Gaga sees a special role reserved for the team of people she surrounds herself with both for organizational and artistic purposes. She therefore conceives of her producers, assistants, managers, stylists, musicians, and other members of the Haus of Gaga as having a protective function. "I think that with fame comes a lot of people that are jealous," she says, "and with success comes people that want things from you. The key to having both is surrounding yourself with people that want good things from you" (in Daily Record 2009).

Conclusion

Born in 1986 in New York City, the singer today known as Lady Gaga enjoyed the benefits of a protective family nurturing the best of her undisputed artistic abilities. From being able to play piano by ear at age four to moving on musically by gradually honing her skills by means of formal education as well as favorable cultural exposure, it seems that the young Italian American was destined for success. Aided by various music industry insiders, she went relatively quickly from being an unknown singer who dropped out of college in 2005 to becoming a global sensation from 2009 onwards. Yet, while surely many try, only few succeed, even with music industry support, as stardom by definition is a highly limited resource. While there can be no doubt that Lady Gaga is specially talented and driven, social factors will also have been at work to accomplish her eventual success and fame.

The fame of Lady Gaga as a sociological subject matter can benefit from the fact that the performer herself has addressed aspects of fame and celebrity at length. Clearly not afraid to actively pursue living in the limelight, Lady Gaga subjectively perceives fame as dichotomous between individual celebrity, which she wishes to avoid, and a socially shared fame, or "the fame" as she calls it, which she embraces. But soon upon achieving a considerable amount of fame after her first hit singles in the spring and summer of 2009, the singer already began to contemplate on the negative aspects of fame and the fame monster that had appeared. Initially drawn to the fame in the naïve way reminiscent of the title track from the 1980 movie *Fame* ("I'm gonna live forever"), Lady Gaga began to realize some of those problematic aspects of fame two of her main muses, David Bowie and John Lennon, were already singing about in 1975 ("Fame, puts you there where things are hollow"). To deal with these issues, Lady Gaga surrounded herself with a support staff of creative and organizational experts. Needless to say, in view of the continued popularity Lady Gaga has enjoyed since her rise to fame, these efforts have largely proven to be successful. And aided by appropriate business strategies, as the next chapter will show, Lady Gaga's success also generated a substantial amount of financial rewards as well.

References

Barton, Laura. 2009. I've Felt Famous My While Life. *The Guardian*, January 20, 2009. http://www.theguardian.com/music/2009/jan/21/lady-gaga-interview-fame

Callahan, Maureen. 2010a. *The Rise and Rise of Lady Gaga*. New York: Hyperion.

———. 2010b. Who's That Lady? *New York Post*, January 21, 2010. http://nypost.com/2010/01/21/whos-that-lady/

CBS News. 2011. Lady Gaga on 'Mastering the Art of Fame'. Transcript. *CBS News*, February 14, 2011. http://www.cbsnews.com/8301-18560_162-7337078.html

Crossfield, Corey. 2008. The Interview: Lady Ga Ga. *Short and Sweet NYC*, July 22, 2008. http://www.shortandsweetnyc.com/2008/07/the-interview-lady-ga-ga/

Daily Motion. 2008. Lady Gaga – Interview. *Daily Motion*, November 1, 2008. http://www.dailymotion.com/video/x79hia_lady-gaga-interview_music

Daily Record. 2009. Lady Gaga Loves to Glam up with Her Disco Glitz. *Daily Record*, July 2, 2009. http://www.dailyrecord.co.uk/entertainment/music/music-news/lady-gaga-loves-to-glam-up-1030522#D8b8ARIsDJ4tTUij.97

Deflem, Mathieu. 2011. Bob Leone and the Sociology of the Fame. Gagafrontrow. blogspot, February 12, 2011. http://gagafrontrow.blogspot.com/2011/02/bob-leone.html

———. 2012. The Presentation of Fame in Everyday Life: The Case of Lady Gaga. *Margin* 1(The Divas Issue): 58–68.

Dockterman, Eliana. 2014. Lady Gaga Unveils Poster for Roseland Ballroom's Last Concerts. *Time*, March 19, 2014. http://time.com/30651/lady-gaga-roseland-ballroom-concert/

Dyball, Rennie. 2010. Former Manager: Lady Gaga Was 'Painfully Shy'. *People Magazine*, October 7, 2010. http://www.people.com/people/article/0,,20432389,00.html

Ferris, Kerry O. 2010. The Next Big Thing: Local Celebrity. *Society* 47: 392–295.

Gagapedia. Website. http://ladygaga.wikia.com/

Goffman, Erving. 1959. *The Presentation of Self in Everyday Life*. Garden City, NY: Doubleday.

Grigoriadis, Vanessa. 2010. Growing Up Gaga. *New York Magazine*, March 28, 2010. http://nymag.com/arts/popmusic/features/65127/

Herbert, Emily. 2010. *Lady Gaga: Behind the Fame*. New York: The Overlook Press (Published in the United Kingdom as *Lady Gaga: Queen of Pop*. London: John Blake).

Lady Gaga. Twitter post. March 28, 2008 (4:14 AM). https://twitter.com/ladygaga/status/778462462

Lester, Paul. 2010. *Lady Gaga: Looking for Fame. The Life of a Pop Princess*. London: Omnibus Press.

Mead, George H. 1934. *Mind, Self and Society from the Standpoint of a Social Behaviorist*, ed. C.W. Morris. Chicago: University of Chicago.

Moody, Nekesa M. 2009. Lady Gaga is a Creation, But an Authentic One. *The Plain Dealer*, June 24, 2009. http://blog.cleveland.com/entertainment/2009/06/lady_gaga_is_a_creation_but_an.html

mrbrendanjay. Instagram post. August 7, 2013. https://www.instagram.com/p/cujIZbvJmf/

OfficialOnDaGrineTV. Lady GaGa's Inspiring Interview in Vancouver Before She Blew It Up Big! *YouTube video*, uploaded July 2, 2010. https://www.youtube.com/watch?v=bXPj99ULyBo

Robinson, Lisa. 2010. Lady Gaga's Cultural Revolution. *Vanity Fair*, September 2010: 280–286, 329–331.

Silva, Horacio. 2010. The World According to Gaga. *The New York Times Style Magazine*, March 4, 2010. http://tmagazine.blogs.nytimes.com/2010/03/04/the-world-according-to-gaga/

SpotOn. 2015. SpotOn Networks Opens Second Central Office In San Francisco. *Press release. SpotOn*, July 8, 2015. http://www.spotonnetworks.com/press-releases/

Stefanimusic. Website (archived). https://web.archive.org/web/ */ http://www.stefanimusic.com

Sullivan, Brendan Jay. 2013. *Rivington Was Ours: Lady Gaga, the Lower East Side, and the Prime of Our Lives*. New York: Itbooks.

Vena, Jocelyn. 2009. Lady Gaga Explains Inspiration Behind Beyonce Collabo, 'Telephone'. *MTV.com*, November 24, 2009. http://www.mtv.com/news/1627050/lady-gaga-explains-inspiration-behind-beyonce-collabo-telephone/

Wikipedia. Lady Gaga Discography. https://en.wikipedia.org/wiki/Lady_Gaga_discography

Williott, Carl. 2016. RedOne Says He Worked on Eight Songs for Lady Gaga's New Album. *Idolator*, May 24, 2016. http://www.idolator.com/7634606/lady-gaga-lg5-redone-new-music-songs

CHAPTER 4

The Business of Lady Gaga

No special exposition in the sociology of capitalism is needed to bring out the relevance of the monetary rewards that come with an attained level of fame, especially in the area of pop culture, which is essentially characterized by its wide mass appeal and associated financial benefits. At the same time, however, the sociological approach of this book does not reduce popular culture to its commercial dimension. A true sociology of the economics of pop culture does not equate pop with money and does not define what is popular as commercial. It is a truism to note that commercial music is subject to economic principles and the usual concerns for profit maximization. However, the notion of commercial music is also often used or understood erroneously to attribute an economy of music to a particular style of music, thereby overlooking that all forms of musical expression have a material basis that may be subjected to commercial exploitation. Properly understood, the sociological question on the business aspects of fame and popular culture should not address itself exclusively to cases like Lady Gaga to be blinded by its synchronicity of wealth and pop, but realize that other cases in entirely different realms of culture are formally similar. Whatever economics of fame apply to Lady Gaga must also apply to Yo-Yo Ma, lest one otherwise would assume the cello to have become an instrument of special appreciation in today's Western music culture.

The business side of Lady Gaga's career has itself been the subject of her fame. Indeed, an essential part of fame in contemporary popular culture under conditions of advanced capitalism is not only that fame generates wealth but also that its wealth becomes a subject of reflection additionally accelerating fame. At various levels of discourse, from mundane comments on the internet to academic analysis, the monetary aspects of Lady Gaga's fame have indeed often been discussed in rather hastily concocted pieces of advice that have been written from within, and purported to be for the benefit of, the marketing world. These marketing tips based on the career of Lady Gaga have found their way in several essays (e.g., Bodnar 2011; Bridges 2015; DePaz 2012; Machan 2011; Peters 2011; Yohn 2012, 2014) and formed the basis for a case study at the Harvard Business School (Nobel 2011) and a book-length treatise (Huba 2013). Typically, these "Gaga marketing lessons" have assumed that motivational aspirations are at work on the part of the singer. Such a psychologistic reading will be avoided in the analysis I offer here in favor of a sociological approach that relates fame to its relation to economic matters at an inter-subjective level. Situated within the broader economics of popular music culture (i.e., the music industry), this chapter first offers an overview of the indicators of the fame of Lady Gaga in monetary terms and subsequently analyzes the business components and marketing strategies that have been employed to organize and build the singer's career.

Music Culture and Music Industry

Based on the sociological understanding of society and (popular) culture adopted in this book, the economic organization of social life is seen as differentiated from other social institutions by virtue of its specialized concentration on the production, distribution, and consumption of goods and services. Conforming to a non-reductionist approach, this conception implies that culture entertains a relationship with economy, politics, and law, but additionally also that music as a cultural phenomenon is itself differentiated along lines similar to those that exist in the wider societal context to distinguish between the industry, policy, values, and norms of music. This brief Parsonian reflection will suffice to further clarify the general role of economy in popular culture before the case of Lady Gaga's business is explored.

It is impossible to disagree with music scholar Simon Frith's (2001) contention the peculiar status of musical sound as a non-material substance (of unsuspecting air molecules behaving as the result of a composer's will, to paraphrase Frank Zappa) that is expressed through a material product and, as a result, subject to economic activities. Unacknowledged by

Frith though, the commercialization of music can pertain to any kind of musical genre. And by extension, indeed, the same mechanisms can apply to fame as well. The music (and fame) culture co-exists with the music (and fame) industry in a relationship of inherent tension as the commercial pursuits and artistic or entertainment values are joined. Whether this connection is perceived as problematic or not must remain an open question. Commercial interests in music range from issues concerning the professionalization of musicians, instruments, and musical scores, to recordings.

To the extent that music is materialized, it becomes a product subject to commodification, with all due possible consequences in the context of a free-market economy. While all social actors involved in the music industry may enjoy musical sound, they are economically divided between producers and consumers and have relatively competing interests as a result. In today's internet age, this demarcation has been elevated to a hitherto unprecedented level, making the case of Lady Gaga's economic success, as one aspect of her fame, precisely of special interest. The role of the marketing of music needs no special clarification. Although its dynamics are subject to considerable changes, marketing concerns the manner in which musicians and performers can effectively reach their audience. Needless to add that the perspective adopted in this book cannot agree with Frith (2001) and other reductionists that the material products of pop music are made "*for* the public as defined *by* the media" (p. 43, my emphases). Instead, no subjective motives can sociologically be attributed to any kind of music beyond its objectives functional consequences. Marketing concerns the meshing of the artistically valuable with the commercially viable, much like any other cultural expression, including a work of scholarship produced in book form.

The underlying business model of the popular music industry is one based on failure, rather than success (Frith 2001). It is treated as a given among music executives that most musicians signed to record deals and other contracts will fail and that only a few will be successful. The success stories of the music business (the stars) are economically profitable to the point that they more than recoup others' losses. Whatever goes wrong in the industry is attributed to the failures of others in a cycle of blame-giving, from the musician to the producer, from the producer to the manager, from management to the recording company, and so on. Under these circumstances of selective blame and fatalism, it becomes even more puzzling to ponder the conditions under which a pop artist like Lady Gaga and other recent success stories did manage to become treated as somebody placed at the center of the music industry's so-called star system.

THE WEALTH OF LADY GAGA

All indications are that even in this day and age of a generally declining music industry, Lady Gaga's fame has come with an impressive measure of commercial success and wealth.[1] In 2010, the year after her first hit songs had reached a global audience, the success of Lady Gaga's fame could already be described as gigantic in a monetary sense. With millions of downloads and CDs sold, hundreds of millions of YouTube views, and sold-out concerts everywhere, the singer has since her rise to fame consistently ranked among the highest earners in entertainment. Based on rankings provided by *Forbes* magazine (Forbes website), Lady Gaga had earned $62 million in the period between June 2009 and June 2010, when she debuted at #4 on the Celebrity 100 list of highest-earning entertainers. The year thereafter, in the wake of strong album sales, a sold-out world tour, and various product endorsements, the singer topped the list, knocking out Oprah Winfrey, at $90 million earned in the prior year (Pomerantz 2011). In 2012, following the release of her *Born This Way* album in May 2011, Lady Gaga ranked second with $52 million earned (Forbes website). Between June 2012 and June 2013, her earnings were estimated at $80 million, mostly as a result of the successful Born This Way Ball concert tour (Forbes website). That income ranked her second among musicians behind Madonna, who grossed $125 million following her highly successful MDNA tour, but highest among celebrities under the age of 30, edging out Justin Bieber who had earned $58 million in the same period (Makarechi 2013; O'Malley Greenburg 2013). In 2014 and 2015, Lady Gaga's earnings stood at $33 million and $59 million, respectively (The Richest website). In 2015, when she ranked somewhat lower at #25 on the celebrities highest earners list, her income was still very impressive considering that in the preceding year she had not even released a new album and had toured only on a relatively small scale with Tony Bennett (Marfil 2015). Revenue in that year was mostly due to business partnerships, indicating the relevance of product diversification in contemporary pop music stardom. By 2015, Lady Gaga's net worth was estimated to be $280 million (The Richest website).

Breaking down the sources of the singer's income, Lady Gaga generates revenue from her music in the form of sales of CDs and downloads as well as concert tours. Lady Gaga's debut album, *The Fame*, was immensely successful, not immediately upon its release but gradually over time as singles drawn from the album became hits. The best-selling debut album of the year in the United States, *The Fame* eventually peaked at number two on the Billboard charts and in many other countries reached the number one spot or was otherwise highly successful, often attaining multiple platinum status. In July 2010, the album was the best-selling digital album download in history, until it was later robbed of that honor by Adele's 2011 album *21*. To date, *The Fame* has sold some 16 million copies worldwide. Because Lady Gaga's second major release, *The Fame Monster*, was issued as an EP as well as a double album re-issue of her first album, sales for that album are counted either as a self-standing EP release or as part of *The Fame*. The album sold nearly 6 million worldwide, more than 1.6 million copies of which in the United States. Lady Gaga's next album, 2011's *Born This Way*, sold over 1.1 million copies in its first week of release, in large part because of a promotion campaign from Amazon which offered the album in download form for only 99 cents. Launched without knowledge on the part of Lady Gaga and her team, the one-week campaign also contributed to a drop of 84 % to only 174,000 copies sold during the album's second week (Newman 2011; Sisario 2011). *ARTPOP*, to date the singer's last pop record that was released in November 2013, sold a comparatively disappointing 250,000 in the United States in its first week of release, but did go on to become the globally ninth best-selling album of the year with 2.3 million copies sold worldwide, more than 750,000 of which in the United States. *Cheek To Cheek*, the duet album with Tony Bennett released in September 2014, has to date sold about 700,000 copies in the United States, which is notable as it is a jazz album. The album also topped the Billboard chart in its first week of release with 131,000 copies sold, making it the third number one album for Lady Gaga and the second for Tony Bennett, who at 88 was the oldest living person to achieve that status. By April 2016, Lady Gaga's album sales in the United States stood at 4.7 million for *The Fame*, 1.6 million for *The Fame Monster* (single-disc version), 2.4 million for *Born This Way*, 757,000 for *ARTPOP*, and 717,000 for *Cheek To Cheek* (Trust 2016).

Lady Gaga's hit singles have propelled much of the chart success of her albums and are especially noted for their high sales in the form of digital download. The debut single "Just Dance" reached number one on the Billboard charts in January 2009, when it held the record for most downloads in one week. It subsequently became a global hit, selling some 10 million copies in digital downloads alone. Even bigger hits were some of Lady Gaga's following single releases in 2009, most notably "Poker Face" and "Bad Romance," which by now have sold, respectively, 14 million and 12 million copies worldwide. "Poker Face" is the most downloaded tune in digital music history in the UK, and worldwide it was the best-selling song of 2009. The single, "Born This Way," of the same-titled album topped the charts in multiple countries around the world upon its release in February 2011 and has to date sold some 9 million copies. It became the 1000th song to hit the number one spot on the Billboard Hot 100. Some Lady Gaga singles released more recently have done less well in sales. Fan favorite "Marry the Night," the fifth single of *Born This Way*, only reached number 29 on Billboard and has to date sold about 700,000 copies in the United States. Lady Gaga's next single, "Applause," the lead single of *ARTPOP* that was released in August 2013, reached number four in the United States, where it has to date sold about 2.5 million copies. The song did not reach the number one spot on any major national chart across the world. At the time of this writing, Lady Gaga's best-selling singles in the United States are "Poker Face" (7.3 million), "Just Dance" (7.1 million), "Bad Romance" (5.6 million), "Born This Way" (4.1 million), and "Paparazzi" (3.5 million) (Trust 2016).

As a final source of a music-related revenue stream, Lady Gaga's concert tours have also generated much income for the singer. The Fame Ball tour in Spring and Summer of 2009 was mostly held at small venues and largely had a promotional function to expose the singer to a wider audience. Lady Gaga's next headlining tour, however, the Monster Ball which began following the release of "Bad Romance" at the theater level and which, taking advantage of Lady Gaga's rise to global fame thereafter, moved to arenas from February 2010 onwards, was enormously successful. While the Fame Ball tour had brought in only about $3 million, the Monster Ball eventually raked in a staggering $227 million on a total of more than 200 shows between November 2009 and May 2011. The tour is the 13th highest-grossing tour of the 2010s decade. Lady Gaga's next world tour, the Born This Way Ball, was originally slated to bring in $200 million, but eventually grossed $168 million when several of its final shows had to be canceled because the singer needed to undergo hip surgery in the Spring of 2013 (Forbes website). Following the commercially somewhat less successful *ARTPOP* album, its accompanying artRAVE tour consisted of 79 shows between May and November 2014 for a gross income of $83 million, ranking seventh among worldwide tours in 2014 (Pollstar 2014).

The Cheek To Cheek concert series with Tony Bennett and Lady Gaga grossed $15 million worldwide, but consisted of only some three dozen shows in theaters and at jazz festivals.

Perhaps an even better indication of the wealth that came with Lady Gaga's rise to fame are some of her known expenditures. Whereas the Fame Ball tour and theater version of the Monster Ball in 2009 were actually not profitable by themselves (but may have helped to generate other forms of income), some of the special costs involved were not only made in view of future earnings but were also due to the singer's lavish spending habits on clothes, staging, uniquely designed television performances, and the likes. In the early years of her fame, Lady Gaga did not own a house or apartment, but lived in expensive hotels unless she stayed with her parents or friends. That situation changed when in 2013 she began renting a reasonably modest, but fairly expensive, two-bedroom apartment on New York's Central Park South. More indicative still of her immense wealth by means of the ability to spend money, in 2014 Lady Gaga bought an ocean-view gated villa in Malibu for $23 million (Beale 2014).

The Lady Gaga Industry

The advent of the internet and, especially, the development of file-hosting websites and the spread of downloading (involving a de-materialization of music as a product) have drastically changed the landscape of the record industry. While recordings in the form of vinyl, cassette, and CD were an essential element of the music industry for almost the entire twentieth century, since recently other avenues have had to be devised to secure the necessary economic basis of a professional music career and its associated fame in pop culture. The fame of Lady Gaga can in this respect serve to analyze how economic success in the world of popular music today is still possible. Pondering on the conditions of Lady Gaga's economic success, the development of the Lady Gaga industry has been enabled by a large team of associates and various ways to monetize her fame beyond the selling of music itself.[2]

The Lady Gaga Team

No artist stands alone. Behind and with Lady Gaga, a team of people are involved who contribute to support and develop her artistry and directly and indirectly enable and secure the economic health of her career.

Reviewing the most important players in the world of Lady Gaga, mention must first be made of her father, Joe Germanotta, who originally set up the company Mermaid Music Inc. in equal partnership with his daughter to represent her in her business dealings. He has since also remained involved in the singer's career, often accompanying her on her concert tours, and also taking on formal duties, for instance as President of House of Gaga Publishing, Lady Gaga's music publishing company. Besides the music producers that helped to create the Lady Gaga sound, such as Rob Fusari, RedOne, and DJ White Shadow, a large number of other important artistic personnel are involved with building Lady Gaga's artistry and indirectly contributing to build and expand her career. Collectively referred to as the Haus of Gaga, they include choreographers, fashion stylists, makeup artists, creative directors, and personal assistants.

In terms of the business aspects of her recording career, Lady Gaga's main associates include Interscope A&R representative Vincent Herbert (who is also the chair of Streamline Records), founder of Cherrytree Records Martin Kierszenbaum, record label owner and singer Akon of Kon Live Distribution, and Interscope co-founder and chairman Jimmy Iovine (replaced in the latter function by John Janick in 2014). Lady Gaga's first album, *The Fame*, was released under the umbrella of Interscope with all three other just mentioned record labels which are imprints of Interscope, which itself is owned by Universal Music Group, one of the four largest international record companies today (Wikström 2009:71–84). Since then, Lady Gaga's subsequent albums were released without involvement from Cherrytree Records, while Kon Live's share was sold to Interscope after the release of the *Born This Way* album.

Indicating the complexity of the music industry today, many other people are involved in a host of business functions associated with Lady Gaga. Examples include legal representatives, tour managers and promoters, concert staging designers, talent agency representatives, and personal managers. Among these, special mention can be made of former and current personal managers, Troy Carter, who worked with Lady Gaga since her discovery by Vincent Herbert in 2007 until November 2013, and Bobby Campbell, who took over after Carter's dismissal. It was while she was managed by Troy Carter that Lady Gaga experienced her rise to fame as her career changed drastically from that of an unknown to a global pop sensation (Sacks 2014). In 2007, Carter formed the management and production company Coalition Media Group, and in 2010 he set up Atom Factory to oversee the career of Lady Gaga and a small number of other lesser-known acts. Among the successful strategies employed during Carter's management, Lady Gaga's career was targeted to be built from the ground up, specifically by initially, in 2008, giving exposure to the singer via a multitude of performances at small clubs in order to reach "the first 50," as the philosophy of finding the first 50 fans was described, and subsequently move up from there (Suster 2016). As that strategy worked, Lady Gaga could gradually move up to performing at the level of theaters and arenas, at the same time relying on an increasing number and variety of media, such as radio, television, and internet (see Chap. 6).

In the years when Lady Gaga's success and fame expanded, the singer's relationship with her personal manager was one she herself described as a friendship and which produced many success stories in terms of album and single sales, concert tours, and related business ventures. According to Carter, his working relationship with Lady Gaga was based on an informal "95–95" principle, meaning that 95 % of the time the manager would not involve himself with creative decisions, while 95 % of the time Lady Gaga would not interfere in the business side of things (TechCrunch YouTube video). Describing the relationship as essentially involving a high degree of trust, the partnership rather suddenly and unexpectedly ended on November 4, 2013, when Lady Gaga fired Carter, just one week before the release of her album *ARTPOP*. The day before, the singer was seen crying during a live performance of her song "Dope" on the YouTube Music Awards, possibly indicating she had reached her decision to dismiss Carter. The reason for the split has not unexpectedly been reported to involve creative differences (Hampp 2013), but Carter's turn toward involving his business ventures more heavily into the direction of investing in technology companies (such as Uber, Spotify, and Dropbox) may also have influenced the break up. On a December 2014 episode of the Howard Stern radio show, Lady Gaga spoke of business decisions Carter had executed unilaterally, in the period when she was recovering from hip surgery, even though her interests were directly involved. Since his hiring in 2013, Lady Gaga's new personal manager (and the singer's former assistant manager) Bobby Campbell has brought the singer under Artist Nation, the management branch of Live Nation, which oversees the careers of more than 350 major artists via over 100 personal managers (Sisario 2014). The move came after Lady Gaga's *ARTPOP* album and accompanying artRAVE tour had failed to attract a wide audience outside of the star's loyal fan base and was also critically not always well received (Sheffield 2014). The jazz tour with Tony Bennett and various performances outside the world of pop and dance throughout 2015 and the early part of 2016 enabled not only a more diverse but also more widely acceptable Lady Gaga (see Chap. 10).

It is useful to ask the question why Lady Gaga could rely on the dedicated support of an obviously great creative and business team even before her career was to take off. Building on the talent of Lady Gaga as a composer, musician, and performer, former manager Carter and current manager Campbell and many others working with the singer have regularly confirmed, that the singer was never promoted as a brand but as a gifted artist, one who is talented, unique, and different. This focused attention to Lady Gaga from before the days of her fame has been enabled by the development of the star system in the music industry, whereby some, very few performers are treated with special consideration while a host of other acts are largely ignored. As musical tastes change and media technologies are constantly changing, the volatility of the popular music market generates a risk-management system whereby a few anticipated blockbuster performers receive particular attention.

From the moment she was discovered by Vincent Herbert and introduced to Troy Carter and Jimmy Iovine, Lady Gaga has indeed been treated as a potential superstar on a worldwide scale, "an artist who should have a 40 or 50 year career," to use the words of manager Carter, for whom it is worthwhile to maintain a "global infrastructure" that operates 24/7 (in LeBlanc 2010). Under the star system, the estimated potential of a special talent leads to concentrate efforts on a few select performers, such as Lady Gaga, not so much to nurture that talent for artistic reasons but to generate spectacular profits to offset losses elsewhere. As such, Lady Gaga not only benefits from the star system to develop her career and enable her fame, she does so by definition at the expense of many others. Success and fame in popular music are part of a zero-sum game. Moreover, in return for the special attention she receives from her record company, Lady Gaga has agreed to a so-called 360 deal, a contract arrangement whereby not only recordings but also touring, merchandising, and other revenue streams are shared (Jurgensen 2010). The agreement specifies that the record company is also involved in investing and supporting revenue-generating activities besides recorded music in return for a share in the profits on these. Also referred to as a "multiple rights deal," this new type of contract has become more popular, at least among record companies, because of dwindling sales in recorded music.

Gaga Company Tie-Ins and Sponsorships

From a profit-generating viewpoint, Lady Gaga does not just make money from the sale of recorded music and concert tickets alone. The singer also entertains so-called tie-ins or brand partnerships with (other) brands and products, which are meant to generate profit and help sell Lady Gaga's artistic products. In the case of Lady Gaga, most of these tie-ins can be said to connect relatively closely with her artistic endeavors and image.[3] Among the many examples that can be mentioned, songs of Lady Gaga's debut album *The Fame* were used in a video game called Tap Tap Revenge. The album was not only released in multiple formats and editions (see Chap. 6) but was also issued on an mp3 player manufactured by Korean company iRiver. In 2009, Lady Gaga teamed up with Monster Cable to sell her own brand of headphones, the so-called Monster HeartBeats, released under the very successful line of headsets called Beats By Dr. Dre. Coinciding with the release of the *Born This Way* album in 2011, the follow-up model HeartbeatsV2 was released.

Brand partnerships with Lady Gaga have also been set up with a variety of media outlets to ensure distribution of her music and videos. Some of Lady Gaga's music videos, for instance, were first aired exclusively on certain television channels (e.g., the video to the song "Telephone" premiered on the E! channel), popular TV shows (e.g., the video of "The Edge of Glory" was first shown on So You Think You Can Dance), and via video games, such as when the *Born This Way* album could first be heard and downloaded via a specially designed GagaVille as part of the FarmVille game released by Zynga. Of all Lady Gaga albums, *Born This Way* received the most lavish sponsorship support when it was released in May 2011, including partnerships with Starbucks, Vevo, HBO television, iTunes, Best Buy, and other companies (Hernandez 2011). A deluxe double-CD edition of the album was also slated to be sold only at Target stores, until the exclusivity of the CD sale was lifted over alleged problems concerning some of the retail company's donations to politicians thought to be unkind toward gay rights (Oldenburg 2011). The *Born This Way* album was successfully promoted by Starbucks, which later also sold a special edition of the *Cheek To Cheek* album with Tony Bennett, as well as via a so-called Gaga Workshop that was set up at Barneys New York. The 2013 album *ARTPOP* was less heavily promoted than *Born This Way* but still enjoyed several company tie-ins, such as with Best Buy which used the "Do What U Want" track in a television advertisement for Beats by Dre and with car manufacturer Kia whose ad for its Soul model featured the *ARTPOP* lead single "Applause."

Many more brand partnerships can be mentioned, ranging from corporate tie-ins related to Lady Gaga's charities and activism (see Chap. 8) to financially lucrative private event concerts, such as a complete artRAVE show that was held as a private event for Microsoft (Brett 2014) and a live performance with Tony Bennett that was organized for *Bloomberg Businessweek* (Garvey et al. 2014). Other brand partnerships are established independently from Lady Gaga's music releases, such as in 2016 when it was announced that Lady Gaga is collaborating with Mattel to create a doll in the singer's likeness as a special limited-edition release in the successful Monster High series. From a purely financial viewpoint, arguably the single most successful sponsorship venture Lady Gaga has engaged in are the fragrances that were launched in association with the singer. Created under the umbrella of Lady Gaga's Haus Laboratories, two fragrances were launched by manufacturer Coty: Lady Gaga FAME in August 2012 and Eau de Gaga in August 2014. The fragrance FAME, marketed as the "first ever black eau de parfum," was introduced via a massive promotion campaign, including a performance art event at the Guggenheim museum, where Lady Gaga was seen sleeping in a giant FAME perfume bottle (and peed in a champagne bottle when she awoke, then got a new tattoo), and via campaigns in Macy's stores in the United States. Within about half a year, the fragrance had sold 30 million bottles, generating a reported $1.5 billion (The Data Lounge).

Closely related to Lady Gaga's prominent presence in online media (Chap. 6), several of the singer's tie-ins have involved technology companies. On March 22, 2011, internet giant Google organized a "Google Goes Gaga" event at the company's headquarters in San Francisco, a video of which was released online later that day (Talks At Google YouTube video). At the 2016 Grammys, moreover, Lady Gaga partnered with technology giant Intel to create a special effects performance of the singer's singing of a medley of David Bowie songs. It is interesting to note that not all of the Lady Gaga-related tie-ins have been effective, either for the singer or for the company with which she has partnered. The best example in this respect is the partnership with famed electronics company Polaroid. In January 2010, it was announced that Lady Gaga would become a creative director for the company and help launch a new series of products seeking to bring instant picture cameras back (Golijan 2011). Announced as a multi-year partnership, specifically planned were a Bluetooth-enabled printer called Polaroid Grey Label, camera glasses, and digital cameras. However, while the printer was released in May 2011, it was not successful and no additional Gaga-related Polaroid products have been released since (Bradley 2014). Likewise, a set of Gaga-branded electronic sunglasses modeled after the ones the performer wore during the Fame Ball tour were never produced (Smillie 2009).

As much as certain products are used to help sell Lady Gaga and her music, the singer herself has also been engaged in the selling of products. Distinct from tie-ins, though accomplished for similar financial reasons, Lady Gaga relies on various forms of business sponsorships whereby companies directly provide revenue to Lady Gaga in return for promotion. By example, the highly successful Monster Ball Tour (2010–2011) was sponsored by Virgin Mobile. The communications company had its logo plastered everywhere possible at the venue where a Lady Gaga Monster Ball concert was held. A Virgin Mobile photo booth was set up to take pictures of fans, a selection of which was placed online at the site ladyvirginmobile.com. Virgin Mobile was also involved in sponsorship for the Born This Way Ball concert tour as was telecommunications company Skype Technologies, which set up a Skype Ball website and held a contest to award a lucky winner the chance to Skype with Lady Gaga (Hampp 2014). Later tour support has come from the Swedish liquor company Absolut Vodka, which supported Lady Gaga's artRAVE world tour of 2014, among other efforts in the form of a bar at the show for meet and greet ticket holders (Live Nation 2014).

Especially noteworthy is the sponsorship Lady Gaga has received in the form of product placement in many of her videos, thereby securing monetary support from companies as diverse as a gambling website, a brand of watches, and a variety of beverages. Some of these consumer goods were apparently chosen because they were thought to have an "organic" connection with Lady Gaga's artistic endeavors (Hampp 2010). But besides headphones, a whole range of other products have been featured in Lady Gaga videos as well, including alcoholic beverages and condiments. Among the companies present in videos from her first album *The Fame* are Beats by Dr. Dre ("Just Dance"), gambling site bwin.com, Beats headphones, Casio watches ("Poker Face," "Eh, Eh"), liquor company Campari ("LoveGame"), and energy drink Neuro Sonic ("Paparazzi"). The video to the song "Telephone," released in March 2010, featured about a dozen such product placements, including technology giant Hewlett-Packard, LG Electronics, the PlentyofFish dating site, and Miracle Whip. As the video was cleverly construed as a commentary on consumerism, it also featured products, such as Wonder Bread and Diet Coke, that were placed in the video for artistic reasons and for which no monetary compensation was received.

Lady Gaga as Product

As with most of all professional musicians that seek to establish their own independent career today, Lady Gaga derives more revenue from touring and merchandising than from recording sales, sharing all accumulated profits with her record company Interscope as part her "360 deal." A wide range of Lady Gaga products, such as t-shirts, posters, costumes, wigs, key chains, phone cases, beach towels, and a toothbrush, can be bought at her concerts or online at her Bravado store. Even as the sales of CDs have dwindled and digital files can easily be shared, Lady Gaga still epitomizes the present-day pop star who knows how to sell merchandise, including CDs and downloads, in the post-record age, a strategy that relates closely to the role of media in the singer's music and fame (see Chap. 6).

Looking at the selling of Lady Gaga products from a business viewpoint, it is critical to observe that what comes to mind when we speak of Lady Gaga are not merely the catchy pop tunes and dance beats she and her producers have created but also the strong visual images and fashion styles the performer has become known for. In view of the construction of her fame, in particular, the image of Lady Gaga is at least as, if not more important than her music. For while all artists intent on building a professional career need to package and present their art in some specific form toward an audience, some artists are clearly more image-minded than others. In this context, Lady Gaga can be seen to present a versatile product that is always more than mere musical sounds alone. Indicating a critical sign of the times since the rise of downloading, especially its legal form via iTunes, and continuing on with the recent popularity of streaming services, the music industry today cannot survive by selling recorded music alone, changing the role of musical storage to the core of a more broadly conceived and diversified product. Along with other pop stars whose careers took off at the time of Lady Gaga's rise to fame since her fist recoded music was released in 2008, Lady Gaga belongs to a new kind of popular music performers for whom more than recorded sound would have to become a product of music.

Intricately connected with Lady Gaga's music, therefore, the singer's public persona also involves her perceived to be shocking fashion choices, her look and her vision, as well as, on a more content-oriented level, her activism, her outspokenness, her sense of being different, and, more generally, her involvement in establishing outreach toward her fans and those she perceives to be deserving of special consideration. As such, Lady Gaga essentially exemplifies product differentiation, the eccentric nature of which has indeed been found to affect appreciation of her work (Van Tilburg and Igou 2014). As discussed in more detail later in this book (Chaps. 6 and 7), Lady Gaga and her team have relied on various media to connect effectively with a truly global audience in many different ways at once, involving both style and substance, and arousing both controversy and support.

Among the more attention-grabbing aspects of the Lady Gaga image, mention can be made of her stage costumes and album covers which seek to break the mold of the traditional young female pop star. Maintaining her sense that she is always Lady Gaga, the singer also dresses in a manner many will perceive as outlandish or shocking. Most famous perhaps in creating the Lady Gaga image was the meat dress she wore at the 2010 MTV Video Music Awards, where she received a record eight awards. Heavily discussed in the media and online communities, the dress itself acquired its own measure of fame, even obtaining its own page on Wikipedia (Wikipedia "Lady Gaga's Meat Dress"). From the viewpoint of the economics of Lady Gaga, the many aspects of the singer's image can be observed to function as a marketing device, even when it may not be intended as such. For whereas the subjective psychology of Lady Gaga in making certain image choices, or even of the music and other art she makes, is not a determinant of her fame, the inter-subjective recognition thereof among her audience surely is. Moreover, Lady Gaga's image also plays an economic role in the origins of her fame inasmuch as the attention it receives can subsequently also be monetized.

The diversification of the Lady Gaga product is also reflected within the realm of her artistry as her work is presented and has been accepted as uniquely diverse because of its multiple styles and expressions. Stylistically, indeed, Lady Gaga's music is primarily situated in the world of pop, but she is there also considered something of an outsider as she emphasizes her unusual route of getting into pop from a more diverse past that includes a classical piano training, a childhood exposure to rock music, and a deliberate adoption of mixed musical styles, ranging from electronic dance to heavy metal and jazz. Lady Gaga is as such essentially presented as a chameleon (see Chap. 10).

The Economics of Lady Gaga

There is no rational way to deny that Lady Gaga has been able to foster a tremendously successful and financially profitable career, a feat all the more remarkable given the often lamented state of the popular music industry today. However, it need therefore not necessarily be concluded, as some analysts have done, that Lady Gaga is a "branding genius" (DePaz 2012) who is "very calculated" (Brown 2010) and has a special "marketing intuition" (Huba 2013:11). It is not clear, after all, that the singer would be motivated by economic concerns more than by artistic ambitions or that, somehow, a career in the arts in an advanced capitalist society would be possible without a measure of organization. Such positions are not only empirically flawed but also betray one of the central shortcomings in a reductionist approach in that it overlooks that even the very best of music, however it is culturally constructed, has to be advertised and sold. Without organization and business support, no art could ever reach its audience and, hence, could never be art. The idea of the starving artist, after all, can only be sustained posthumously when a lucrative celebrity industry connects itself with someone selected from among the dead. The very notion of popular music as a form of commercial entertainment exemplifies the co-existence of economics and art. Likewise, there can be no fame attained and no revenue acquired in any career based on artistic or other accomplishments unless there is an appropriate supporting infrastructure. Even Mozart had to eat. And, judging from the sheer monetary success of her career alone, Lady Gaga must be eating very well.

However, no matter the talent and skills of Lady Gaga as a performer and no matter the supporting contributions from various members of her artistic team, it would be foolish to claim that there are no economic aspects of marketing involved in promoting her work. Whatever lessons that can be learned from the marketing of Lady Gaga's fame for other artists or other, altogether different products can only be the subject of speculation. The singer's success as a factual outcome does not necessarily imply that it has been largely controlled by the singer and her team, rather than having been facilitated by favorable circumstances. Moreover, the relative singularity of Lady Gaga to launch a globally successful music career at a time when the popular music industry was in decline prevents any wild speculations on what can be learned from her case for the benefit of other artists, let alone for other products. Proposing marketing lessons from Lady Gaga may well reflect a component in the success of her marketing, rather than being a reflection thereon.

Although it can perhaps never be known if or to what extent Lady Gaga herself is driven in whole or in part by financial motivations and commercial intent, the question can be asked to what extent she herself has a role in the marketing of her work and to what extent, conversely, she relegates such activities to her managers and the other members in her organizational support team. There are some objective indications that Lady Gaga is not only a talented artist with a great musical education but also has at least a voice in many of her career decisions. Her former manager Troy Carter has in interviews said that Lady Gaga herself is involved in the business decisions in part because she has some knowledge of the business side of popular music based on her prior work in the music industry and her knowledge of social media (Bloomberg 2015). As an aspiring artist, indeed, Stefani Germanotta worked as an intern at Viacom's Famous Music Publishing in early 2006 (Deflem 2011). Given the success of her father's business career, also, and the close working relationship he has entertained with his daughter, it is more than likely that Lady Gaga has at least a more than average knowledge of the inside workings of the popular music industry.

Especially in today's fragile state of popular music, it can be assumed that all artists will need some business sense to maintain a professional career. What is peculiar about Lady Gaga is how she has embraced such an organizational sense of thinking as part of, rather than despite, her artistic ambitions. Reminiscent of other artists whose popularity has often been misunderstood to imply they were working in entertainment rather than in art, Lady Gaga practices a sense of art where success and authenticity are meant to go hand in hand. For example, despite the concerns that are made over product placement in music videos in terms of its impact on young adults (Eagle and Dahl 2015), Lady Gaga will at once rely and comment on consumerism, as in the "Telephone" video. Similarly, whereas some critics dismiss the "Lady Gaga spectacle" as pure show "with the music an odorless, colorless, almost unnecessary additive" (Caramanica 2009), Lady Gaga and her team emphasize that her work "comes from the heart," to use the words of manager Campbell, even when it generates money as well (Rys 2016). In this context, the best marketing device Lady

Gaga and her team have employed is the one of not having and not needing any marketing device.

Conclusion

The aim of this chapter was not to explore, from a practical viewpoint, which if any marketing lessons can be learned from Lady Gaga, but was instead focused on analyzing the business dimensions of the singer's career sociologically. In view of the spectacular economic success of Lady Gaga, there can be no doubt that the fame of the singer is in some measure associated with the application of a successful business model, specifically by being able to rely on a well-functioning team of collaborators, company tie-ins and sponsorships, and a diversified product of multiple artistic contributions and of Lady Gaga herself in all of her manifestations, including a combination of popular appeal and authenticity.

Lady Gaga's understanding of a commercially viable and artistically authentic self re-connects with what was said in Chap. 3 about the role she sees reserved for her support team in the attainment of fame. But there are limits placed on this collaborative ideal. It is striking in this respect, indeed, to note that while many members of the Lady Gaga team will emphasize their respective role in creating Lady Gaga, the singer will always counteract any such idea and instead emphasize her sense of control over all aspects of her work. Against the notion that others were responsible for her success, she has said, "I am completely self-invented" (in Van Meter 2011) and "ate shit until somebody would listen" (in Grigoriadis 2010). Judging from the dozens of collaborators who have seen their employment with the star terminated in the relatively few years since her rise to fame, the Haus of Gaga clearly has a back door, especially for its members who err in thinking they work *with* Lady Gaga rather than *for* her. The firing of personal manager Troy Carter, who had been with the singer since 2007 all the way through her global stardom, is the most striking example, particularly because it resulted from the star's own decision, the impact of which for her career and fame still remains to be seen (Callahan 2013).

In an interview with *Harper's Bazaar* in 2011, Lady Gaga said, "What means something to me is my music. I don't want to make money; I want to make a difference" (in Blasberg 2011). Whether the statement is accurate is sociologically irrelevant to the fact that Lady Gaga strives to rely on an audience that perceives her to be genuine and anything but calculated. Introducing her song "Money, Honey" at the Monster Ball shows, Lady

Gaga could always be heard to proclaim that she hated money. But, later in the show, she also stated to hate the truth even more. Subjective intentions aside, in terms of the objective consequences of the success of Lady Gaga's career and her conception of art and money as well the singer's own role therein, the fame of Lady Gaga can be observed to have generated economic privileges of such proportions that a considerable form of closure is created as a measure of interpersonal privilege (Kurzman et al. 2007). The elevated status of fame thereby also creates the additional need to attain and secure a special legal privilege to protect acquired goods and rights.

Notes

1. Numerical data in this chapter draw from cited sources as well as selected pages on Gagapedia (Gagapedia website), Forbes.com (Forbes website), The Richest (The Richest website), and the Lady Gaga albums and singles pages on Wikipedia (Wikipedia "Lady Gaga Discography").
2. Selected materials drawn from two small essays on the business of Lady Gaga have been incorporated in this section (Deflem 2012, 2013).
3. Information about all mentioned Lady Gaga-related product tie-ins and endorsement deals was retrieved from Gagapedia (Gagapedia website).

References

Beale, Lauren. 2014. Lady Gaga Buys $23-Million Malibu Estate with Stables, Bowling Alley. *Los Angeles Times*, October 25, 2014. http://www.latimes.com/local/westside/la-fi-hotprop-20141026-story.html

Blasberg, Derek. 2011. Lady Gaga: The Interview. *Harper's Bazaar*, April 13, 2011. http://www.harpersbazaar.com/celebrity/latest/news/a713/lady-gaga-interview/

Bloomberg. 2015. Lady Gaga's Longtime Manager Troy Carter on the Split. Video. *Bloomberg.com*, December 8, 2015. http://www.bloomberg.com/news/videos/2015-12-09/lady-gaga-s-longtime-manager-troy-carter-on-the-split

Bodnar, Kipp. 2011. Marketing Lessons From Lady Gaga. *HubSpot*, May 11, 2011. http://blog.hubspot.com/blog/tabid/6307/bid/13715/Marketing-Lessons-From-Lady-Gaga.aspx

Bradley, Diana. 2014. Polaroid Splits with Creative Director Lady Gaga. *PR Week*, October 2, 2014. http://www.prweek.com/article/1315548/polaroid-splits-creative-director-lady-gaga

Brett, Jennifer. 2014. Lady Gaga Performs Private Concert for Microsoft in Atlanta. *AJC.com*, July 28, 2014. http://www.accessatlanta.com/weblogs/buzz/2014/jul/28/photos-lady-gaga-performs-private-concert-microsof/

Bridges, Frances. 2015. Celebrity Substance: Lady Gaga. *Forbes*, December 31, 2015. http://www.forbes.com/sites/francesbridges/2015/12/31/celebrity-substance-lady-gaga/#37151119672f

Brown, Frederick M. 2010. Lady Gaga's Revelations Calculated? *CBSNews*, September 12, 2010. http://www.cbsnews.com/news/lady-gagas-revelations-calculated/

Callahan, Maureen. 2013. What Happened to Lady Gaga? *The New York Post*, December 14, 2013. http://nypost.com/2013/12/14/what-happened-to-lady-gaga/

Caramanica, Jon. 2009. An Artist Whose Chief Work Is Herself. *The New York Times*, May 3, 2009. http://www.nytimes.com/2009/05/04/arts/music/04gaga.html

Deflem, Mathieu. 2011. Bob Leone and the Sociology of the Fame. *Gagafrontrow.blogspot*, February 12, 2011. http://gagafrontrow.blogspot.com/2011/02/bob-leone.html

———. 2012. Marketing Monster: Selling the Fame of Lady Gaga. In *The Wicked Twins: Fame & Notoriety*. Exhibition catalogue, Paul Robeson Galleries, a program of Rutgers, 30–35. The State University of New Jersey.

———. 2013. Four Truths About Marketing Lady Gaga Lies. *The European Business Review* 70–72.

DePaz, Keisha L. 2012. Brand Marketing: What Startup Founders Can Learn From Lady Gaga. *Under30CEO.com*, December 10, 2012. http://under30ceo.com/brand-marketing-what-startup-founders-can-learn-from-lady-gaga/

Eagle, Lynne, and Stephan Dahl. 2015. Product Placement in Old and New Media: Examining the Evidence for Concern. *Journal of Business Ethics*. http://download.springer.com/static/pdf/786/art%253A10.1007%252Fs10551-015-2955-z.pdf

Forbes. Website. http://www.forbes.com/

Frith, Simon. 2001. The Popular Music Industry. In *The Cambridge Companion to Pop and Rock*, eds. Simon Frith, Will Straw, and John Street, 26–52. Cambridge, UK: Cambridge University Press.

Gagapedia. Website. http://ladygaga.wikia.com/wiki/Gagapedia

Garvey, Marianne, Brian Niemietz, and Oli Coleman. 2014. Tony Bennett and Lady Gaga Bring Their 'Cheek'-y Act to Michael Bloomberg's Business Week Bash. *New York Daily News*, December 2, 2014. http://www.nydailynews.

com/entertainment/gossip/confidential/tony-bennett-lady-gaga-big-business-gig-article-1.2029584

Golijan, Rosa. 2011. This is What Happens When Polaroid Lets Lady Gaga Design Something. *Jezebel*, January 7, 2011. http://jezebel.com/5727101/this-is-what-happens-when-polaroid-lets-lady-gaga-design-something

Grigoriadis, Vanessa. 2010. Growing Up Gaga. *New York Magazine*, March 28, 2010. http://nymag.com/arts/popmusic/features/65127/

Hampp, Andrew. 2010. How Miracle Whip, Plenty of Fish Tapped Lady Gaga's 'Telephone'. *AdvertisingAge*, March 13, 2010. http://adage.com/article/madisonvine-news/miracle-whip-plenty-fish-tap-lady-gaga-s-telephone/142794/

———. 2013. Lady Gaga-Troy Carter Split: What Happened, the Future and Why it's Business as Usual for Now. *Billboard*, November 08, 2013. http://www.billboard.com/biz/articles/news/legal-and-management/5785549/lady-gaga-troy-carter-split-what-happened-the-future

———. 2014. Skype, Live Nation Team For 'Ones To Watch' Concert Series At House of Blues (Exclusive). *Billboard*, February 6, 2014. http://www.billboard.com/biz/articles/news/5900934/skype-live-nation-team-for-ones-to-watch-concert-series-at-house-of-blues

Hernandez, Brian Anthony. 2011. How Lady Gaga Created a Web Marketing Spectacle for Born This Way. *CherylWaller.com*, May 24, 2011. http://www.cherylwaller.com/blog/2011/05/24/how-lady-gaga-created-a-web-marketing-spectacle-for-born-this-way-pics/

Huba, Jackie. 2013. *Monster Loyalty: How Lady Gaga Turns Followers into Fanatics*. New York: Portfolio/Penguin.

Jurgensen, John. 2010. The Lessons of Lady Gaga. *The Wall Street Journal*, January 29, 2010. http://www.wsj.com/articles/SB10001424052748704094304575029621644867154

Kurzman, Charles, Chelise Anderson, Clinton Key, Youn Ok Lee, Mairead Moloney, Alexis Silver, and Maria W. Van Ryn. 2007. Celebrity Status. *Sociological Theory* 25: 347–367.

LeBlanc, Larry. 2010. Industry Profile: Troy Carter. *CelebrityAccess*, June 7, 2010. http://www.celebrityaccess.com/members/profile.html?id=515

Live Nation. 2014. Absolut Goes Gaga. Press release. May 1, 2014. http://investors.livenationentertainment.com/news-center/news-center-details/2014/ABSOLUT-GOES-GAGA/default.aspx

Machan, Dyan. 2011. Lady Gaga: Small Business-Icon. *Smart Money*, October 4, 2011. http://www.smartmoney.com/small-business/small-business/lady-gaga-smallbusiness-icon-1315005144884/

Makarechi, Kia. 2013. Lady Gaga, Forbes' Highest-Earning Celebrity Under 30, Beats Justin Bieber For Title. *Forbes*, July 23, 2013. http://www.huffingtonpost.com/2013/07/23/lady-gaga-forbes-highest-earning-celebrity-under--30_n_3639410.html

Marfil, Hannah Raissa. 2015. With $59 Million, Lady Gaga Ranks High on Forbes List of Top Earners for 2015. *International Business Times*, June 30, 2015. http://www.ibtimes.com/59-million-lady-gaga-ranks-high-forbes-list-top-earners-2015-1989772

Newman, Melinda. 2011. What Lady Gaga's Falling 'Born This Way' Sales Numbers Tell Us. *HitFix*, June 23, 2011. http://www.hitfix.com/blogs/the-beat-goes-on/posts/what-lady-gagas-falling-born-this-way-sales-numbers-tell-us

Nobel, Carmen. 2011. HBS Cases: Lady Gaga. *Harvard Business School*, September 26, 2011. http://hbswk.hbs.edu/item/6812.html

O'Malley Greenburg, Zack. 2013. The World's Highest-Paid Musicians 2013. *Forbes*, November 19, 2013. http://www.forbes.com/sites/zackomalleygreenburg/2013/11/19/the-worlds-highest-paid-musicians-2013/

Oldenburg, Ann. 2011. Lady Gaga Ends Deal with Target over Gay Issues. *USA Today*, March 9, 2011. http://content.usatoday.com/communities/entertainment/post/2011/03/lady-gaga-ends-deal-with-target-over-gay-issues/1#.Vz3edWMqQ7k

Peters, Georgina. 2011. Lady Gaga, Guru: More Than Meets the Eye? *Business Strategy Review* 22(2): 69–71.

Pollstar. 2014. *2014 Pollstar Year End Top 20 Worldwide Tours*. http://www.pollstarpro.com/files/charts2014/2014YearendTop20WorldwideTours.pdf

Pomerantz, Dorothy. 2011. Lady Gaga Tops Celebrity 100 List. *Forbes*, May 18, 2011. http://www.forbes.com/2011/05/16/lady-gaga-tops-celebrity-100-11.html

Rys, Dan. 2016. 'What Can We Help You Achieve?' Lady Gaga's Manager and Branding Experts Mull the New Normal. *Billboard*, March 17, 2016. http://www.billboard.com/articles/business/7263735/sxsw-2016-branding-lady-gaga-mac-presents

Sacks, Danielle. 2014. Troy Carter: Fired by Lady Gaga and Loving It. *FastCompany*, January 13, 2014. http://www.fastcompany.com/3024171/step-up-troy-carter

Sheffield, Rob. 2014. Lady Gaga's Live Artflop: NYC Ghosts and Flowers. *Rolling Stone*, May 14, 2014. http://www.rollingstone.com/music/news/lady-gagas-live-artflop-nyc-ghosts-and-flowers-20140514

Sisario, Ben. 2011. In Lady Gaga's Album, Evidence of a New Order. *The New York Times*, June 1, 2011. http://www.nytimes.com/2011/06/02/arts/music/lady-gagas-born-this-way-shows-albums-new-role.html?_r=1

———. 2014. Lady Gaga Becomes a Live Nation Client. *The New York Times*, June 11, 2014. http://www.nytimes.com/2014/06/12/business/media/lady-gaga-becomes-a-live-nation-client.html

Smillie, Dirk. 2009. The Business of Lady Gaga. *Forbes*, November 25, 2009. http://www.forbes.com/2009/11/25/lady-gaga-music-business-entertainment-marketing.html

Suster, Mark. 2016. Spotting, Nurturing and Mentoring Talent – The Power of Troy Carter. *Both Sides of the Table*, February 26, 2016. http://www.bothsideofthetable.com/2016/02/26/spotting-nurturing-and-mentoring-talent-the-power-of-troy-carter/
Talks At Google. Lady Gaga: 'Google Goes Gaga' | Musicians at Google. *YouTube video*, uploaded March 22, 2011. https://www.youtube.com/watch?v=hNa_-1d_0tA
TechCrunch. Atom Factory's Troy Carter on Music Technology | Disrupt NY 2013. *YouTube video*, uploaded April 30, 2013. https://www.youtube.com/watch?v=jOQTgNtscrE
The Data Lounge. Lady Gaga FAME Sells 30million, Grosses $1.6billion! https://www.datalounge.com/thread/12450526-lady-gaga-fame-sells-30million-grosses-1.6billion!
The Richest. Website. http://www.therichest.com/
Trust, Gary. 2016. Ask Billboard: Lady Gaga's Sales & What's the Longest Streak for Americans Atop the Hot 100? *Billboard*, April 17, 2016. http://www.billboard.com/articles/columns/chart-beat/7334121/ask-billboard-lady-gagas-sales-whats-the-longest-streak-for
Van Meter, Jonathan. 2011. Lady Gaga: Our Lady of Pop. *Vogue*, February 10. http://www.vogue.com/865458/lady-gaga-our-lady-of-pop/
Van Tilburg, Wijnand A.P., and Eric R. Igou. 2014. From Van Gogh to Lady Gaga: Artist Eccentricity Increases Perceived Artistic Skill and Art Appreciation. *European Journal of Social Psychology* 44(2): 93–103.
Wikipedia. 2016a. Lady Gaga Discography. https://en.wikipedia.org/wiki/Lady_Gaga_discography
———. 2016b. Lady Gaga's Meat Dress. https://en.wikipedia.org/wiki/Lady_Gaga%27s_meat_dress
Wikström, Patrik. 2009. *The Music Industry: Music in the Cloud*. Cambridge, UK: Polity.
Yohn, Denise Lee. 2012. What You Can Learn from Lady Gaga. *QSR Magazine*, June 2012. http://www.qsrmagazine.com/denise-lee-yohn/what-you-can-learn-lady-gaga
———. 2014. Lady Gaga Is Still Schooling Marketers. *Forbes*, July 16, 2014. http://www.forbes.com/sites/deniselyohn/2014/07/16/lady-gaga-is-still-schooling-marketers/

CHAPTER 5

The Laws of Lady Gaga

It is a distinct sign of the relative poverty of celebrity studies, as it often is of any specialty field that is defined in terms of its material subject matter rather than an appropriate analytical outlook, that other areas and perspectives of inquiry are not adequately taken into account, even when their relevance is unquestionable. Thus, fame and celebrity scholars will know a lot about relevant social dimensions and mechanisms without connecting their findings with other specializations of study to make sense of what is known. For that reason alone, it was important in the context of this book to set up this sociological study of the fame of a pop star, not in terms of research on the fame of other pop sensations but in terms of perspectives and questions in the sociology of popular culture and music. Because closely connected to the business theme addressed in the previous chapter there are legal issues involved in the entire process of fame, it is therefore also necessary to entertain theoretical perspectives in the sociology of law, or the broader field of law and social science, in order to make sense of the role of law in society, in general, and the role of law in the world of entertainment, in particular.

Different avenues can be pursued in the sociology of law to address the quantitative and qualitative shifts that pertain to the legal dimensions of fame in popular culture, from the classical approaches of Max Weber and Emile Durkheim to the modern sociological understanding of law from the wide variety of theoretical pluralism that, for better or worse, marks sociology until today (Deflem 2008). Sociologists can learn from Weber the need to focus on the procedural aspects of law to guarantee law under specified conditions (of due process) and from Durkheim the development of legal norms under conditions of substantive cultural changes (of increasing individualism). Importantly, and harmonizing with the general analytical approach that is adopted in this book on fame and music, the sociological study of law always implies a study of law in society, not of law as such. This attention to the study of the social dimensions of law is among the central characteristics that sets the sociology of law as a social science apart from jurisprudence as the internal study of law (such as it practiced in law schools).

Taking the best of what sociology's founders and modern developers have had to offer, the theory of law that has been developed by Donald Black may count among the sharpest manifestations of what a distinctly sociological approach to law has to offer, especially when it comes to analyzing the conditions of the behavior of law, both quantitatively and qualitatively (Black 1976). Today most commonly referred to as pure sociology, Black's approach will be relied upon in this chapter, not to test the theory at a general level but to make sense of the case of Lady Gaga's legal entanglements that began to manifest themselves alongside of her rise to fame. I will first present a basic introduction to the perspective of the pure sociology of law and indicate its most useful propositions for the study of law and fame. I will then explain the most important legal issues and lawsuits Lady Gaga has encountered from the beginning of her career to her standing as a commercially successful pop sensation, and subsequently unravel its course and dynamics from the stated theoretical perspective.

The Behavior of Law in Society

Donald Black's pure sociology of law formulates a theory on the behavior of law as a social phenomenon as part of a science of study understood, appropriately indeed, as the study of empirical variation in social life (Black 1976, 1995, 1998). In line with the general sociological perspective adopted in this book, pure sociology does not entertain any normative value judgments on its subject manner, say on the relative merit of certain artistic contributions or on what constitutes art, and instead, externally observes any social event or cultural construct within its location in society. The contextual nature of social phenomena is referred to as their social geometry. The goal of a pure sociology of law, then, is to analyze the conditions under which law behaves within society.

Among the central strengths of Black's approach is its integrative power to bring various strands of sociological thinking together in an encompassing framework of a multi-dimensional social space. As such, the theory can lead to predictions on multiple aspects of law or, as in this chapter, to make sense of the case of the legalities involved with Lady Gaga's rise to fame within a more encompassing framework. The dependent variable of law is measured both quantitatively in terms of its amount and qualitatively in terms of kind. In the case of the legal activities surrounding an increasingly famous and successful pop star like Lady Gaga, the amount of law that is attracted can be expected to increase as more law is involved in the very constitution of a professional musician (as a legal entity) and legal actions become more likely because of increased visibility. Qualitatively, law can vary in kind, such as in the form of criminal law oriented at punishment or as civil law involving monetary compensation. For reasons of its location in the lucrative free market of pop music, the case of Lady Gaga may be assumed to attract law that has financial repercussions, for which reason civil litigation rather than criminal prosecution can be expected as the primary form of fame-related law.

The predictions on the quantitative and qualitative direction of legal activity surrounding Lady Gaga may not be surprising, but, importantly, the explanatory framework from a pure sociology viewpoint is decidedly placed at the social rather than individual level. Indeed, rather than relying on a psychology of motives and intentions, the social geometry of law analyzes the location and direction of legal behavior along the lines of the social characteristics of stratification, morphology, culture, organization, and social control (Black 1976, 1998:158–162). Briefly explained in general terms, stratification refers to the vertical space in social life, which can be more or less equal or unequal, positioned higher and lower, and downward and upward in direction. Referring to the horizontal dimension of society, morphology implies the degree of differentiation and differences in terms of relative intimacy and distance. Culture is the symbolic space of society in relation to knowledge, ethics, and aesthetics, which can be more or less conventional and closely related or not, while organization or corporate space refers to the extent to which a community is formally organized. Social control is the normative aspect of society to handle cases of right and wrong through both more and less formal mechanisms.

From the viewpoint of the social geometry perspective, various propositions can be developed to order reality in terms of all similar cases of law and conflict resolution, whether they be formal law in Western societies or informal forms of normative regulation in small communities (Black 1976). Hence, the theory is meant to be a general one, accounting for variation among all cases of similar phenomena, such as law, art, and ideas, yet it should also be capable of accounting for the dynamics of each social phenomenon on the basis of its within-case characteristics in terms of its location in social space. In this chapter, I will use the legal activities surrounding Lady Gaga as an illustration of the perspective of the social geometry of law. Because of its illustrative status relative to the employed theory, the case of the legalities surrounding Lady Gaga will first be empirically described, after which an appropriate model of explanation will be developed.

Litigating Lady Gaga

Lady Gaga is not only a performer and, from the viewpoint of law, is not even primarily a performer but a legal entity as well. As mentioned in the previous chapter, for business-related contractual purposes, Lady Gaga is legally constituted as the domestic limited liability company Mermaid Music, LLC. Initially formed in March 2005 under GuestWifi, the Wi-Fi business of Lady Gaga's father Joe Germanotta, the company was introduced as Mermaid Music a year later, right before the singer then-named Stefani Germanotta would go on to sign her first production deal with Rob Fusari. Related Lady Gaga companies are Mermaid Touring, Inc., which was established in April 2008 with Stefani Germanotta as Chief Executive Officer (CEO), and Mermaid Music Management, Inc., which was set up in March 2014 with father Germanotta as CEO.[1] The latter company was established since newly hired personal manager Bobby Campbell brought Lady Gaga under the management division of Live Nation. Further, the trademark rights of Lady Gaga are since 2010 represented by Ate My Heart, Inc., while her publishing interests are overseen by House of Gaga Publishing. Since 2010, several dozen legal cases have taken place that concern various interests of Lady Gaga, including some 35 trademark filings, about half a dozen cases of copyright infringement, and at least eight lawsuits involving various contractual matters concerning the singer. Reviewing these cases thematically will allow their main dynamics to be revealed in terms of the behavior of fame-related law.

Trademark: Securing thy Gaga Name

Trademark laws regulate central aspects of the name that is Lady Gaga. The right of trademark is legally defined as a form of a property right whereby the owner can exercise certain rights to have a name associated with certain products. In the United States, the trademark must be applied for and approved by the US Patent and Trademark Office in the Department of Commerce. To assure the right to use the name of Lady Gaga and some of its associated names on a variety of products, Ate My Heart has to date successfully been granted about 50 trademarks (Trademarkia website). They include the right to use the name "Lady Gaga" for at least five categories of products, including audio and video recordings, lipsticks, fragrances and personal care products, and various types of clothing. They further include the names of several Lady Gaga song titles, such as "Bad Romance," "Monster," and "ARTPOP," for several goods and services such as tote bags and T-shirts as well as many other consumer products varying from the streaming of audio and video to soaps, jewelry, furniture, wine, perfume, and personal care products for pets that are trademarked for such names as "Haus of Gaga" (the name of Lady Gaga's creative team), "Little Monsters" (the name she coined for her fans), "Jo Calderone" (a male performance alter ego of the singer), and "Miss Asia Kinney" (the name of her dog).

Between March 2010 and December 2015, at least 35 trademark claims were filed by Ate My Heart against various companies.[2] These filings concern the use of several names, including "Gagafit," "Lady Agha," "Gaga's Garden," and "Golden Gaga," for various product categories, such as clothing, skin care products, ball chain bracelets, telephones, and footwear. Only a few of these cases have received any kind of public attention and most, if not all, seem to have been judged in favor of Lady Gaga's Ate My Heart as the plaintiff or claimant. A closer look at the cases that have received some attention in the news media or on which more information could be retrieved offers an interesting glimpse into some of the issues involved.

In 2011, a trademark filing by Ate My Heart was issued against Mind Candy and Moshi Music over a song by a character called "Lady Goo Goo" that was part of the online children's game Mind Candy (Sweney 2011). It was ruled that the song could not be released on iTunes. In the same year, trademark was claimed against the ice cream brand "Baby Gaga" that prides itself on selling ice cream made from breast milk (Kaplan

2011; United States Patent and Trademark Office 2013). The filing was based on the notion that the terms "Baby" and "Lady" were so similar that the ice cream would be understood by consumers to be connected to and endorsed by the singer, additionally charging that the waitress serving the treat is dressed in one of the fashion styles Lady Gaga is well known for. As Lady Gaga's company lost the case, Baby Gaga ice cream is being sold until this day.

Another trademark case of 2011 concerned a case brought on behalf of Lady Gaga, named as Stefani Germanotta, against the domain owner called "Oranges arecool XD" for maintaining the domain name "ladygaga.org" (Lipman 2011; National Arbitration Forum 2011). The case is interesting because it involved a claim against a private person who was a fan of the singer as well as because Lady Gaga lost the case. While Lady Gaga's lawyers argued that the site was maintained in bad faith to profit from the singer's fame, the holder of the domain counterargued that the webpages were operated as an unofficial fan site without any commercial benefits. A three-member arbitration panel ruled that no case could be made that the site owner would not have a legitimate interest to the domain name because operating a fan page is a bona fide reason to own the domain. The motion on behalf of Lady Gaga was therefore denied.

Other cases involve products unrelated to music which Lady Gaga is interested in potentially selling herself. In September 2011, a case was filed against Excite Worldwide, LLC for trademark infringement for selling jewelry and cosmetics carrying the Lady Gaga name and for attempting to trademark the names "Lady Gaga" and "Lady Gaga LG" as it relates to its products (Finn 2011). While the resolution to the case is not known, the Excite company presently does not carry any products with the Lady Gaga name. In 2012, it was revealed that Lady Gaga had twice failed to register thy Gaga name for cosmetics products because the trademark "Gaga Pure Platinum" had already been set up for that product category in 2000 (Sciarretto 2012). For the same reason, also, Lady Gaga has not filed trademark claims against the company Too Faced Cosmetics which in 2016 launched a foundation called "Born This Way" to which name the company has since 2013 owned a trademark. In 2013, a claim of trademark violation was brought by Ate My Heart against a brand of jeans called "GA GA Jeans," which was denied on the assumed ground of causing confusion between the brand name and Lady Gaga (RadarOnline 2013; United States Patent and Trademark Office 2015).

Finally, at least two cases have involved trademark issues concerning Lady Gaga that took place outside the United States. In 2013, the Supreme Court of Japan affirmed a decision of the Japan Patent Office to reject the trademark "Lady Gaga" for music recordings and downloads and videos (International Trademark Association 2014). In 2014, a decision by the Hong Kong International Arbitration Centre concerned a claim brought on behalf of Lady Gaga against a domain owner of a website in China (Hong Kong Lawyer 2014). It was ruled that the domain name had been registered in bad faith, to create the illusion of official endorsement, and therefore had to be transferred to the claimant.

Copyright: Protecting Gaga Products

Copyright law concerns the legal right to use and distribute an original creative work. In the United States, copyright is regulated by federal law in the 1976 Copyright Act under Title 17 of the US Code to apply to any work that is fixated in a tangible medium of expression that is relatively permanent or stable (United States Copyright Office). In the case of popular music, copyright thus most clearly applies to the music and videos produced by a performer in the form of records, CDs, and digital downloads.

House of Gaga Publishing has been involved as one of several plaintiffs on behalf of the artistic works of Lady Gaga in half a dozen cases of copyright infringement filed as class action suits by Broadcast Music, Inc. (BMI).[3] Along with ASCAP (American Society of Composers, Authors and Publishers) and SESAC (Society of European Stage Authors and Composers), BMI is one of the main performing rights organizations in the United States that collects licensing fees and distributes artists' royalties. Lady Gaga has all of her original songs as writer and co-writer registered with BMI under the name of Stefani Germanotta.[4] All of the six copyright cases that were filed by BMI between 2013 and 2015 with explicit mention of House of Gaga Publishing as one of the involved parties concerned protected music that was used publically by third parties without a proper license. All were judged in favor of the music publisher and involved the payment of fees and statutory damages.

Besides the BMI copyright complaints, an additional three cases have concerned copyright violations claimed over specific songs recorded by Lady Gaga. In August 2011, a copyright case was brought against Lady Gaga herself, when in August 2011 Rebecca Francescatti filed a suit against Lady Gaga and sound engineer Brian Gaynor in a federal district court in Illinois for copyright infringement of the Francescatti composition "Juda" (Donoghue 2014; United States District Court, Northern District of Illinois 2014). Arguing that the "Juda" song was substantially similar to Lady Gaga's recording "Judas" from the *Born This Way* album, it was claimed that the song had been copied by way of the fact that engineer Gaynor had worked on both recordings. On June 17, 2014, the Court ruled that no substantial similarities could be found.

Two other copyright case concerning Lady Gaga recordings were not brought against the singer but against some of her collaborators. In November 2013, singer and producer Teddy Riley filed a lawsuit in a California federal court to request a jury trial over copyright infringement and copyright fraud involving the Lady Gaga song "Teeth" from the singer's album *The Fame Monster* (Bychawski 2013; Gardner 2013; United States District Court, Central District of California 2013). Strikingly, the lawsuit was filed by Riley against his own daughter Taja Riley, because she would have received, without authorization, a co-writing credit on "Teeth" which Riley himself claimed to be entitled to. Riley sought to receive all monies earned from the song, attorney's fees, and statutory damages. The outcome of the case is not known, but the absence of information on a ruling likely indicates that the case was not judged in Riley's favor.

Another copyright claim over a Lady Gaga song was brought against producer Rob Fusari in July 2011, when Calvin Gaines filed a suit before the US District Court of New Jersey against Fusari over unacknowledged co-authorship of several songs released on *The Fame*, including the global smash hit "Paparazzi," for which Gaines had provided programming (United States District Court, District of New Jersey 2012, 2013; Jaccarino 2011). Following Gaines's claim, Fusari filed a third-party complaint against Lady Gaga so that she would become involved in the lawsuit as co-author and co-producer, to which the singer in turn responded by filing a motion to dismiss the complaint. Lady Gaga's motion was accepted by the federal district court of New Jersey and the case moved on without her (Rufo 2013).

Closely related to copyright issues, mention should also be made of a plagiarism case concerning Lady Gaga that was filed by French artist Orlan in Paris in 2013 over the video for the 2011 song "Born This Way" (Piettre 2013). Orlan claimed that the image of a disembodied head of Lady Gaga that at some point appears in the video would be an imitation of a sculpture Orlan had created in 1996 called "Woman With Head." Orlan also argued that the cover art for Lady Gaga's "Born This Way" single would be extremely similar to her 1989 sculpture "Bumplode." Orlan was therefore seeking 7.5 % of the proceeds from the Lady Gaga video, which would total to some $37.1 million. While the case in France was still ongoing, in January 2016 motions were filed in a district court in New York to subpoena two witnesses in the United States, including Lady Gaga's former fashion director Nicola Formichetti who worked on the video (Ghorashi 2016).

Contract Disputes: Suing Lady Gaga

The legal cases involving Lady Gaga that have been most discussed in the media involve contractual issues and related cases where the singer has been sued for large amounts of money. Two of these cases involve contractual obligations between the singer and two of her former collaborators, producer Rob Fusari and personal assistant Jennifer O'Neill. The case with Fusari began in March 2010, when the producer filed a suit against Team Love Child and Mermaid Music for breach of contract, seeking $30.5 million (Duke 2010; Supreme Court of the State of New York 2010a). Mermaid Music is the company representing Lady Gaga, which is owned equally by the singer and her father Joe Germanotta, while Team Love Child is the company that was set up with Fusari as a result of their agreement, which is owned by Mermaid for 80 % and by Fusari for the remaining 20 %. In the suit, producer Fusari revealed both personal and business-related details about his partnership with Lady Gaga, recounting how he met the singer through Wendy Starland, began working with her on songs, mutually agreed on collaboration contracts in May and September of 2006, and along the way also engaged in a romantic relationship with the almost 20-year junior Stefani Germanotta, an affair that would have ended after the singer had been dropped by Def Jam late 2006. Fusari also claimed to have introduced the singer to both manager Laurent Besencon and A&R representative Vincent Herbert. In the lawsuit, Fusari asserts that he was withheld payment per the terms of his contract with Lady Gaga. In response, Lady Gaga immediately countersued Fusari, claiming that his contracts with her were unlawful (Farley 2010; Supreme Court of the State of New York 2010b).

In September 2010, the case between Fusari and Lady Gaga was settled out of court for an undisclosed amount of money. Once that settlement was announced, Wendy Starland, who had originally introduced Stefani Germanotta to Fusari, sued the producer over breach of the terms of an oral contract for her to find a singer for him to work with (Lynch 2014; United States District Court, District of New Jersey 2015). Even though Starland was not part of the formal contracts between Germanotta and Fusari, she argued that she had a verbal agreement with the producer that the profits derived from her discovery of a female singer would be shared equally. In part based on Lady Gaga's testimony backing up Starland's request against Fusari, in November 2014 a jury awarded Starland $7.3 million in damages as well as 50 % of all future revenue that Fusari and his companies would receive from their deals with Lady Gaga (O'Sullivan 2015; Ross 2013; Zambito 2014). Yet, on appeal in September of 2015, a judge ruled that testimony regarding Fusari and Germanotta's personal relationship was improperly admitted at the Starland trial, and a new jury trial was ordered. Lawyers working on behalf of Lady Gaga have been successful in keeping the details of her personal relationship with Fusari from becoming public, while Starland has not yet been able to receive any monies from Fusari, who reportedly transferred some of his assets, for which reason she filed another lawsuit against him (RadarOnline 2016; United States District Court, Southern District of New York 2015; Zambito 2015). Fusari was said to have been admitted to a rehabilitation facility following the initial judgment against him and has since embarked on a singing career. After filing for bankruptcy, he reached a settlement with Starland for $3.2 million, an arrangement which might involve a controversial sale of his rights in songs he co-wrote with Lady Gaga and others (Gardner 2016).

Another interesting contractual dispute between Lady Gaga and a former collaborator involved the case of Jennifer O'Neill, who filed a lawsuit against Lady Gaga in December 2011, seeking $400,000 in lost wages for overtime hours as the singer's personal assistant (Duke 2013; United States District Court, Southern District of New York 2013). O'Neill was originally hired as Lady Gaga's personal assistant in early 2009 after having been friends with Lady Gaga since sometime before 2008, then resigned and then was re-hired in 2010. O'Neill claims she had to work 24/7 every day with no entitlement to breaks. In a videotaped testimony, Lady Gaga responded to O'Neill's claims that the former assistant was a "f—king hood rat" who was just out to profit from the star (Golding 2013). The case was settled out of court in October 2013, just days before a jury trial was set to begin. O'Neill was reported to have signed a contract to write a tell-all book about her time as Gaga's assistant, but no such book has as yet appeared (Michaels 2014).

One additional contract dispute involving Lady Gaga took place in July 2012, when MGA Entertainment, the company that makes so-called Bratz dolls, sued Lady Gaga for more than $10 million on breach of contract charges (Bell 2012; Supreme Court of the State of New York 2012). Lady Gaga would have failed to approve a line of dolls created in her image even though MGA Entertainment had agreed on the manufacture and distribution of such a doll with Bravado. The case was eventually withdrawn after an undisclosed agreement was reached out of court (Dolmetsch 2012).

RICO Charges: Gangster Gaga?

On June 24, 2011, the arguably strangest lawsuit against Lady Gaga was filed when an individual named Caitlin Demetsenare sued the singer and several of her associated companies (including Ate My Heart, Mermaid Music, and Live Nation Merchandise) on behalf of herself and others similarly situated over charges relating to the Racketeer Influenced and Corrupt Organizations (RICO) Act, the Consumer Protection Act, and unjust enrichment. The reasons behind the case was that Lady Gaga would have illegally profited from the sale of the so-called Pray for Japan wristbands which the singer had offered for sale to fans in order to raise money for aid to send to Japan following the March 2011 earthquake and tsunami in that country (Hughes 2011; United States District Court, Eastern District of Michigan 2011). Part of the Organized Crime Control Act of 1970, the RICO Act was originally drafted to deal with organized crime and, applied to a variety of cases, allows for both criminal and civil procedures. The case against Lady Gaga and associated companies was filed as a class action lawsuit on the grounds that some of the monies of the $5.00 bracelet were withheld and that the charge for shipping to mail the bracelets were in excess of the actual shipping cost, so that not all 100 % of the proceeds would have been donated to Japanese charities as advertised. The case went to trial and the judge ordered Lady Gaga and her associates to pay $107,500, money that would be donated directly toward Japanese earthquake relief (Harrison 2012).

THE GEOMETRY OF LADY GAGA

Analyzing the legal cases Lady Gaga has been involved in, two descriptive observations can be immediately made that affirm the centrality and general character of law in modern societies. As both a famous and wealthy person, Lady Gaga has been subject to a considerable amount of legal activity, an amount that can surely be assumed to be greater than most, lesser known members of society. In a qualitative sense, moreover, the legal cases concerning Lady Gaga all involve compensatory styles of law in civil procedures rather than criminal prosecution. While these findings may not be surprising, the perspective of social geometry developed by Donald Black (1976) can lead to develop a distinctly sociological explanation of their relevant characteristics. Although here serving as an illustration to the validity of Black's theory, this analysis can also contribute toward developing the building blocks of a general theory of law and fame. Such a theory must be made up of testable propositions that are valid under conditions of control, that is, all other conditions being equal (Black 1995). On the basis of the discussed legal cases, the relevant location of Lady Gaga in society can be explained in terms of the five dimensions of social space originally outlined by Black (1976).

In terms of the qualitative style of law as a function of the location of Lady Gaga in vertical space, the complete absence of any criminal proceedings involving the singer illustrates the validity of the general proposition that upward law tends to be compensatory, especially when the defendant is wealthier and, by extension, more famous than the plaintiff (Black 1976:29). Quantitatively, the case of Lady Gaga shows that law varies directly with stratification (Black 1976:13). Thus, the high differentiation of modern society in terms of vertical space, whereby wealth, power, influence, and indeed fame are unevenly distributed, generally accounts for the fact that Lady Gaga attracts law. If they can, people will sue Lady Gaga. Needless to say, they rarely can, but nonetheless Lady Gaga will be more likely a target of legal claims, especially involving monetary stakes, than anyone who is not famous and wealthy. Claimants as varied as former collaborators (Fusari, O'Neill), other artists (Orlan, Francescatti), and more random individuals (Demetsenare) have sued the singer. Perhaps an even more striking indication of the quantity of law generated by fame is the multitude of trademark filings that have been made on Lady Gaga's behalf. Fame increases law, especially of a monetary kind, again showing the centrality of the economics of popular culture. These findings lead to defend the general proposition that law varies directly with fame.

Additionally, stratification is an important dimension of social space because law varies directly with rank (Black 1976:17). In the case of Lady Gaga, the validity of this proposition is demonstrated by the fact that the singer has much better access to justice by being able to pay more and better lawyers as her fame has come with great wealth, part of which can be diverted to legal protection. In today's society, the association between wealth and justice is almost so obvious that it would be banal to dwell upon or even mention it, were it not for the fact that it runs completely counter to the legal principle of equality before the law. Yet, although that principle is explicitly embedded in modern legal systems, it is rarely if ever attained in practice (Black 1995, 1998). Hence, Lady Gaga has won most of all legal cases she has been involved with because she is Lady Gaga, a person of high rank. More striking yet, some of the cases Lady Gaga lost have been inconsequential toward her privilege. For instance, the fan site ladygaga.org is presently not operational, despite Lady Gaga losing a case over the domain name against a fan.

In terms of the upward or downward direction of law, the legalities surrounding Lady Gaga law show that downward law can indeed be said to be greater than upward law (Black 1976:21). Specifically, the downward direction of law in the case of Lady Gaga is revealed from the abundance of trademark and copyright claims against any and all who are seen to intrude on the right that seek to protect the Lady Gaga brand, even when the person infringing on that right is a fan, such as in the case of the ladygaga.org domain name. Moreover, in the case of financially lucrative rights, Lady Gaga and her representatives can be seen to file relatively many cases without attracting much public attention. The argument can be made that fame tends to attract relatively quiet, undiscussed forms of law, while whatever law attracted by fame that does get much attention, especially in the media, is less likely to occur. The settlement in the Fusari case, for instance, involves several millions of dollars, but that amount will be dwarfed by the revenues that are generated from protecting the Lady Gaga trademarks that are associated with all kinds of commercial products. Also, in terms of the direction of law, as predicted (Black 1976:21–22), lawsuits brought against the singer (as cases of upward law) are not only much fewer than the amount of filings made by her or on her behalf but are also more difficult to win when they do occur.

Turning to the dimension of horizontal space, a basic general proposition on the quantity of law is that the relationship between law and relational distance is curvilinear (Black 1976:41). In the case of Lady Gaga's legal life, this curvilinear relationship is indicated by the fact that the majority of lawsuits brought against or in relation to Lady Gaga have come from people that work in the music industry, such as producer Rob Fusari and singers Teddy Riley and Wendy Starland. To some extent, these claimants are close to Lady Gaga as fellow professionals in the same industry, while, to another extent, they are also removed from her as no longer or never having been on friendly terms with her. They are, as such, neither too close to nor too far removed from Lady Gaga to initiate legal proceedings against or concerning her.

The remaining three dimensions of social life outlined by Donald Black (1976) in his original formulation (culture, organization, and social control) harmonize with what was said about vertical and horizontal space. At the most general level, law is predicted to vary directly with culture and organization and inversely with social control (Black 1976:63, 86, 107) inasmuch as culturally more complex and formally more organized societies have more law when other forms of social control are missing. In the Lady Gaga case, the culture of fame-related law itself is an indication of this relationship as the legal cases involving Lady Gaga are highly complex and contain all due legal jargon and a multitude of references to statutes and precedents. Culturally, moreover, the proposition that law varies directly with conventionality (Black 1976:68) can be observed from the fact that Lady Gaga, as a legally constituted professional, is involved with a relatively wide variety of legal issues, such as trademark, copyright, plagiarism, and breach of contract. Located within the music industry, also, the main players in these legal cases share similar cultural values. No matter the outsider role Lady Gaga often attributes to herself (see Chap. 8), the legalities of her career are in and of themselves an indication of the conventionality of her position at the very center of society.

Organizationally, the proposition that litigiousness is higher among individuals who are well organized (Black 1976:91) is shown from the fact that Lady Gaga's interests are often legally framed as part of a larger, multiorganizational effort, such as by means of the representation of House of Gaga Publishing in BMI copyright claims. The same principle applies to some of Lady Gaga's legal adversaries as they too seek organizational strength by soliciting the support of entertainment law firms. The case of the lawsuit against Lady Gaga over concerns with her selling a charity bracelet for Japan is most striking in this respect because the lawsuit originated from a legal company called "1-800-LAW-FIRM" (Hughes 2011). Whatever publicity-generating aspect was initially tied to the case cannot be known, but the organizational strength of the claimant functioned as a central factor in Lady Gaga losing the case.

With respect to social control, finally, the proposition that law varies directly with other forms of conflict management (Black 1976:112) can be observed from the fact that the outcome of cases can vary in terms of Lady Gaga being on the winning or losing side, but that all cases invariably take place within a specified formal legal framework. In the case of trademark, for example, Lady Gaga's interests were as readily protected in the case of the "Lady Goo Goo" song, because the singer possesses trademark over audio and video recordings that are posted on iTunes, as they were not attained in the case of Gaga Pure Platinum cosmetics when trademark was already accorded to someone else. Even Lady Gaga cannot fight the law. At the same time, Lady Gaga is much better, as a famous and wealthy person, at fighting others with the law.

Conclusion

The findings in this chapter on the legalities surrounding Lady Gaga generally support the relevance of legal privilege in the study of fame articulated in the theoretical framework described in Chap. 2 and harmonize with the perspective of the behavior of law and its foundations in the sociology of law. Specifically, great attention is observed to be paid in Lady Gaga's legal cases to procedural requirements, as Max Weber predicted, while restitution rather than punishment is the goal of relevant lawsuits, as Emile Durkheim observed (Deflem 2008). While these findings are not especially surprising, the perspective of social geometry can formulate a sociological explanation of observed variations in reality, removed from any psychological interpretation, to make sense of seeming inconsistencies in Lady Gaga law when the focus would be merely on the winning or losing of cases.

In the world of popular music, fame generates wealth as well as law as an additional powerful resource. In fact, the argument can be made that fame in popular music is especially noteworthy because it combines the prestige that comes from cultural fame with economic wealth and the accompanying normative influence and power that exists legally. The force of law in the case of Lady Gaga is shown not only from its visible but also from its more hidden side. Law is only one form of social control, and other mechanisms of control can be invoked before law can even take place, precisely in order to avoid law. The examples in the Lady Gaga case are indicative of the true scope of the legal privilege of fame. Indeed, not only are the most lucrative and impactful forms of law in the case of Lady Gaga rarely discussed and generally not well known (trademark, copyright) but also the cases that have received most debate in the media (contract disputes) have actually diverted attention from those forms of social control which Lady Gaga and her representatives do not want to be widely known. The case of Lady Gaga suing a fan over a fan site received little attention and was perhaps not as controversial, but it is telling that the singer was able to avoid involvement as a third party in the copyright case brought against Fusari over songs she co-wrote and released under her name. More striking yet was Lady Gaga's ability to keep potentially embarrassing details of her personal life that had been entered in the Starland case against Fusari from being revealed. Reportedly, the suppressed materials details would include "sensitive, private and personal information" that could cause "great harm to Germanotta's personal and professional reputation" (Ross 2013). Those details might have shed more light on the contracts Fusari had with Germanotta in 2006 as well as the singer's romantic entanglement with guitarist Tommy Kafafian, whom she dated before Fusari, and his role in contributing to songs released on *The Fame* (Callahan 2010:54–58).

Moreover, several former collaborators of Lady Gaga have been reported to have received legally arranged payouts and have otherwise been diverted from formal proceedings. By example, singer Wendy Starland, who introduced then Stefani Germanotta to producer Fusari and claims to have had a role in developing her career in those early days, never could get her work formalized in any contract (Callahan 2010:111–112). The mere mention of lawyers strained her relationship with Germanotta. Similarly, Bob Leone, who unofficially managed the singer in 2006, has said he was promised compensation for his efforts in getting young Stefani exposure and landing the deal with Fusari, but eventually received nothing (Boyle 2013). When Leone tried to sell some Lady Gaga discs with unreleased songs via an auction website a few years later, he was duly contacted by Lady Gaga's lawyers, withdrew the auction, and accepted a $10,000 settlement. The power to divert attention from law is perhaps the greatest legal privilege of all. It also shows how Lady Gaga and her team have been successful in using a variety of media to cultivate a public perception of the singer that may or may not be in line with her private identity, but that has in any case been useful in building a successful career.

Notes

1. See the Company Detail website and the New York State website for basic information on the Lady Gaga-related companies mentioned in this chapter.

2. See the United States Patent and Trademark Office website for the data mentioned in this section.
3. The copyright cases involving House of Gaga Publishing can be retrieved via a search on the website Law 360 (Law 360 website).
4. A listing of all songs (co-)written by Stefani Germanotta that are registered at BMI are available online via the BMI website (BMI Repertoire website).

References

Bell, Crystal. 2012. Lady Gaga Sued: Toymakers MGA Entertainment Files $10 Million Lawsuit Against The Singer. *The Huffington Post*, July 25, 2012. http://www.huffingtonpost.com/2012/07/25/lady-gaga-sued-toymakers-mga-entertainment_n_1701299.html

Black, Donald. 1976. *The Behavior of Law*. New York: Academic Press.

———. 1995. The Epistemology of Pure Sociology. *Law and Social Inquiry* 20(3): 829–870.

———. 1998. *The Social Structure of Right and Wrong*, Revised edn. San Diego, CA: Academic Press.

BMI Repertoire. Website. http://repertoire.bmi.com/startpage.asp

Boyle, Simon. 2013. Penniless and Living with His Elderly Mother, the Mentor Cruelly Dumped by Lady Gaga after He Helped Transform Her into World Superstar. *Daily Mail*, August 24, 2013. http://www.dailymail.co.uk/tvshowbiz/article-2401543/Bob-Leone-ex-manager-Lady-Gaga-penniless-living-elderly-mother.html

Bychawski, Adam. 2013. Lady Gaga 'Sued by Teddy Riley Over "The Fame Monster" Track'. *New Musical Express*, November 2, 2013. http://www.nme.com/news/lady-gaga/73590

Callahan, Maureen. 2010. *The Rise and Rise of Lady Gaga*. New York: Hyperion.

Company Detail. Website. http://www.company-detail.com

Deflem, Mathieu. 2008. *Sociology of Law*. Cambridge, UK: Cambridge University Press.

Dolmetsch, Chris. 2012. MGA Entertainment Withdraws Motion in Lady Gaga Dolls Suit. *Bloomberg*, August 23, 2012. http://www.bloomberg.com/news/articles/2012-08-23/mga-entertainment-withdraws-motion-in-lady-gaga-dolls-suit-1-

Donoghue, R. David. 2014. Lady Gaga's 'Judas' Does Not Infringe Copyright. *Chicago IP Litigation*, November 14, 2014. http://www.chicagoiplitigation.com/2014/11/lady-gagas-judas-does-not-infringement-copyright/

Duke, Alan. 2010. Ex-Boyfriend Sues Lady Gaga for $30.5 Million. *CNN*, March 19, 2010. http://www.cnn.com/2010/SHOWBIZ/Music/03/19/lady.gaza.lawsuit/

———. 2013. Lady Gaga Avoids Trial; Settles Pay Dispute with Former Assistant. *CNN*, October 29, 2013. http://www.cnn.com/2013/10/29/showbiz/lady-gaga-lawsuit-settled/
Farley, Christopher J. 2010. Lady Gaga vs. Rob Fusari: Inside Her Countersuit. *The Wall Street Journal*, March 22, 2010. http://blogs.wsj.com/speakeasy/2010/03/22/lady-gaga-vs-rob-fusari-inside-her-countersuit/
Finn, Natalie. 2011. Lady Gaga Wants 'Lady Gaga' All to Herself. *EOnline*, September 28, 2011. http://www.eonline.com/news/266565/lady-gaga-wants-lady-gaga-all-to-herself
Gardner, Eriq. 2013. Lady Gaga Producer Sues His Own Daughter for Claiming Songwriting Credit. *The Hollywood Reporter*, January 15, 2013. http://www.hollywoodreporter.com/thr-esq/lady-gaga-producer-sues-his-412327
———. 2016. Are Copyright Shares to Songs by Destiny's Child and Lady Gaga About to Be Auctioned? *The Hollywood Reporter*, April 27, 2016. http://www.hollywoodreporter.com/thr-esq/are-copyright-shares-songs-by-888113
Ghorashi, Hannah. 2016. Orlan Reopens $31.7 M. Lawsuit Against Lady Gaga in New York. *Art News*, January 8, 2016. http://www.artnews.com/2016/01/08/orlan-reopens-31-7-m-lawsuit-against-lady-gaga-in-new-york/
Golding, Bruce. 2013. Lady Gaga Rants Under Oath in Pay Battle with Former Personal Assistant. *New York Post*, February 1, 2013. http://nypost.com/2013/02/01/lady-gaga-rants-under-oath-in-pay-battle-with-former-personal-assistant/
Harrison, Lily. 2012. Judge Orders Lady Gaga to Pay Over $100,000 to Settle Japan Bracelet Lawsuit. *Celebuzz*, October 25, 2012. http://www.celebuzz.com/2012-10-25/judge-orders-lady-gaga-to-pay-over-100000-to-settle-japan-bracelet-lawsuit-exclusive/
Hong Kong Lawyer. 2014. Ate My Heart Inc. v 林清茂. *Dispute Resolution*. http://www.hk-lawyer.org/content/ate-my-heart-inc-v-林清茂
Hughes, Sarah Anne. 2011. Lady Gaga Responds to Japan Charity Wristband Lawsuit. *The Washington Post*, June 29, 2011. https://www.washingtonpost.com/blogs/celebritology/post/lady-gaga-responds-to-japan-charity-wristband-lawsuit/2011/06/29/AG5NtVqH_blog.html
International Trademark Association. 2014. *Opinion to the Supreme Court of Japan Relating to the Final Appeal of IP High Court Decision*. Case No. 2013 [Gyo-Ke] 10158. http://www.inta.org/PDF%20Library/Japan%20Supreme%20Court%20Brief%202.pdf
Jaccarino, Mike. 2011. Producer Files Suit Against Lady Gaga's Rob Fusari, Says He Was Cheated Out of Credit for 4 Songs. *New York Daily News*, June 16, 201. http://www.nydailynews.com/entertainment/gossip/producer-files-suit-lady-gaga-rob-fusari-cheated-credit-4-songs-article-1.130925

Kaplan, Don. 2011. Gaga: You Breast Stop Copying Me. *The New York Post*, March 7, 2011. http://nypost.com/2011/03/07/gaga-you-breast-stop-copying-me/

Law 360. Website. http://www.law360.com/

Lipman, Melissa. 2011. Lady Gaga Caught In Bad Romance With Fan Site. *Law360.com*, September 23, 2011. http://www.law360.com/articles/273481/lady-gaga-caught-in-bad-romance-with-fan-site

Lynch, Joe. 2014. Lady Gaga Talent Scout Feels 'Validated' After Winning $7.3 Million in Lawsuit. *Billboard*, November 19, 2014. http://www.billboard.com/articles/news/6320051/lady-gaga-wendy-starling-rob-fusari-lawsuit-interview

Michaels, Sean. 2014. Lady Gaga's Former Assistant Writing Tell-All Book. *The Guardian*, July 18, 2014. http://www.theguardian.com/music/2014/jul/18/lady-gaga-former-assistant-writing-book-fame-monster-jennifer-oneilll

National Arbitration Forum. 2011. *Ms. Stefani Germanotta v. oranges arecool XD*. Trademark claim, Claim number: FA1108001403808. http://www.adrforum.com/domaindecisions/1403808.htm

New York State. Website. http://www.ny.gov

O'Sullivan, Jeannie. 2015. Music Producer Gets New Trial In Lady Gaga Breach Case. *Law360.com*, September 30, 2015. http://www.law360.com/articles/709499/music-producer-gets-new-trial-in-lady-gaga-breach-case

Piettre, Celine. 2013. Why Is French Artist Orlan Suing Lady Gaga? A Rundown on the Lawsuit. *BlouinArtInfo*, June 1, 2013. http://www.blouinartinfo.com/news/story/916090/why-is-french-artist-orlan-suing-lady-gaga-a-rundown-on-the

RadarOnline. 2013. On The Warpath! Lady Gaga Threatens Legal Action to Stop Manufacturing Of 'Easy Access' Jeans Bearing Her Name. *RadarOnline*, October 8, 2013. http://radaronline.com/exclusives/2013/10/on-the-warpath-lady-gaga-threatens-legal-action-to-stop-production-of-easy-access-jeans-bearing-her-name/

———. 2016. Bad Romance! Lady Gaga Pays Ex-Boyfriend $12 Million After Refusing To Share Profits. *RadarOnline*, April 21, 2016. http://radaronline.com/celebrity-news/lady-gaga-pays-ex-boyfriend-millions-secret-settlement/

Ross, Barbara. 2013. Secrets About Lady Gaga's Financial and Personal Life to Be Kept Under Seal: Judge. *New York Daily News*, August 5, 2013. http://www.nydailynews.com/entertainment/gossip/secrets-lady-gaga-financial-personal-life-seal-judge-article-1.1417927

Rufo, Anthony. 2013. Lady Gaga: She's No Copyright Monster. *Trademark and Copyright Law*, May 17, 2013. http://www.trademarkandcopyrightlawblog.com/2013/05/lady-gaga-shes-no-copyright-monster/

Sciarretto, Amy. 2012. Lady Gaga Battling Cosmetics Company Over Trademark. *PopCrush*, June 29, 2012. http://popcrush.com/lady-gaga-cosmetics-company-trademark/

Supreme Court of the State of New York. 2010a. *Robert Fusari Productions LLC v. Team Love Child LLC and Mermaid Music LLC*. Index No. 650179/2010.

———. 2010b. *Stefani Germanotta and Mermaid Music LLC v. Rob Fusari and Rob Fusari Productions Inc. and Rob Fusari Productions Limited Liability Company.* Index No. 650183/2010.

———. 2012. MGA *Entertainment, Inc. v. Bravado International Group Merchandising Services, Inc.* Index No. 652547/2012 NYSCEF.

Sweney, Mark. 2011. Lady Gaga Wins Injunction Against Lady Goo Goo. *The Guardian*, October 13, 2011. http://www.theguardian.com/music/2011/oct/13/lady-gaga-injunction-lady-goo-goo

Trademarkia. Website. http://www.trademarkia.com/

United States Copyright Office. Copyright Law of the United States. http://www.copyright.gov/title17/

United States District Court, Central District of California. 2013. *Edward Theodore Riley, Adida Music Inc. v. Taja Riley, EMI Publishing, EMI Virgin Music Inc, Sony/ATV Music Publishing Acquisition.* Case 2:13-cv-00158-SS. https://www.scribd.com/doc/120358477/Gov-uscourts-cacd-551682-1-0

United States District Court, District of New Jersey. 2012. *Calvin Gaines v. Rob Fusari and Rob Fusari Productions LLC*. Civil action, No. 2:2011cv04433 - Document 47 D.N.J. 2012. http://law.justia.com/cases/federal/district-courts/new-jersey/njdce/2:2011cv04433/262547/47/

———. 2013. *Calvin Gaines v. Rob Fusari and Rob Fusari Productions LLC. and Stefani Germanotta aka Lady Gaga.* Opinion, No 2:2011-cv-04433-WJM-MF Document 85 D.N.J. 2013. http://law.justia.com/cases/federal/district-courts/new-jersey/njdce/2:2011cv04433/262547/85/

———. 2015. *Wendy Starland v. Rob Fusari et al.* No. 2:2010cv04930 - Document 583 D.N.J. 2015. http://law.justia.com/cases/federal/district-courts/new-jersey/njdce/2:2010cv04930/247026/583/

United States District Court, Eastern District of Michigan. 2011. *Caitlin Demetsenare v. Stefani Germanotta et al.* Case 2:11-cv-12753-BAF-LJM. http://bitterqueen.typepad.com/files/complaint-against-lady-gaga.pdf

United States District Court, Northern District of Illinois, Eastern Division. 2014. *Rebecca Francescatti v. Stefani Joanne Germanotta p/k/a Lady Gaga, et al.* Legal case, No. 11, CV 5270. http://www.leagle.com/decision/In%20FDCO%2020140618A52/FRANCESCATTI%20v.%20GERMANOTTA

United States District Court, Southern District of New York. 2013. *Jennifer O'Neill v. Mermaid Touring Inc. and Stefani Joanne Germanotta, a/k/a 'Lady Gaga'.* No. 11 Civ. 9128 PGG. http://www.employmentandlaborinsider.com/wp-content/uploads/sites/328/2013/09/Blog.9.13.13.ONeill-v.-Mermaid-Touring1.pdf

———. 2015. "Wendy Starland v. Rob Fusari Productions, LLC." Case: 1:15-cv— 1408-VSB. http://radaronline.com/wp-content/uploads/2016/04/starland-lawsuit-court-docs-signed.pdf

United States Patent and Trademark Office. Website. http://www.uspto.gov

United States Patent and Trademark Office. 2013. Ate My heart Inv. v. Adam Swan. *Opinion*, mailed May 24, 2013. http://ttabvue.uspto.gov/ttabvue/ttabvue-91202493-OPP-10.pdf

———. 2015. Ate My Heart Inc. v. GA GA Jeans Limited. *Opinion*, mailed March 10, 2015. https://e-foia.uspto.gov/Foia/RetrievePdf;jsessionid=69B46358B713A98D156BFFE016E223B4.prod_cidmext_jboss1_jvm2?system=TTABIS&flNm=91205110-03-10-2015

Zambito, Thomas. 2014. Lady Gaga Backs Friend in Lawsuit against N.J. Record Producer. *NJ.com*, September 24, 2014. http://www.nj.com/news/index.ssf/2014/09/lady_gaga_backs_friend_in_lawsuit_against_nj_record_producer.html

———. 2015. Record Producer Who Lost in Lady Gaga Case in Rehab, Withdrew Millions from Accounts, Lawyer Claims. *NJ.com*, May 12, 2015. http://www.nj.com/news/index.ssf/2015/05/record_producer_who_lost_in_lady_gaga_case_in_reha.html

CHAPTER 6

Gaga Media: From Internet to Radio

The role of media in the case of fame in the world of popular music is at least twofold inasmuch as music, as sound, is communicated in the form of particular recording media, such as tapes, records, CDs, and downloads, while an attained position of fame in music, as in any other social realm is also communicated toward an audience through various media of communication, both to transmit music or other objects around which fame can be established and to communicate ideas and information more or less related to the public persona to whom fame is ascribed. It is mostly with respect to the media of the production and distribution of musical sound that important technological changes have taken place that have greatly affected music culture and music industry over the past decades. The transformation from vinyl records to CDs and digital downloads has also been accompanied by radical changes that have been brought about by technological developments, ushered in with the advent of the current digital age, concerning the ways in which musicians can and need to engage with their audience, from the more established means of print, radio, and TV to the online avenues of the no longer new but nonetheless still expanding social networking sites. This chapter explores how Lady Gaga's rise to fame has been facilitated by the role various media have played in her career, both as a musician and as a public person of fame.

In the study of fame, the role of media—as of the audience or publics to which these media are connected (the topic addressed in the next chapter of this book)—is fundamental inasmuch as fame in modern society can otherwise not be established. Specifically in the context of complex societies, face-to-face interactions are far too limited to establish fame through the gossip of old, at least if such fame is to reach beyond the bounds of a local celebrity subculture (Ferris 2010). Yet, the development of mass media allows for communications and interactions that extend far beyond any more or less confined locales. Congruent with the cultural perspective of fame articulated in this book, I will first develop a sociological conceptualization of the relationship between media and fame, and subsequently analyze relevant dimensions in the case of Lady Gaga, especially how the singer became a favorite topic of attention, involving a multitude of positions ranging from adulation to vilification, across multiple media. Against an all-too-readily accepted wisdom of a more or less popular kind, I will argue that the internet has not been primarily responsible for Lady Gaga's rise to stardom.

Media of Fame and Music

As suggested in Chap. 2, cultural expressions are by definition symbolically mediated in specific forms, including words, sights, and sounds that can be materially produced and re-produced by various means, such as print and video and audio recordings. As an aspect of the study of culture, a sociological theory of media must apply to fame as well as to music. Harmonizing with the constructionist perspective adopted in this book, fame and music are culturally constructed as particular relationships of interaction. From this understanding, it follows that the role of media in establishing these relationships is of basic importance. The major theoretical positions on the role of media in culture and society that have been defended by sociologists will by now be familiar and can be briefly explained before an application to fame and music will be developed.

As with the study of popular culture, the role of media in society has traditionally been relatively neglected and framed in reductionist terms when addressed. The works of Horkheimer and Adorno and of C. Wright Mills can again be mentioned as prototypical. The Marxist persuasions of Horkheimer and Adorno (1944) are perhaps sharpest of all in reducing modern forms of media of communication to their presumed hegemonic qualities. "Films, radio, and magazines," the Frankfurt Schoolers write, "make up a system which is uniform as a whole and in every part" (p. 120). And what the industry has to offer, the argument goes, is not much more than a predictable hit song, a movie filled with clichés, and other commodity forms of simplified culture that serve market interests. C. Wright Mills (1956:298–324) articulated a similar reductionist viewpoint with respect to the industry of fame and celebrity and the role played therein by the media in creating what he called a mass society. Based on his radical sociological leanings, Mills argues that in modern societies like the United States the media function such as to create a market of consumers, not a public interested in ideas. The very expression "mass media" is indicative of the widespread nature of the unquestioned manner in which such an absolute position is accepted, although, of course, it need not be.

In modern sociology, reductionist perspectives on the media of fame are at times still stubbornly defended, not least of all in connection with popular music. David Marshall (1997), for example, conceives of fame in the world of pop music as an "industrial construction" and consequently attributes the popularity of the boy band New Kids On The Block in the late 1980s to a cleverly devised media machinery that made the group to be nothing but "a brand name for a commodity" (pp. 150, 181). With the turn toward "taking culture seriously" in the social sciences, however, sweeping and bland statements on a political economy of mass society and fame can no longer be maintained (Gamson 1994:200–203). A cultural approach will emphasize the extent to which the various participants in media communications are active relative and toward one another. The meanings that are attributed to cultural expressions need not be uniform, but can and often do vary among segments of society or across dimensions of space and time. Furthermore, avoiding a perspective of technological determinism, the increasing variation of media forms and the ability of participation in them, from personal audio recorders to laptops with wireless capabilities, must lead to conceive of the role of media in more differentiated terms of relative participation which a simplistic consumer model cannot capture.

It must be noted that even some critical theorists have accepted at least the idea of the liberating power of media. The best example of such a perspective for the study of culture is Jürgen Habermas's (1962) historical study of the public sphere. Habermas argues that the modern forms of an open public debate have been subjected to commercial exploitation (public opinion), but he also holds on to the idea that critical potentials remain embedded in these institutions, especially under conditions of a democratic political culture. This perspective does not imply that the world of popular music and fame will be the center of political or even cultural upheaval, but it does introduce the idea that relationships established through various media are of a more dynamic nature than an orthodox hegemonic perspective would lead to suggest. While some contemporary scholars hold on to the reductionist notion that celebrity is a function of media industry forces (Couldry 2016), it is noteworthy that even musicologist Simon Frith (2001), who conceives of popular music in terms defined by the media, has to acknowledge that the professionals of the music industry lack at least some control over those media and therefore must partly also respond to musical tastes as they emanate from the community.

In the context of this examination on the media of Lady Gaga, a very brief overview of the most important media of mass communication and of music production and distribution may suffice. In terms of the history of communications media, technological advances were instrumental in developing print media in the form of newspapers and magazines on a scale reaching mass populations from the nineteenth century onwards when technologies of transportation began to reach beyond local and national borders (Gorman and McLean 2009). In the next century followed the development of film and radio and, after the Second World War, commercial television expanded as arguably the most important media for many decades. From the 1980s onwards, new technological innovations in the electronic and digital realm would gradually enable the spread of more and more media for personal use, ranging from home videotape players to DVDs and today's massively popular handheld mobile phones, revolutionizing communications media as never before.

It requires little argument to realize that the technological changes that mark communications media in general have had special repercussions for the world of music as the role of technology in musical production, reproduction, and distribution cannot be underestimated (Théberge 2001, 2015). Especially in the realm of popular music, technology plays a key role, even in the creation of musical sound itself, from its capturing through microphone on tape to its transmission by means of amplification, resulting in the central roles accorded to audio engineers and producers. The main material forms of music registration evolved from magnetic tape recordings in professional studios to today's digital media which can produce high-quality sound at relatively low cost. The means of music reproduction and its various media of distribution likewise increased in quality of sound and ease of use, from vinyl records to tapes, CDs, digital downloads, and on-demand streaming.

The digital age has had ramifications in the world of music perhaps more acutely and lastingly than in any another area of cultural life (Wikström

2009). Especially since the rapid expansion of the internet, the value of recorded music as such has decreased, even though the role of music in everyday life has arguably expanded. Popular music can today even more be said to be everywhere even though it is bought much less as a product in itself (Leyshon et al. 2005). As a tangible product associated with music is less discernable since the expansion of legal download formats, especially following the popularization of iTunes through the iPhone, music distribution has also become less oriented toward the sale of recorded music in favor of live concert performances and other music-related goods, such as merchandise and video games. In Chap. 4, the economic repercussions of these transformations for the career of Lady Gaga were already discussed. In the following pages, the focus is on how Lady Gaga has adapted to the technological changes in the mass communications landscape and in the music industry by seeking to reach and establish her audience through a variety of media.

Media Gaga

There is no doubt that Lady Gaga is among the first pop stars to have attained global fame in the internet age. Yet, as the following analysis will clarify, the internet is far from the only medium through which Lady Gaga has reached stardom. In fact, even though Lady Gaga's recording career did not begin until 2008, at a time when various social networking sites were already fairly well established, her fame was initially attained by promoting her recorded music, which itself was made available in various media formats, through the conventional means of radio, television, magazines, and newspapers, as well as through multiple online media.

Lady Gaga Recordings

The fame of Lady Gaga is based on, though surely not to be reduced to, her music, especially in its various recorded formats that are made available to the public. As mentioned in Chap. 3, early on in her career, the singer self-released two discs under her birth name, *Words* and *Red and Blue*, which she sold at shows in 2006, but which did not serve their intended promotional intent. The Lollapalooza appearance of August 2007 was also accompanied by a promotional disc of five songs issued by manager Besencon for industry insiders, but it too failed to garner any notice.[1] Since 2008, Lady Gaga has officially released music through her record company, initially in the form of the single "Just Dance" and her debut album *The Fame*, followed by additional singles drawn from that album. Her next major release, *The Fame Monster* in 2009 was likewise preceded by a lead single, "Bad Romance," and followed by additional single releases, similar to the release of lead single "Born This Way" of the same-titled album of 2011 and an additional four singles from that album as well as lead single "Applause" of 2013's *ARTPOP* and its additional two single releases. The duet album with Tony Bennett, *Cheek To Cheek*, was also accompanied by two singles. All Lady Gaga singles featured music videos, with the exception of the *ARTPOP* song "Do What U Want," which had its video pulled, despite various announcements by Lady Gaga herself, possibly over concerns with director Terry Richardson and co-singer R. Kelly, who both have faced sexual assault charges (TMZ 2014).

Lady Gaga's recorded music is available for purchase in multiple forms, including downloads, CDs, vinyl records, USB flash drives, deluxe and standard albums, and special editions and re-releases. Beginning with her debut album *The Fame* and continuing on until her latest albums, multiple international editions of the physical CD versions of Lady Gaga albums have been released across the world. By example, *The Fame* is available in about 40 different international versions, usually containing minimal differences in artwork and occasionally featuring selected bonus songs. Released shortly after the breakthrough of digital music formats, the album was also made available on USB flash drive and as a download card from the now defunct Platinum Music Pass service. Lady Gaga's second major release *The Fame Monster* was issued as a single-disc EP, a double-disc re-issue of *The Fame*, as well as in deluxe and super deluxe formats with different artwork and extra merchandise. In 2011, *Born This Way* was released in standard and deluxe editions, while 2013's *ARTPOP* was issued in slightly differing artwork formats, such as an edition on metallic foil paper and censored versions featuring less nudity on the cover, as well as in the form of a digital download app for iPhone and android devices. The collaboration album with Tony Bennett, *Cheek To Cheek*, was released in a standard edition, a deluxe version with extra songs, in editions exclusive for retailers such as Target, and as a special collector's box set with extra merchandise items.

Several strategies are used to ensure sales of Lady Gaga's music recordings even in this day and age when music itself has become less of a commodity. Whereas the releases of *The Fame* and *The Fame Monster* were still based on the notion of Lady Gaga as an up-and-coming pop sensation, the *Born This Way* album in 2011 enjoyed a very wide and massive release reserved for a star who has already arrived and who can be pushed to the next level. Already in the Spring of 2010, at the beginning of the arena version of the Monster Ball tour, Lady Gaga spoke of music for a new album that was being recorded during the tour itself. During her acceptance speech at the MTV Video Music Awards (VMAs) in September 2010, she announced the title of the new album, which had already been speculated among fans. Then on January 1, 2011 at 12:01 am, Lady Gaga took to Twitter to formally announce the release of the "Born This Way Single" on February 13 and the *Born This Way* album on May 23 (Lady Gaga Twitter post).

The strategy to tease and discuss the *Born This Way* album repeatedly and considerable time in advance allowed the massively successful Monster Ball tour to be extended throughout the Spring of 2011 and to create a hype for the new album thereafter (Elberse 2013:65). According to former Lady Gaga manager Troy Carter, this so-called long lead strategy followed the idea of the release a blockbuster summer movie and was based on a similar approach by Taylor Swift, who announced her 2010 album *Speak Now* a relatively long time in advance after having worked on the album over a purported two-year period. Like *Born This Way*, Lady Gaga singles are also typically announced several weeks in advance, and subsequently issued as a download and then as a video, as a CD, and as part of a remix or gift bundle, all in order to guarantee a prolonged stay on the charts. In the case of the *Born This Way* album, the strategy may have inadvertently created unrealistic expectations and hurt album sales and the singer's reputation, to wit that later Lady Gaga recordings have been released without a huge amount of advance notice. It is to be noted, moreover, that this change in strategy came about after the continued decommodification of music and the increasing popularity of streaming services in most recent years. The most effective adjustment to the new music industry landscape has in fact been the exact opposite approach to the blockbuster rollout of *Born This Way* when R&B singer Beyoncé released her self-titled album by total surprise in December 2013, a mere month after Lady Gaga's *ARTPOP* had appeared (Robinson 2014).

Additionally conceived as useful from the viewpoint of adapting to the changing media landscape, several Lady Gaga albums have been released in edited or clean as well as explicit editions. The albums *The Fame Monster* and *Born This Way*, in particular, were released in edited formats that muffled the sound of certain words deemed offensive. With record stores disappearing, this self-censorship strategy was voluntarily enacted by Lady Gaga's record company to assure album sales in US retail outlets, such as Wal-Mart and Best Buy, to which the vast majority of disc sales has shifted since the decline of traditional record stores but where explicit editions of music albums are not sold. In the case of *The Fame Monster*, the strategy left fans to listen to Lady Gaga singing about herself as a "free bit" rather than the intended "free bitch." The album was later released in an unedited version as well, though only on iTunes and the USB flash drive format. An unedited CD version of the album has only been selectively available, such as in Australia where the CD is sold with a warning sticker. As album sales shifted even more toward digital downloads away from retail, the 2013 album *ARTPOP* was simultaneously released in both edited and unedited versions.

Radio and TV

The releases of Lady Gaga's recordings in the form of singles, albums, and videos in themselves have followed established forms of music production and distribution that have been around for several decades. It will therefore perhaps also cause no surprise that the more established media of radio and television have been heavily relied upon to promote the singer's music, especially early on in her career. The presence of Lady Gaga's music on radio developed relatively slowly at first as her music was initially considered too urban and too dance oriented. Specifically, the single "Just Dance," released in April 2008, initially was judged not to fit mainstream radio stations, where programmers, according to manager Troy Carter, thought it "was too much of a dance song" (in Elberse 2013:61).

Holding on to the strategy to reach an audience through radio, however, the medium would soon play an instrumental role in Lady Gaga's rise to fame. One important factor in Lady Gaga's radio popularity was the favorable reception the singer gradually received on pop and dance music-friendly radio stations, especially in larger metropolitan markets, such as San Francisco and New York, which served as a "launching pad," to use the words of Interscope's Jimmy Iovine, for a national campaign (in Elberse 2013:62). This radio popularity also benefited from the singer's increasingly successful exposure among some special target groups, such as the gay community and the dance scene, which were especially reached through small club live performances throughout 2008 (see Chap. 7). Additionally important was the decision to launch Lady Gaga's debut album in Canada first because that country was judged more favorable toward the reception of her music, allowing her success there (and elsewhere in the world) to subsequently enable a successful return to the United States. For that reason, manager Carter sought out a radio station in the city of Buffalo (close to the Canadian border) to play the "Just Dance" single and have a buzz created around the up-and-coming star (Vitez 2013; Suster 2016).

Needless to say, the presence of Lady Gaga's music has steadily increased from her first hit singles on until her rise as a successful pop star. By 2010, Lady Gaga had become among the most played artists on many a country's radio stations, and since then radio has remained important for the promotion of her work. In 2011, by example, radio was an intrinsic part of the huge launch of the *Born This Way* album as the same-titled single from the album premiered on radio worldwide at 6:00 am EST on February 11, several months prior to the album's release on May 23, and was subsequently released as digital download later that day (Vena 2011). Radio has remained an important element in Lady Gaga's popularity and fame ever since, for even though chart positions are presently also based on sales and streaming plays, the role of radio airplay has remained important. Even though single releases are nowadays also available on streaming services and via other online sites such as YouTube and iTunes, they are until today also released to radio and remain acknowledged as important to Lady Gaga's success. For instance, when the single "Yoü and I" was released in August 2011, it was in the United States issued in several dozen different versions that were distributed to local radio stations with the lyrics edited so as to hear Lady Gaga referencing the names of various cities and states. In the Fall of 2013, the Lady Gaga single "Applause" became the singer's most played song on the radio, even supplanting her major hit "Bad Romance" of 2009 (Sciarretto 2013b).

The rise of Lady Gaga's radio presence was accompanied by several, increasingly more high profile and fame-generating television appearances. Especially in the case of a visual performer as Lady Gaga, television has the added advantage of marketing not only the sounds but also the many sights that come with the singer and her performances. The television campaign for Lady Gaga began soon after the release of the "Just Dance" single in 2008, initially leading to possibly even more success, especially on an international level, than its radio counterpart (Lester 2010:75–76). Corresponding to the launch of Lady Gaga in selected markets outside of the United States, several early television performances took place abroad, where "Just Dance" became a hit on TV even before the song would attain chart success.[2] Among the more notable television appearances of Lady Gaga in 2008 are her performances of "Just Dance" on the US television show So You Think You Can Dance in July, at the Miss Universe beauty pageant in Vietnam (where Lady Gaga wrote the line notes for her debut album *The Fame*) broadcast by NBC the same month, on the Canadian station MuchMusic and the Swedish show Sommarkrysset in August, and at the NRJ Music Tour in France in September. Lady Gaga's first US television appearance was on the Logo channel's NewNowNext Awards show in May 2008, followed by performances of "Just Dance" on Jimmy Kimmel Live in October and on The Ellen DeGeneres Show and during the third hour of The Today Show in December.

Once Lady Gaga's debut single became a hit in the United States in January 2009 and took off globally along with her following smash hits like "Poker Face" and "Paparazzi," the singer's presence on television accelerated right along with her increasing popularity and fame at a rate that kept the singer constantly moving from one television show to another along with radio appearances and live shows. In the United States and elsewhere, Lady Gaga appeared on an increasing number of high-profile shows on mainstream television stations, often in non-music-related programs with wide audiences. Whereas the singer appeared on about 20 television shows in 2008, that number had increased to more than 60 in 2009. Among the more notable TV performances in the United States are a memorable all-live rendition of "Just Dance" on the Tonight Show in January 2009, followed by appearances on The View in March, American Idol in April, and a return to both the Ellen DeGeneres Show and Dancing With The Stars in May. Over the same period, alongside of touring worldwide, the singer also appeared on many television shows elsewhere in the world, including popular music programs and talk shows in various countries in Europe and in Japan. In the month of April 2009 alone, Lady Gaga appeared on television shows in the UK, Germany, Italy, The Netherlands, and France.

By the Fall of 2009, Lady Gaga was literally everywhere where stars can be seen on television, including performances on the shows hosted by Ellen DeGeneres and Jay Leno and the singer's first appearance on the popular comedy show Saturday Night Live. The following year continued Lady Gaga's dominance on television, with multiple appearances either or both in the form of song performances and interviews on such popular programs as The Oprah Winfrey Show in January, the Today Show, and Good Morning America in February, American Idol in May, Larry King Live in June, and The Today Show in July. For the latter broadcast, an estimated 20,000 fans gathered near the NBC studios at Rockefeller Plaza in New York City for a free five-song concert performance by Lady Gaga and her band, who were that week playing four sold-out Monster Ball shows at Madison Square Garden.

The television history of Lady Gaga from 2011 onwards will be well known for obvious reasons of her accelerated fame. What is noteworthy to observe is that the singer has sought the television limelight less frequently in the years since the release of *Born This Way*, but has shifted to more high-profile events. The attempt at saturating the television airwaves with Lady Gaga in 2009 and, to a somewhat lesser extent, in 2010 was followed by more targeted efforts befitting a star who has arrived. Following repeat appearances on TV shows hosted by Ellen DeGeneres and Oprah Winfrey, the release of *Born This Way* was preceded by an HBO airing of a live concert performance of the Monster Ball at Madison Square Garden recorded earlier that year as well as appearances on American Idol, Saturday Night Live, The View, David Letterman, and Good Morning America. In November 2011, the television station ABC aired a 90-minute special, "A Very Gaga Thanksgiving," demonstrating Lady Gaga's now unquestionable star status. The release of *ARTPOP* in 2013 was somewhat less spectacular in its promotional support, but nonetheless also featured various television appearances, including another Thanksgiving special on ABC in which Lady Gaga performed with the popular Muppets characters.

Over the past few years, Lady Gaga has remained a mainstay on television in the United States and elsewhere. Yet, although the hype of the singer as the newest pop sensation could evidently not be maintained once her career was more established, it has perhaps been most striking in more recent years that Lady Gaga has broadened her reach to appear not only as a pop star, but also in the context of artistic endeavors in other styles. Especially noteworthy is the attention from television to the singer's jazz performances with Tony Bennett, which anticipated and followed the release of their album *Cheek To Cheek* and its accompanying live concert series, including a concert special recorded at New York's Lincoln Center that aired on PBS in October 2014. Since then, Lady Gaga's television appearances have involved memorable performances at the Oscars, Super Bowl, and other mainstream shows, showcasing, as further discussed in Chap. 10, that her vocal abilities and musical talents extend well beyond the world of dance and pop to incorporate a broad variety of styles.

News Media

It has in many respects become absurd to attempt to differentiate between news media in their print and online versions. Since some years now, indeed, most all print media also exist in an online version, either in truncated form or in full, while many other contemporary news media exist exclusively online, on a subscription basis or supported by revenue streams from advertising. In the news media, especially in newspapers and magazines, the presence of Lady Gaga has mirrored her growing popularity on radio and television. As the traditional news outlets have largely lost the more central role they once enjoyed, these appearances mostly followed the presence of Lady Gaga elsewhere to solidify her position as an up-and-coming and eventually more established star. Among the more memorable times when Lady Gaga appeared in news sources during her rise to fame, mention can be made of articles specifically devoted to her, often with the singer's image on the cover, in such notable outlets as *Rolling Stone* (Hiatt 2009, 2011; Strauss 2010), *Vanity Fair* (Robinson 2010, 2012), and *Vogue* (Van Meter 2011, 2012). Accompanied by pictures of Lady Gaga in variously impactful outfits, these features often included exclusive interviews with the singer, allowing her to explain, from her viewpoint as subject, certain aspects about her work and her fame, or to leave matters of public curiosity unexplained and introduce more confusion, thereby fueling additional speculation and attention.

Additionally, much has been written in the news media about Lady Gaga as the object of attention. In words and images, Lady Gaga thus gradually got to be discussed and seen everywhere across a wide range of news media on the cover of magazines and in the pages of newspapers all over the world. As much as Lady Gaga at the height of her rise to fame around the Spring of 2011 had come to dominate the internet, she then also dominated newspapers and magazines (Greenslade 2011). Besides discussing her music and art more generally, much news attention was specifically devoted to the fame and success of Lady Gaga, initially to reveal amazement over who this new lady really was and what her intentions and aspirations could be, including stories on her childhood and years before and during her rise to fame (e.g., Barton 2009; Callahan 2010). From then on, the singer was discussed as a newly established pop sensation, who, it was especially argued, had become extremely successful, wealthy, and influential (e.g., Bauer 2010). By example, in 2013, *Time* magazine listed Lady Gaga second on its list of 100 most influential people in the world, behind Myanmar politician Aung San Suu Kyi (James 2013), while *Forbes* has since 2010 listed the singer on its list of highest-paid celebrities (Forbes website). The fame of Lady Gaga itself became the topic of an attention that in turn contributed to generate that fame.

As is the case with other media as well, the news media and Lady Gaga promote one another in a symbiotic relationship. As Lady Gaga's fame rises, so do reports on her and so do the outlets that do the reporting. Especially once her star as the new "it girl" in pop music had risen, everybody wanted a piece of Lady Gaga. Likewise corresponding to Lady Gaga's attained fame at the high point of her career after *Born This Way* has been the relative fatigue that later set in among the news media, especially following the relative underperformance of *ARTPOP*. In most recent years, however, it has been most striking that the news media have once again been paying more attention to Lady Gaga and have also been more kind to her, especially since her work with Tony Bennett and the general diversification of her styles and artistic accomplishments, even speaking of a return to "cultural dominance" (Russoniello 2016).

The Internet

It should not come as a surprise that the internet had an important role in Lady Gaga's rise to fame, for the straightforward, if not altogether simple reason that fame outside the context of the internet has in contemporary society become impossible as all of social life itself has now been firmly established in the cyber world as well. The very idea of the internet as a new medium of interaction has become absurd. Nonetheless, the case of the origins of Lady Gaga's fame enjoys a special relationship to the internet, which can readily be surmised in a general sense from the fact that the singer went from an almost completely unknown talent in 2008 to a household world in the few years that followed. More specifically, furthermore, Lady Gaga was among the first performers in popular music to fully embrace and exploit the then up-and-coming social networking sites. Given their current centrality to pop culture and social life, the novelty of Lady Gaga's approach to the internet may by now, in the few years that have passed since her rise to fame, already be difficult to understand but cannot be overlooked.

The very beginning of Lady Gaga's career, even before her discovery and recording contract with Interscope, was already intimately related to the internet. When she still performed under her birth name, Stefani

Germanotta had an online presence by means of her own website (stefanimusic.com), which was maintained sometime between 2005 and 2006, and which from 2007 onwards redirected to her page on MySpace, then among the most popular social networking sites, especially for musicians. The singer's MySpace page was maintained since 2005 and especially active throughout 2008, since when it has remained in operation but is only occasionally updated as MySpace generally has declined (Lady Gaga MySpace). As an unsigned artist, the singer also maintained a page on the PureVolume website, where music could be uploaded by participating musicians as a free streaming service to fans.[3] First as Stefani and subsequently as Lady Gaga, the singer maintained a PureVolume page between 2006 and 2007, and would regularly upload songs she was then recording, especially with producer Rob Fusari.

The early availability of Lady Gaga's music on MySpace and PureVolume aided the singer's initial exposure in the club scene as well as through the occasional listener being directed to her web presence by means of word-of-mouth among fans in the world of dance and pop music. After having been told about the singer then called Stefani Germanotta, producer Rob Fusari first heard her music on her PureVolume page (Cooper 2016). Even more important perhaps from the viewpoint of Lady Gaga's professional career, Interscope talent scout Vincent Herbert was introduced to her music via her MySpace page. The singer's earliest internet presence, upon her signing with Interscope, was also heavily supported by her own website (ladygaga.com), which has been maintained since shortly after the release of the "Just Dance" single in April 2008. In its earliest incarnation, the site included a blog called Haus of Gaga with behind-the-scenes information on her music and early live shows as well as various pieces of news and pictures for and with her earliest fans. The website also hosted several promotional videos, such as for the song "Beautiful, Dirty, Rich" and a "The Fame, Part One" video introduction to her debut album *The Fame*. Since then, the ladygaga.com website has been redesigned following every new album release, although it has generally decreased activity as other social networking sites have gained in importance. In its early years, the site still maintained a popular forum for discussion among fans, but it has since been discontinued.

A particularly popular item on ladygaga.com for Lady Gaga to connect with her fans, absent other media exposure in the early days of her career, were the so-called Transmission Gagavision videos. These webisodes consisted of short videos documenting Lady Gaga's musical journey as she traveled the world in search for fame and stardom. The videos were originally hosted on the now defunct social media service imeem as well as on YouTube, where they can still be viewed today. Forty Transmission Gagavision videos were released between June 2008 and March 2009. In April 2011, shortly before the release of *Born This Way*, the video series was briefly resurrected. Discontinued after only four episodes, the series was briefly active again in 2014 with two videos. A similar video series called "Monstervision" was launched in 2012, but was operational for only a few episodes.

Among the reasons why the ladygaga.com website has lost much of its centrality to promote Lady gaga online is the appearance and popularity of many social networking sites and the gradual diffusion of Lady Gaga across the internet. While a host of fan sites sprung up to support Lady Gaga during her rise to fame, the singer herself also expanded her cyber presence in an exponential fashion across multiple online media. As MySpace declined in popularity, Facebook became one of Lady Gaga's central mechanisms to connect with her audience, along with a YouTube channel and accounts on Twitter, Instagram, Tumblr, in addition to the development of her own dedicated website littlemonsters.com and official record company webpages in several countries. The scope and complexity of these websites and their evolving nature make it difficult to draw an accurate picture of Lady Gaga's many presences on the internet today, which itself may be an important indication of the path and scope of her fame. A brief overview of the most important aspects of Lady Gaga's extensive participation in various online media may indicate its relevance to her career and rise to global stardom.

To communicate music, Lady Gaga as other musicians today need not rely on the sale of recordings but can also post her music on sharing sites. Via her own YouTube channel and her accompanying Vevo account, Lady Gaga can deliver her videos and music freely and directly to her fans. Since early on in the singer's career, also, YouTube has been the primary venue for her videos, rather than MTV and other media, a strategy that proved very successful (Rao 2010). By April 2010, the video to "Bad Romance," released just a few months prior in 2009, was the most viewed video on YouTube with 180 million views (Dybwad 2010). The video had attracted almost 300 million views by October, at which time Lady Gaga became the first musician to gather one billion views on all her YouTube videos combined, beating out teen idol Justin Bieber, even though the video to his song "Baby" had overtaken "Bad Romance" in total number of views

(Barnett 2010; Kaufman 2010). Since then, other artists and individual videos have surpassed Lady Gaga's early records, but her YouTube presence overall remains strong, with the artist presently ranking 17th among the most-viewed Vevo channels with over 3.7 billion views.

On social networking sites, the most notable aspects of Lady Gaga's online presence include the singer's Facebook account. Active since April 2008, the singer's Facebook pages have attracted many fans from all corners of the globe throughout her career, serving as an important indicator of her fame. Overtaking Barack Obama, Lady Gaga set a Facebook record in the Summer of 2010 with 10 million likes, a number that had risen to almost 25 million by the end of that year (Warman 2010). By 2012, she had garnered more than 53 million likes, even though she was by then surpassed by Eminem and Rihanna (Johnson 2012). Not surprising given Facebook's continuingly growing popularity, the networking site has remained a central point to disseminate Lady Gaga news, photos, and videos until his day. At the time of this writing, Lady Gaga's Facebook page had received more than 61 million likes.

Next to Facebook, Twitter is arguably the other major social networking site the relevance of which can today not be ignored. Among the first entertainers to join Twitter in March 2008, Lady Gaga used the site only rarely that year, but began to be very active from January 2009 onwards, tweeting a plethora of messages about her music and a variety of other issues relating to fashion, activism, and more. By November 2009, Lady Gaga's Twitter account had 1.6 million followers (Smillie 2009). With the number of her followers steadily increasing in 2010, Lady Gaga took to YouTube in August 2010 to declare herself "Twitter queen" when she had about 5.7 million followers (Rose 2010). Indicating her sharp rise in popularity, by November 2011, the singer had 16 million followers, a number that stood at 28 million by August 2012 (Johnson 2012). In 2013, Lady Gaga had garnered more than 39 million Twitter followers, but lost her Twitter queen status to Katy Perry, who had almost 40 million followers, while "Twitter king" Justin Bieber had over 42 million (Sciarretto 2013a). By June 2016, with her Twitter account having attracted more than 60 million followers, Lady Gaga ranked eighth in the most-followers list, with Katy Perry, Justin Bieber, and Taylor Swift occupying the top-3 spots.

In part related to the increasing popularity of Twitter and the declining impact of the now defunct (non-affiliated) companion site Twitpic, Lady Gaga joined the increasingly popular photo-sharing site Instagram in June 2012. Her account has since garnered more than 16 million followers.

Other networking sites Lady Gaga is or has been active on include Tumblr (where the singer briefly maintained a fashion blog called Amen†Fashion in June and July of 2012), Ping (the networking site associated with iTunes that was introduced by Lady Gaga in 2010, but that is no longer operational since 2012), Google+ (where the singer has over 10 million followers), and various music websites, such as Last.fm and SoundCloud, where Lady Gaga's music can be heard in addition to Pandora, Spotify, and other streaming services.

Perhaps most remarkable, and surely unique among entertainers, has been the development of LittleMonsters.com, a dedicated website designed by Lady Gaga and her team specifically for the benefit of her own fan community. The site was created after Lady Gaga had seen the movie *The Social Network* about Facebook founder Mark Zuckerberg, and called her then-manager Troy Carter with the idea to develop a website exclusively dedicated to her fans (Sutphen 2013). The website was launched in May 2011 allowing fans to sign up for a beta version of the site that eventually started in February 2012. The fully operational version of the littlemonsters.com website was subsequently launched in July 2012. Based on free registration, users of the site can post content in the form of messages and pictures. The site has been used by Lady Gaga to reach out to her fans and allow registered users advance sales of concert tickets. By April 2016, littlemonsters.com had almost 1 million registered users.

The Public Sphere of Lady Gaga

The role of media in Lady Gaga's rise to fame cannot be undervalued for the very fact that fame is established in interaction with an audience in ways that are always mediated in some form or another. Harmonizing with the cultural perspective of fame defended in this book, the general observation can be made that Lady Gaga as a fame-attaining pop star has benefited from media in ways that are partly conventional, partly novel, and that in some ways reflect the established mechanisms and formats of the existing media institutions, yet that also penetrated into those media in creative ways newly and uniquely devised by Lady Gaga and her team. The media landscape does not reflect a wholly conservative force of hegemonic cultural dominance, for it would not need nor allow a character like Lady Gaga to appear along the many more orthodox performers that are always available in the world of popular music. Yet, at the same time, even Lady Gaga must play along in and with the media as they are already formed in the world in which she seeks to establish a career. As such, the public sphere of Lady Gaga to some extent involves an adaptation to the existing structures of pop culture, yet to another extent shows the power of disruption and innovation that she and her collaborators relied upon.

Much like Lady Gaga's music is stylistically in some ways conventional and in other ways genre-bending (see Chap. 10), the method of its production and distribution also reflects the central duality that marks the Lady Gaga media landscape. On the one hand, Lady Gaga has consistently released music in the form of singles and albums, accompanied by videos, abiding to a structure that has been firmly established since at least the 1960s, when single and album formats became popular, and the 1980s, when MTV and other music television stations normalized the music video as an indispensable medium of popular music. On the other hand, the approach to the distribution and selling of Lady Gaga's music is firmly rooted in the post-2008 climate in which it was made. Rather than only relying on CDs and downloads, Lady Gaga's recorded music is available in every conceivable and available format, digital and online or otherwise, in a wide range of different editions. The product diversification that marks Lady Gaga merchandise and her public persona as a whole (as discussed in Chap. 4) is as such also reflected in the commodity of her recorded music. It is also reflected in the release of the singer's music through various media, from retail stores to streaming services, executed on the basis of various strategies that involve more or less lead time on a more or less wider scale.

The dual strategy of adaptation and innovation is most clearly revealed in the manner in which Lady Gaga has relied simultaneously on a wide variety of media in a number of different ways. To be sure, former manager Troy Carter is right when he refers to Lady Gaga as a "digital baby" (in Rao 2010) as the singer has indeed used the avenues of online media arguably more effectively than any other artist before her. In the distinctiveness of her rise to fame at the very beginning of the now normalized era of the smart phone and social networking sites, Lady Gaga is rivaled perhaps only by teen sensation Justin Bieber, who likewise reached global stardom after the once new online technologies were already in place and established, though not yet adequately recognized by music industry insiders.

The novel nature of Lady Gaga's online media strategy was, of course, partly due to the fact that the internet had not nearly been as developed as it was in the years before the time when Lady Gaga began her recording career. Yet, the approach to take advantage of the internet to build Lady

Gaga's career was otherwise also characterized by its decidedly relentless and diversified approach across multiple platforms, including the singer's own website, the various popular social networking sites, especially Twitter and Facebook, and the littlemonsters.com website that is specifically devoted to the Lady Gaga fan community. The scope of outreach on the internet is potentially global and can be controlled more independently by Lady Gaga and her team. The use of online media will additionally have benefited from the fact that former manager Carter is extensively involved in the world of tech companies and that Lady Gaga herself had an early awareness of the impact of the internet via her own relevant online experience as an unsigned singer and her father's background in Wi-Fi technologies. Striking also is the great attention that is paid to the integrity of the news and information that is shared via Lady Gaga's networking sites. Lady Gaga's accounts on Twitter and Instagram, in particular, are until this day maintained exclusively by the singer herself.

Lady Gaga's embrace of the internet has not stood alone—far from it, in fact—as she has also benefited greatly from a penetration in the time-honored media of radio, television, and news, in its both print and online versions. Especially early on in her career, the traditional medium of radio was relied upon to get Lady Gaga's music out to wider audiences, in addition to promoting her heavily in smaller clubs and, from then on, gradually through increasingly elaborate tours (see Chap. 7). The centrality of the role of radio is affirmed by the fact that online networking sites were initially explored by Lady Gaga and her team "out of desperation," to use the words of manager Carter, precisely because radio could not readily be reached when it was understood that radio had to be reached (TheLeapTV YouTube video). Along with television, radio has the advantage of being able to reach a much broader audience than only the most dedicated fans of the music of Lady Gaga. And for the establishment of her fame, in that sense, the more conventional media are more important than any online platforms, some of which until this day remain secondary to a large segment of the population as sources of information relative to radio and television. The role of the media in the case of Lady Gaga should therefore not be reduced, as some have done (Bennett 2014; Click et al. 2013), to the audience of her most ardent fans alone. To the establishment of Lady Gaga's fame, after all, it matters less whether a dedicated audience likes her or her music as that a wide general public knows her and, in whichever form, pays attention to her, whether they like to or not. As such, the liberating force of Lady Gaga's successful penetration of the media landscape across the board indicates its emancipatory potentials against any pre-structured market directives.

Finally, based on the changing nature of Lady Gaga's media presence in recent years, at least two observations can be made that indicate the changing nature of the singer's fame in quantitative as well as qualitative respects. Whereas Lady Gaga was all the rage in the media in the central years of the establishment of her fame in 2009 and 2010, she has since been less of a topic of obsessive discussion, though far from neglected, and has lost some of the centrality she once enjoyed in popular culture. For example, on *Billboard* magazine's Social 50 chart, which estimates the activity musicians enjoy on the major social networking services, Lady Gaga spent a total of no less than 11 weeks in the top spot in 2011, but she ranked only 38th in the Spring of 2016 (Billboard "Charts: Social 50"). The many fan sites that were once devoted to the singer, likewise, have by now dwindled to a mere dozen.

To some extent, the decrease in active attention Lady Gaga has recently received, no doubt, is a function of the development of her fame from its rise to its arrival and continuation, but it may have especially affected the singer as she embraced and entertained the notion of (the) fame so resolutely. Further, precisely because Lady Gaga's once relatively novel use of online media proved to be successful, those strategies have since been adopted by a great many artists and have also generally increased in popularity outside the world of popular music. Even in the relatively few years since Lady Gaga's rise to fame, it is now already difficult to grasp that the singer's early use of the social networking sites, in particular, was relatively unprecedented right until 2009, when record companies were still generally hostile toward any internet media, which were seen as the primary cause of the music industry's decline. But the trailblazing role of Lady Gaga on the internet has been so successful that, ironically, today her presence in the cyber world has become less central. In the now saturated online world of popular music and other realms of popular culture, attention goes to so many at once that fewer can get the standout attention that can lead to fame.

From a qualitative viewpoint, moreover, it has been striking that Lady Gaga has already been discussed as an established star who has in more recent years experienced a few bumps in the road. Some criticisms of fatigue and an alleged lack of originality had already accompanied her 2011 album *Born This Way* (Anderson 2011; Newman 2011), but it was especially in 2014 that more than the occasional media report appeared to question whether, or even proclaim that, the singer's career and fame had come to a halt (Dorval 2014; Duca 2014; George 2014). At that time, Lady Gaga had just fired her manager Troy Carter, who had been with her from the start, and her *ARTPOP* album and its accompanying tour were said to underperform. The release of *ARTPOP* was accompanied by an app that was originally announced as "the future of album," but eventually never released in its complete intended version (Vitez 2013). In April 2016, the company Backplane that was set up and supported by Troy Carter, Lady Gaga, Google chairman Eric Schmidt, and others to create the littlemonsters.com website filed for bankruptcy (Constine 2016). Nonetheless, the reports of Lady Gaga's demise were not only greatly exaggerated, but they also showed that the singer remained in the news and thereby ironically maintained her fame. Moreover, since then, especially following her critically acclaimed work with Tony Bennett and several very well-received artistic contributions outside the world of pop, Lady Gaga has been greeted with a new kind of respectability that may indicate a favorable media environment for her upcoming music releases and the continuation of her fame, although the long-term success and fame of Lady Gaga must remain, of course, an open question.

Conclusion

It is not true, this chapter has shown, that the internet has been primarily responsible for Lady Gaga's success. Instead, what is most special about the singer's fame, in view of its reliance on a wide variety of media, is that Lady Gaga has creatively exploited the new media of the internet while at the same time also successfully relying on the traditional media of radio, television, and news. On the basis of the distribution of Lady Gaga's recorded music as well as various aspects of her public persona, a multitude of media were pursued to build a fan base and, on the basis of that core following, subsequently reach a wider audience via the exploitation of many additional media. Importantly, then, Lady Gaga has not neglected the traditional media. By appearing in print as well as on radio and TV and, in this way, attract a broad audience, Lady Gaga has been exposed in terms of both her many sounds and her equally, if not even more, striking visions. Hence, Lady Gaga's success and, more broadly, her fame have relied on the singer's inversion of the historical precedence of radio over internet to move from internet to radio (and other traditional media) and effectively establish a presence in any and all media.

It may reflect an idealized notion of the power of social networking sites and other online communication forms to assume that the present media landscape is no longer characterized by the hierarchies that marked the pre-internet era. In fact, Lady Gaga herself once defended such an objectively untenable position in a piece entitled "Extreme Critic Fundamentalism" that was originally published for *V Magazine* in 2011. "The reality of today's media," she wrote, "is that there are no echelons … And the hierarchy is embalmed—for us all to remember nostalgically, and honor that it once was modern, but is now irrelevant" (in Cheung 2011). It is not only remarkable to read such a statement when it is obviously false, but especially that it is Lady Gaga who challenges the existence of echelons when her career has proven, not only that there still are echelons but also that she has taken full advantage of the existing structures of the media hierarchy and has continued to do so until this day. It is perhaps not only a result of a misplaced romanticism that the simultaneous exploitation of a wide variety of media contributing to the rise of Lady Gaga's career has not readily been acknowledged. Likewise, a scholarly outlook, such as the one adopted in this book, should not lead to overlook that the various factors of the origins and dynamics of fame can only be isolated for analytical purposes. Sight should never be lost of the fact that these factors happen at once in shaping the direction and level of fame. The role of the media, more specifically, relates closely to the dynamics of the audience Lady Gaga has managed to attract and receive attention from.

Notes

1. As with many other Lady Gaga songs from before her rise to fame as well as other songs that have not been officially released since then, the promotional disc from the Lollapalooza days leaked to the public and is now readily available online (Ryan 2009).
2. A list of Lady Gaga's television appearances up until 2011, from which information for this section is taken, is available on Gagapedia (Gagapedia "Television Appearances").
3. Though no longer maintained, the PureVolume pages of Stefani Germanotta and Lady Gaga are still available (Lady Gaga PureVolume; Stefani Germanotta PureVolume).

References

Anderson, Kyle. 2011. Lady Gaga Calls Madonna Comparisons 'Completely Ridiculous' in NME Interview. *Entertainment Weekly*, April 21, 2011. http://www.ew.com/article/2011/04/21/lady-gaga-madonna-comparisons

Barnett, Emma. 2010. Lady Gaga Attracts Over One Billion Video Views on YouTube. *The Telegraph*, October 25, 2010. http://www.telegraph.co.uk/technology/google/8085980/Lady-Gaga-attracts-over-one-billion-video-views-on-YouTube.html

Barton, Laura. 2009. I've Felt Famous My While Life. *The Guardian*, January 20, 2009. http://www.theguardian.com/music/2009/jan/21/lady-gaga-interview-fame

Bauer, Nancy. 2010. Lady Power. *The New York Times*, June 20, 2010. http://opinionator.blogs.nytimes.com/2010/06/20/lady-power/

Bennett, Lucy. 2014. Fan/Celebrity Interactions and Social Media: Connectivity and Engagement in Lady Gaga Fandom. In *The Ashgate Research Companion to Fan Cultures*, eds. Linda Duits, Koos Zwaan, and Stijn Reijnders, 109–120. Farnham, Surrey: Ashgate.

Billboard. Charts: Social 50. http://www.billboard.com/charts/social-50

Callahan, Maureen. 2010. Who's That Lady? *New York Post*, January 21, 2010. http://nypost.com/2010/01/21/whos-that-lady/

Cheung, Nadine. 2011. Lady Gaga Attacks New York Times Fashion Critic. *PopCrush*, September 2, 2011. http://popcrush.com/lady-gaga-attacks-new-york-times-fashion-critic

Click, Melissa A., Hyunji Lee, and Holly W. Holladay. 2013. Making Monsters: Lady Gaga, Fan Identification, and Social Media. *Popular Music and Society* 36(3): 360–379.

Constine, Josh. 2016. Lady Gaga's Startup Backplane Burns Out and Sells Assets. *TechCrunch*, April 11, 2016. http://techcrunch.com/2016/04/11/too-close-to-the-sun/

Cooper, Michael. 2016. Ex Lady Gaga Producer Rob Fusari Reflects on Their Work and on His New Single. *Examiner*, April 8, 2016. http://www.examiner.com/article/ex-lady-gaga-producer-rob-fusari-reflects-on-their-work-and-on-his-new-single

Couldry, Nick. 2016. Celebrity, Convergence, and the Fate of Media Institutions. In *A Companion to Celebrity*, eds. David P. Marshall and Sean Redmond, 98–113. Chichester, UK: Wiley Blackwell.

Dorval, Sophia. 2014. Bored This Way: The Loss of Lady Gaga's Relevance in Pop Culture. *Highbrow*, January 3, 2014. http://www.highbrowmagazine.com/3410-bored-way-loss-lady-gagas-relevance-pop-culture

Duca, Lauren. 2014. The Rise and Fall of Lady Gaga. *The Huffington Post*, March 18, 2014. http://www.huffingtonpost.com/2014/03/18/lady-gaga_n_4978752.html

Dybwad, Barb. 2010. Lady Gaga's "Bad Romance" Takes Over #1 Most Viewed Video on YouTube. *Mashable*, April 14, 2010. http://mashable.com/2010/04/14/lady-gaga-bad-romance-youtube/
Elberse, Anita. 2013. *Blockbusters: Hit-making, Risk-taking, and the Big Business of Entertainment*. New York: Henry Holt and Company.
Ferris, Kerry O. 2010. The Next Big Thing: Local Celebrity. *Society* 47: 392–295.
Frith, Simon. 2001. The Popular Music Industry. In *The Cambridge Companion to Pop and Rock*, eds. Simon Frith, Will Straw, and John Street, 26–52. Cambridge, UK: Cambridge University Press.
Forbes. Website. http://www.forbes.com/
Gagapedia. Television Appearances. http://ladygaga.wikia.com/wiki/Television_appearances
Gamson, Joshua. 1994. *Claims to Fame: Celebrity in Contemporary America*. Berkeley, CA: University of California Press.
George, Kat. 2014. Drowning, Not Waving: The Slow and Bitter End of Lady Gaga's Career. *Noisey*, April 2, 2014. http://noisey.vice.com/blog/drowning-not-waving-the-slow-and-bitter-end-of-lady-gagas-career
Gorman, Lyn, and David McLean. 2009. *Media and Society into the 21st Century: A Historical Introduction*, 2nd edn. Malden, MA: Wiley-Blackwell.
Greenslade, Roy. 2011. Lady Gaga Dominates Magazine Covers. *The Guardian*, January 4, 2011. http://www.theguardian.com/media/greenslade/2011/jan/04/lady-gaga-magazines
Habermas, Jürgen. 1989 (1962). *The Structural Transformation of the Public Sphere: An Inquiry into a Category of Bourgeois Society*. Cambridge, MA: The MIT Press.
Hiatt, Brian. 2009. Lady Gaga: New York Doll. *Rolling Stone*, June 11, 2009. http://www.rollingstone.com/music/news/lady-gaga-new-york-doll-rolling-stones-2009-cover-story-20090611
———. 2011. Deep Inside the Unreal World of Lady Gaga. *Rolling Stone*, June 9, 2011. http://www.rollingstone.com/music/news/deep-inside-the-unreal-world-of-lady-gaga-20110609
Horkheimer, Max, and Theodor W. Adorno. 1972 (1944). *Dialectic of Enlightenment*. New York: Herder and Herder.
James, Nicole. 2013. Lady Gaga Is 'Time' Magazine's Second Most Influential Icon of the Decade. *Fuse*, April 17, 2013. http://www.fuse.tv/2013/04/lady-gaga-time-magazine-second-most-influential-icon
Johnson, James. 2012. Lady Gaga Loses Facebook Followers Record to Eminem. *Inquistr*, August 1, 2012. http://www.inquisitr.com/290567/lady-gaga-loses-facebook-followers-record-to-eminem/
Kaufman, Gil. 2010. Justin Bieber Beats Lady Gaga In YouTube Video Popularity – For Now. *MTV.com*, July 16, 2010. http://www.mtv.com/news/1643829/justin-bieber-beats-lady-gaga-in-youtube-video-popularity-for-now/

Lady Gaga. MySpace. https://myspace.com/ladygaga
Lady Gaga. PureVolume. http://www.purevolume.com/ladygaga
Lady Gaga. Twitter post, January 1, 2011 (12:01 AM). https://twitter.com/ladygaga/status/21068576639160320
Lester, Paul. 2010. *Lady Gaga: Looking for Fame. The Life of a Pop Princess.* London: Omnibus Press.
Leyshon, Andrew, Peter Webb, Shaun French, Nigel Thrift, and Louise Crewe. 2005. On the Reproduction of the Musical Economy After the Internet. *Media, Culture & Society* 27(2): 177–209.
Marshall, P. David. 1997. *Celebrity and Power: Fame in Contemporary Culture.* Minneapolis, MN: University of Minnesota Press.
Mills, C. Wright. 1956. *The Power Elite.* New York: Oxford University Press.
Rao, Leena. 2010. Lady Gaga's Manager: We Make Music Videos For YouTube. *TechCrunch*, May 26, 2010. http://techcrunch.com/2010/05/26/lady-gagas-manager-we-make-music-videos-for-youtube/
Robinson, Lisa. 2010. Lady Gaga's Cultural Revolution. *Vanity Fair*, September 2010, 280–286, 329–331.
———. 2012. In Lady Gaga's Wake. *Vanity Fair*, January 2012, 50–61, 111–113.
Robinson, Peter. 2014. Beyoncé Has Reinvented How to Release an Album. Over to You, Adele. *The Guardian*, January 1, 2014. https://www.theguardian.com/music/2014/jan/01/beyonce-redefined-release-album-adele
Rose, Lacey. 2010. Lady Gaga, Twitter Queen. *Forbes*, August 23, 2010. http://www.forbes.com/sites/laceyrose/2010/08/23/lady-gaga-twitter-queen/
Russoniello, Matt. 2016. Talent Always Wins: How Lady Gaga Monster-Clawed Her Way Back to Cultural Dominance. *Celebuzz*, February 9, 2016. http://www.celebuzz.com/2016-02-09/lady-gaga-super-bowl-comeback/?utm_source=sc-tw&utm_medium=ref&utm_campaign=ladygaga
Ryan, Chris. 2009. Song You Need To Know: Lady Gaga, 'Kandy Life'. *MTV.com*, December 28, 2009. http://www.mtv.com/news/2294898/song-you-need-to-know-lady-gaga-kandy-life/
Sciarretto, Amy. 2013a. Katy Perry Has More Twitter Followers Than Lady Gaga! *PopCrush*, July 26, 2013. http://popcrush.com/katy-perry-twitter-followers-lady-gaga/
———. 2013b. 'Applause' Becomes Lady Gaga's Biggest Radio Hit. *PopCrush*, October 21, 2013. http://popcrush.com/applause-lady-gaga-biggest-radio-hit/
Smillie, Dirk. 2009. The Business of Lady Gaga. *Forbes*, November 25, 2009. http://www.forbes.com/2009/11/25/lady-gaga-music-business-entertainment-marketing.html
Stefani Germanotta. PureVolume. http://www.purevolume.com/stefanilive
Strauss, Neil. 2010. The Broken Heart and Violent Fantasies of Lady Gaga. *Rolling Stone*, July 8, 2010. http://www.rollingstone.com/music/news/the-broken-heart-and-violent-fantasies-of-lady-gaga-20100708

Suster, Mark. 2016. Spotting, Nurturing and Mentoring Talent – The Power of Troy Carter. *Both Sides of the Table*, February 26, 2016. http://www.bothsidesofthetable.com/2016/02/26/spotting-nurturing-and-mentoring-talent-the-power-of-troy-carter/

Sutphen, David. 2013. Troy Carter: Taming the Fame Monster. *Brunswick Review*, (7) Summer 2013. http://www.brunswickgroup.com/publications/brunswick-review/issue-7/troy-carter-taming-the-fame-monster/

Théberge, Paul. 2001. 'Plugged In': Technology and Popular Music. In *The Cambridge Companion to Pop and Rock*, eds. Simon Frith, Will Straw, and John Street, 3–25. Cambridge, UK: Cambridge University Press.

———. 2015. Digitalization. In *The Routledge Reader on The Sociology of Music*, eds. John Shepherd and Kyle Devine, 329–338. London: Routledge.

TheLeapTV. Troy Carter | Atom Factory | 2015. *YouTube video*, March 11, 2015. https://www.youtube.com/watch?v=MVYdt3A6MQM

TMZ. 2014. Lady Gaga Music Video Pulled Reportedly Because of Sexual Assault Claims. *TMZ*, June 19, 2014. http://www.tmz.com/2014/06/19/lady-gaga-music-video-sexual-assault-do-what-u-want/

Van Meter, Jonathan. 2011. Lady Gaga: Our Lady of Pop. *Vogue*, February 10. http://www.vogue.com/865458/lady-gaga-our-lady-of-pop/

———. 2012. Dream Girl: Lady Gaga Graces the September Issue of *Vogue*. *Vogue*, August 21, 2012. http://www.vogue.com/865316/dream-girl-lady-gaga/

Vena, Jocelyn. 2011. Lady Gaga 'Born This Way' Release Details Unveiled. *MTV.com*, February 10, 2011. http://www.mtv.com/news/1657636/lady-gaga-born-this-way/

Vitez, Michael. 2013. At His Lowest, Troy Carter Found a Perfect Match: Lady Gaga. *Philly.com*, February 26, 2013. http://articles.philly.com/2013-02-26/news/37291180_1_lady-gaga-troy-carter-clubs

Warman, Matt. 2010. Lady Gaga Most 'Liked' on Facebook. *The Telegraph*, December 31, 2010. http://www.telegraph.co.uk/technology/facebook/8233650/Lady-Gaga-most-liked-on-Facebook.html

Wikström, Patrik. 2009. *The Music Industry: Music in the Cloud*. Cambridge, UK: Polity.

CHAPTER 7

The Audience of Lady Gaga: Beyond the Little Monsters

It is impossible to be famous without an audience. But it is possible to be famous without fans. It is perhaps because of some of the unique or, at least, most outstanding and widely recognized aspects of Lady Gaga's fame that a differentiation between the singer's fans and her audience is not always carefully drawn. Yet, studying the audience of Lady Gaga as of any other person of fame, it is more than insightful to differentiate among its various segments as they each contribute to the rise and development of fame differently, in ways that are conceptually not necessarily on the same level of analysis. Specifically, in connection with the dynamics of fame in the world of popular music, as I will show in this chapter, the fandom of a famous pop star must be conceived as one element in the attraction which that star receives from a much wider and quite differently connected audience.

My observations in this chapter relate closely to what was said in the previous chapter on how media engage a plurality of publics in multiple ways. Even more than in the case of media, investigations on the role of the audience are elementary to the scholarly study of fame, as has long been recognized (Lewis 1992; Marshall 1997:61–71), and can be approached from a variety of disciplinary angles and theoretical perspectives. Fitting the orientation of this book, the central focus is on the role of the publics of Lady Gaga in the origins of her fame and, furthermore, how members of the various segments of the Lady Gaga publics interact with the star as well as with one another. A great many other questions, of course, could and need to be asked toward the development of a general sociological theory of the audiences of fame, but, as with the other conditions of fame analyzed in this book, their relevance must be brought out analytically relative to a specific disciplinary outlook and an appropriate theory developed therein. In this chapter, I will first briefly outline the contours of a theoretical perspective that by now will be familiar inasmuch as it forms a central part of the cultural framework introduced in Chap. 2 and closely connects to what was said in the previous chapter about the role of media. Against a reductionist perspective, the constructionist approach to the publics or audiences of fame can, in the case of Lady Gaga and other popular music stars, be most fruitfully elaborated on in terms of the ways in which the dimensions of time and space relate to the distribution of music and related artistic expressions as the core of fame. On the basis of this model, it will make sense to analyze the role of the fans of Lady Gaga and of the other members of her audience and how they connect with her and with one another, including the interactions they enjoy at live concert events. Against an all-too-popular misconception, I will argue that the fan community of Lady Gaga's so-called Little Monsters should not primarily be considered part of the audience that bestows attention to her in the constitution of her fame. Instead, Lady Gaga's most devoted fans contribute to the singer's rise to fame as part of the attraction she enjoys, as a cultural phenomenon, from other and much wider segments of her audience.

The Publics of Fame and Music

Sociologically understood, as explained in Chap. 2, fame involves a relationship between a person or group to whom attention is given, on the one hand, and the members of the audience who bestow that attention. Despite its centrality from an inter-subjectivist perspective which no sociology can avoid, the conceptualization of the publics of fame has theoretically received less consideration than the role of the media. This relative neglect of the public has been due to the focus in so-called critical-theoretical circles on media forces as an industry that is based on a market model in which (active) producers can determine the taste of (passive) consumers. In Horkheimer and Adorno's (1944) work on the culture industry, the uniformity of popular culture is said to be accomplished because its recipients are conceived to be passive consumers, capable only "to accept what the culture manufacturers offer" (p. 124). In his contemplations on fame, C. Wright Mills defends a similarly reductionist perspective of celebrity in terms of money and power. However, Mills also introduced an important conceptual distinction between public and mass to bring out the variable connection between the producers and recipients of mediated culture, including the ratio of the number of communicators to the number of listeners, the possibility of two-way communication, the relation of opinion to action, and the relative autonomy of the citizenry (1956:302–303). Yet, while Mills thus offered important methodological tools for the study of the role of media in culture, his theoretical position remained wholly reductionist and deterministic. Indeed, in the case of a modern society like the United States, Mills famously argued, the trend was toward the development of the antithesis of a free society and the "ascendancy of the cheerful robot" (1959:171).

The cultural turn in the social sciences has implied the adoption of a constructionist perspective that allows to bring out the role of agency on the part of the various participants in the practice of their culture. In the context of the study of fame, this re-orientation can bring out the constitutive role of the audience in the creation of fame. This conceptualization has recently benefited from the increased opportunities in contemporary society through which celebrity and audience can interact in ways that are indeed less one-sided than Mills once envisioned. In today's age in which a measure of decentralization of media, though far from complete, is at least more real than ever before in the form of the widespread availability of mobile digital devices, new opportunities are available for many more social actors to participate in celebrity culture, not necessarily to become famous, but surely to participate more actively in its construction (Turner 2016).

In the study of popular culture, the participation of an audience is inevitable, albeit it variable, as some of its cultural forms can indeed be more popular than others. In the case of popular music, obvious sociological attention therefore goes to the audience of music, its composition, age, location, level and mode of organization, and other relevant characteristics. Taking my cues from insights in the sociology of music concerning the role of audiences, a model can be introduced to study the publics of Lady Gaga's fame on the basis of the relevance of the dimensions of space and time in the world of music and popular culture (Bennett 2015; Straw 2001). No special clarification will be needed of the specialty field of historical-comparative sociology to bring out the relevance of space and time in social life generally, but their relevance in the case of popular music and, by extension, fame, especially as it is acquired in the area of music, can be especially illuminating.

In terms of space, popular music can be said to be more or less everywhere as a routine part of everyday life. The role of technology in the dissemination of music across society is not the recent invention of the internet, but dates back to the medium of radio, which allowed for a wide-scale participation in music from the privacy of one's home. The advent of television and various media of music distribution, especially vinyl records and, later compact discs and downloads, expanded these opportunities to create a mass audience. Historically, live concert tours by the performers of popular music grew alongside the ever-expanding reach of radio, indicating the relevance of the interrelationship among various media which, as the previous chapter showed, Lady Gaga critically relied upon in the development of her career.

The relevance of live concert performances today is amplified by the fact that revenue from the sale of recorded music has declined sharply. In the world of popular music, tours were traditionally organized to promote a new record release or, in the case of established "nostalgia" acts, to promote an existing catalog. In more recent years, an important reversal has taken place as recorded music releases nowadays mostly serve to promote concert tours, which, along with merchandise, have become the main source of revenue. From the viewpoint of the audience, live concerts are of special significance as they allow for interaction with the performing artist as well as with other fans. Through other avenues, too, both online and in the physical world, music fans can communicate with one another and create a collective dimension to their fandom (with other fans) and, at an individual level, establish identity (of self) at both local and wider levels of interaction. In the case of fame in the world of popular music, the audience incorporates the totality of all fans (who admire the star), anti-fans (who are highly critical of the star), and non-fans (inasmuch as they express not to be interested in the star).

Turning to the dimension of time, the world of popular music as of other manifestations of popular culture is typically marked by a wave of styles that grow in and out of fashion. In the case of pop music, in particular, success and popularity can be very fleeting and, based on the notion of hits and weekly charts, is often a matter of a moment rather than a period. Also changing over time are the age groups popular music's audiences are primarily drawn from. The world of popular music has traditionally been associated with teenagers, adolescence, and youth culture, but is today demographically more broadly represented and duly marketed across various age groups, ranging from pre-teens to senior citizens, who are involved in music and its associated lifestyles. This broad participation has a commercial aspect in terms of the age categories that are more or less likely to have the financial means to buy music (in the form of recorded music, merchandise, or tickets for live concerts), but also more broadly applies to other forms of involvement in the reception of music, including participation in all kinds of interactions and communications regarding recording and performing musicians, thus contributing to their success and fame. Technological advances have brought about that recorded music as well as the media through which fame is generated is now more readily available than ever before. The means to participate in the social world of music as well as to establish fame are now held in people's hands.

The Demography of Lady Gaga

It is a truism to observe that Lady Gaga has done wonders in connecting with her fans, but she has also more broadly been able to bring her music to multiple segments of the public, many of whom may not even be fans of her or her work. From early on in her career, Lady Gaga has been able to take her music and herself successfully to the public and has been effective in opening up channels of communication and attention, especially, as discussed in Chap. 6, by establishing a formidable presence on social networking sites and at the same time being present in all possible media to reach a wide variety of publics at the level of the global population.

Gaga Fandom and Audience

Lady Gaga found her earliest commercial success as a recording musician in selected avenues of pop music on the internet and, in the physical world, in the dance club scenes, especially among the gay community. Special attention in discussing the Lady Gaga fan base must therefore go to the favorable reception her music has enjoyed in the gay scene. Particularly early on during the establishment of her career from the Spring of 2008 on, Lady Gaga could count on the gay clubs as among the first places where her music was favorably received, the relevance of which Lady Gaga herself had also recognized. "The turning point for me was the gay community," she has said, adding that this early support was instrumental in giving her exposure which subsequently enabled her to move into radio and reach other publics (Vena 2009a). By August 2009, the LGBT magazine *Out* called Lady Gaga pop music's "newest and gayest superstar" (Out 2009). The support and recognition Lady Gaga enjoyed from the gay community also continued once the singer became a global star. Following the move of her career and fame toward broader audiences and across more places, Lady Gaga has likewise continued to acknowledge her indebtedness to the support she has received from the gay community and continued to make gay-friendly artistic choices in her music and take on gay-rights-related activism issues as an explicit part of her work (see Chap. 8).

At the time of her early popularity in the club scene, including the musical cultures connected to the gay community, as well as on the internet, the majority of Lady Gaga's earliest audiences in the totality of her demography were mostly made up of relatively young urban pop and dance music fans. Early exposure in foreign markets, such as Canada and Sweden, added an international dimension, but it was especially from the time of her early global career success onward that Lady Gaga's audience became as big as it was diverse. Since her singles of 2009 became smash hits across the world and the airwaves and other media became saturated with an incessant attention to the performer, it has become almost literally true that everybody knows Lady Gaga. More specifically related to her fans (those who like her music and other aspects of her persona), Lady Gaga's appeal can be seen to cut across generations, ranging from teenagers to senior citizens, displaying various levels of intensity in their devotion. The relatively broad range of Lady Gaga's audience, in general, but also of her fan base, more specifically, may indicate, as the singer herself proclaimed during the early phase of her success, that her presence in pop culture served to fill a void, specifically by bringing pop music and the idea of the larger-than-life pop star back. "People are truly hungry for this," the singer maintained while her career was taking off in the Spring of 2009, arguing that the culture of pop music "is back. I promise you. It's happening right now" (in Montgomery 2009).

As Lady Gaga's popularity grew over the course of her continued successful music career, especially from the Monster Ball tour onward through to the release of *Born This Way* in 2011, both the audiences of her fame as well as the fan base of her music and persona continued to grow in size and diversity. Besides a young urban crowd, also drawn to various aspects of Lady Gaga's presence were many other social categories, including females who saw in the singer a strong role model, popular music fans from all walks of life who recognized her artistic talents, as well as all those who proclaimed not to enjoy anything about the singer at all. Whatever the nature of the emotional energy that has been invested in Lady Gaga following her successful grab for pop stardom and the attention that creates fame, the centrality of the singer's place in pop culture, once it was achieved, could not rationally be denied. By August 2011, Lady Gaga was ranked 11th on the world's 100 most powerful women list published by *Forbes* magazine, ranking her in the top spot in the "Celebrity Power" category (Skarda 2011). After a period of relative withdrawal from the center of global pop attention following the release of *ARTPOP* in 2013, it has not only been noteworthy that the singer has come back strong, especially thanks to her collaborative work with Tony Bennett in the world of jazz, but also that this renewed success and fame diversified her audience and fan base once again, as especially an older generation warmed up to the singer's recent artistic ventures outside the world of pop and dance music.

The Little Monsters

Lady Gaga has a specific and distinct understanding of her fans, whom she refers to as Little Monsters, an expression the singer herself coined during her 2009 summer tour, using the term for the first time on May 9, 2009 during a live performance at the Wango Tango Festival in Irvine, California. At the time, Lady Gaga was preparing the release of her album *The Fame Monster* and professed to a fascination with monsters. The Little Monsters designation has since been adopted by many of her most devoted fans as well as by other members of the Lady Gaga audience referring to that particularly dedicated segment of her wider fandom. In an interview with Larry King in 2010, the singer explained the origins of the term. Talking about how she saw her fans behaving at her shows, she said that it appeared to her they were "salivating at the mouth," that "they were rabid," and "they just behaved like monsters" (in CNN 2010). Lady Gaga at the time sang about monsters and related themes of fright, fear, and death, such as in her song "Monster" and in "Bad Romance" where she references three Alfred Hitchcock movies, and she more broadly displays a theme of monstrosity in her work, defying gender stereotypes (Chap. 9).

The Little Monsters designation has become widely adopted among Lady Gaga's most devoted followers, aided by the singer's own continued use of the term in interviews and at concerts. During the arena version of the Monster Ball in 2010 and 2011, the singer could be heard to narrate a so-called Manifesto of Little Monsters that was also included in the booklet accompanying the super deluxe version of *The Fame Monster* album. Since then, it has also become popular among fans to refer to Lady Gaga as "Mother Mother," a term the singer introduced and devoted its own "Manifesto of Mother Monster" to during the Born This Way Ball tour. Further strengthening the collective identity of her most devoted fan base, Lady Gaga also gave her Little Monsters a unique gesture of greeting and identification, the so-called monster claw. The gesture was introduced by Lady Gaga at her live shows in December 2009 after she had seen one of her fans greeting another fan using the hand gesture that was originally part of the choreography in the video to "Bad Romance."

Several distinct qualities characterize Lady Gaga's Little Monsters and their community as a whole. Most strikingly perhaps is the peculiarly strong sense of commitment and loyalty that exists in the Lady Gaga fan community, both on the part of the fans and Lady Gaga herself. Lady Gaga has on many occasions expressed her connection to and appreciation of her fans, a special sense of empathy that was already presented on her first album *The Fame* in the form of its underlying message of a notion of a shared fame (see Chap. 3). With the release of *The Fame Monster*, Lady Gaga expressed this shared sense of fame more explicitly still, specifically in the "Manifesto of Little Monsters" in which she introduced a role reversal by describing her fans as "the kings" and "the queens" while she herself would be only "something of a devoted jester" (Gagapedia "Manifesto of Little Monsters"). In most all of her interviews during her rise to fame and at the height of her career as well as time and time again in her online communications, Lady Gaga can be heard to extol the virtues of her fans and her undivided loyalty to them.

Lady Gaga also makes sure to practice the special bond she sees with her fans through interactions in both the virtual and physical world, in a general sense by communicating with her fans, not just about them, through various media and, more specially, by such concrete actions as taking pictures with fans, giving them autographs, asking for their feedback, and otherwise conversing with them in more or less direct ways. At times the singer also engages with fans on an individual level, such as when she allowed a ten-year old fan to play piano with her on stage, had a fan she had known for some time listen to songs from *Born This Way* before the album was officially released, and donated the wheelchair she used while recovering from hip surgery to a disabled fan (Vena 2011; Johnson 2013; Wood 2013).

Corresponding to their idol's devotion, Lady Gaga's Little Monsters in turn express their loyalty and dedication in many concrete ways, including waiting in line for long hours to go to multiple shows on her tours, participating actively in online forums and on social networking sites, setting up specialized fan websites, organizing local Lady Gaga events and birthday parties, displaying their loyalty by means of tattoos, clothing, and other aspects of visual style, and otherwise spending time, energy, and money on participating in Lady Gaga's music and buying merchandise, concert tickets, and music releases of the singer.

The strength of the connection with Lady Gaga among her most loyal fans is not only extensive, it is also intense on an emotional level. Displaying a fan experience that is essentially affective (Dilling-Hansen 2015), the devotion Lady Gaga enjoys among her Little Monsters does not just focus on the singer's music, fashion, image, and related artistic expressions, nor even on her philosophical ideas, but nothing less than the totality of the person of Lady Gaga. This existential connection is also proclaimed by Lady Gaga herself and is expressed in many ways, from the tattoos she has of the Little Monsters name and the monster claw to her many public statements on the role of her fans, not just for her career, but for her life. Often seen crying while talking about her fans, Lady Gaga shows herself as unequivocally committed to devoting her life and her work to her fans who, as she once said, are "the center" (in Van Meter 2012). "My fans care so much," she explains, "that I can't stop caring" (in Maher 2011). In the "Manifesto of Little Monsters," likewise, the singer expresses the emotional nature of the bond with her fans when she states, "when you're lonely, I'll be lonely too" (Gagapedia "Manifesto of Little Monsters").

In turn, the psychology of many of Lady Gaga's most dedicated fans is such that they will typically say to "love Lady Gaga," not just to like her or her music, and credit the singer for giving them strength and confidence, even for saving their lives (Samson 2011). They also proudly declare themselves to be Little Monsters as an all-encompassing identity that defines the whole of their life and which, they proclaim, will also last a lifetime. Corresponding to Lady Gaga's notion of the fame as a sense of belonging, Little Monsters define their community as a culture which, in the words of one of its members, "does not value fame, but community and identity above all" (JezebelAgogo Twitter post).

The strongly emotional nature of the bond among the Little Monsters as well as with Lady Gaga at times also functions as a source of hostility, aggression, and general negativity. Various forms of conflict can take place among Lady Gaga fans, as evinced from the occasional online bickering among themselves in the Little Monster community in sexist, racist, ageist, and other prejudiced language and the arguments and even fights that can take place among self-proclaimed dedicated fans who have been waiting in line for many hours under a sweltering sun in hopes of getting to their favorite spot on the front row of a Lady Gaga concert. Negative attitudes from Lady Gaga fans have also been directed at other pop stars who are seen as competing with the singer as well as to their fans and others outside the fan community. When singer Adele's album *21* was overtaking Lady Gaga's *Born this Way* in popularity and awards in 2011, the British singer received a number of hateful tweets from Lady Gaga fans referencing her weight (Owen 2011). Hostile communications from self-professed Little Monsters have at times even involved alleged death threats against such celebrities as Kelly Osbourne, Deadmau5, and Perez Hilton.

Even in the Lady Gaga fan community itself it is generally known that the Little Monsters can be among the most intolerant and arrogant of all pop culture fan bases today. But it is much less acknowledged how Lady Gaga herself has contributed to the problem by not adequately dealing with it and only rarely intervening. At one point, the singer wrote an open letter to her fans that she does not support hateful and abusive behavior, leading to the impression that she actually had to tell her fans that "sending death threats to people maybe isn't the best idea" (Williott 2013). On another occasion, Lady Gaga intervened on behalf of one of her fans who had been bullied online by other fans of hers because the singer would have shown special attention to him (Watkins 2012). Ironically, the special dedication Lady Gaga receives from some of her most ardent fans can at times also transform into hostility toward the singer herself, such as when once dedicated super fans turn against the star because of a bad song or subpar video, as the result of a poorly organized meet and greet, or in protest to the singer's unexplained withdrawal from being active online in the period following her recovery from hip surgery.

Most remarkably, negativity in behavior has at times also been displayed by Lady Gaga herself, such as when she once began blocking and admonishing fans on Twitter, earning her the nickname of "internet policewoman Lady Gaga" (Wass 2013). Some former collaborators have at times also expressed less than flattering statements about the singer's conduct. A former tour crew member once called the singer "a bully and a monster herself" for her alleged abusive behavior toward some of her staff (Samson 2013). Similarly, when Lady Gaga had received the Woman of the Year Award from Billboard in December 2015, a former guitarist on the theater version of the Monster Ball tour tweeted that she is "not a good person" because the alopecia-suffering musician had been "fired for not having long hair" and that she had "fat shamed" her former drummer (Shmeeans Twitter post).

The Geography of Lady Gaga

During and since her ascend to pop royalty, Lady Gaga is everywhere all the time, in all the media as well as in everyday life and in the specialized places for music and art, particularly the dance clubs and performance theaters and arenas. In order to establish contact with her fans in the physical world of the performance of her art, Lady Gaga and other artists of popular music continue to rely on the centrality of live concert shows. In the current digital age, moreover, live shows have taken on additional significance as the sale of recorded music has decreased sharply. But from a sociological viewpoint, too, there are special aspects involved with the connection that an artist like Lady Gaga can establish with her fans and broader segments of her audience during her live shows.

Before her recording career, as discussed in Chap. 3, the singer now known as Lady Gaga performed at open-mic nights and at small-club performances in her native New York City. Following her discovery and signing with Interscope, Lady Gaga went from doing as many as possible shows at small clubs to performing on large tours as a support act for other music star to eventually headlining her own shows at small, then ever bigger venues, in North America and selected countries and, eventually, all over the world. Briefly reviewing the live shows of Lady Gaga's professional touring career, her small-club performances in 2008 involved typically not more than a medley of two or three songs. Based on a model then-manager Troy Carter knew to have been effective in the world of hip hop and rap music, Lady Gaga performed at club after club on as many days as possible for several months to get a buzz going and subsequently move into the mainstream (Sacks 2014). Additionally, in selected markets in the United States and abroad, longer one-hour shows were organized where Lady Gaga was accompanied by two or three dancers and a DJ, with the performer singing live to a pre-recorded track of about eight songs from the debut album *The Fame*. The same set also formed the basis for Lady Gaga's support slot on arena tours with New Kids On The Block in North America in November 2008 and with the Pussycat Dolls in Europe and Oceania in January and May of 2009. In the Spring of 2009, the Fame Ball Tour is held as Lady Gaga's first headlining tour in relatively small venues in North America. Over the Summer, the tour moves to countries in Europe, Asia, and Oceania, where the singer also performs at festivals.

The Monster Ball tour, organized following the release of the album *The Fame Monster*, showed Lady Gaga performing at the highest level of global pop stardom. Beginning on November 27, 2009 in Montreal, the shows were in their original run organized for theater-sized venues. The decision to hold the initial series of concerts in theaters rather than in larger arenas was based on the idea to "not skip a step" in building the career of Lady Gaga, who at the time was "in the middle of an album cycle" of the newly released *The Fame Monster* (LeBlanc 2010). Originally, Lady Gaga had been slated to co-headline a tour called Fame Kills with Kanye West, but the shows were canceled following West's much-publicized interruption of Taylor Swift during her acceptance speech at the 2009 MTV Video Music Awards (Goodman 2009). From February 2010 onward, the Monster Ball continued at the arena level, ending in May 2011 with two stadium shows in Mexico City. In its arena version, the show involved some 120 people, including a 12-piece live band and as many dancers, 30 trucks, and 17 buses. The decision to present the theater and the arena versions of the Monster Ball shows as part of one tour was also strategically oriented at increasing the scope of the concert series as well as the accompanying gross revenue, in which terms the tour is among the most successful of all time. Lady Gaga's next world tours, the Born This Way Ball (2012–2013) and the artRAVE (2014), took place on a similarly grand scale, while smaller and, for jazz, more appropriate theaters were primarily chosen for the 2015 concert series that supported the *Cheek To Cheek* album with Tony Bennett.

The live shows of Lady Gaga, especially those involving performances of her pop music in arenas, are designed to be artistic in both musical and visual ways, consisting of songs drawn from the singer's various albums, accompanied by elaborate sets, costume changes, and video interludes, and additionally displaying a thematic story component that is modeled on the format of musical theater. The Monster Ball, in particular, Lady Gaga presented as "the first ever pop-electro opera" that aspired to take "the form of the greatest post-apocalyptic house party that you've ever been to" (in Vena 2009b). Substantively, Lady Gaga's live shows have a theme and involve a story line and various ideas, and at times even carry a message. The Monster Ball recounted the evolution of Lady Gaga in her journey to fame and was devoted to spreading her message of liberation and freedom. The shows were also presented in terms of Lady Gaga connecting with her fans in a space where they belong and engage, as she said, in a "celebration of shame" (in CNN 2010). Extending from this message, the Born This Way Ball portrayed the singer as an alien who had landed on earth to spread love, music, and fashion, while the artRAVE tour emphasized the joy of an all-night rave party. In the current era of dwindling album sales, it is to be noted, Lady Gaga's live shows have also become central sites to sell merchandise and for fans to meet their idol in arranged and oftentimes sponsored meet and greets, or by having Lady Gaga call them up on stage or to spontaneously meet her backstage after the show. The economics of such efforts co-exist with their emotional significance on the part of the fans and the fame-generating qualities that result from the star's assumed generosity.

In terms of the audiences Lady Gaga has managed to attract over the course of her touring career, several important changes have taken place. From an initial focus on her dedicated fan base in the small shows from the beginning of her career up until the Fame Ball, the audience of the Monster Ball had grown far beyond the fans of Lady Gaga alone to include what music fans typically refer to as the "general public" (or "GP"). The size of the audiences Lady Gaga reached with the Monster Ball (an estimated 1.5 million) was matched by their diversity, including people from across age groups and musical tastes as well as Little Monsters who added to the spectacle others could see. The Born This Way Ball tour was also highly successful in terms of concert attendance and additionally attracted the occasional controversy that furthered Lady Gaga's fame. In some countries, such as China and Korea, several of Lady Gaga's songs have been subjected to government censorship efforts, which also affected her concert performances (Shadbolt 2014). In Korea, by example, the Born This Way Ball concert was restricted to an adults-only crowd of 18 and older, whereas the planned show in Jakarta was canceled altogether after police failed to issue a permit following threats by a radical Islamist group known as the Islamic Defenders Front that is known for committing acts of violence against Christians and humanitarian aid workers (Bychawski 2012; Deflem 2012).

Whereas Lady Gaga's Born This Way Ball tour drew crowds similar in size to the Monster Ball, the artRAVE witnessed a drop to about 900,000 attendants at 76 shows. The artRAVE tour took place over the course of a

204-day period that was interspersed with a relatively high number of days off, presumably as a result of some days being left unfilled as additional shows in the same venue were not organized. Also striking was that the artRAVE concerts, absent any strong hit singles drawn from the *ARTPOP* album, drew more Little Monsters and a new generation of die-hard fans, as that group had in the meantime grown, but was much less successful among the general public, forcing Lady Gaga to reconceptualize the tour as an underground movement. Not surprisingly, the concert series with Tony Bennett in 2015 did find great favor among a general public largely unfamiliar with Lady Gaga's pop music, drawn from a mostly older generation of concertgoers and jazz aficionados, with many Little Monsters not attending the shows. The quest to reach a broader audience in the most recent years of Lady Gaga's fame has continued on, such as with her performances at the Oscars and at the Super Bowl in 2016, but it will still have to reveal its impact in terms of her 2016 pop album, *Joanne*.

THE SYMMETRY OF LADY GAGA

Given the level of popularity Lady Gaga has come to enjoy in the world of popular music, it is not particularly remarkable to observe that the audience of her music and her fame is demographically both extensive and diverse, geographically extending across the globe at a level difficult to attain in less popular art forms. The choice to perform pop and dance music, in itself, has ramifications for the level of fame that can be expected and, as I will show in Chap. 9, may have directly influenced Lady Gaga, especially in view of her gender. Though certain waves can already be detected in the popularity of Lady Gaga's career, it is clear that her fame involves a world audience. The Lady Gaga fandom, moreover, is especially significant in its constitution as an identifiable community with its own name and other identifiable symbols. But the role of the Little Monsters and the nature of the relationships Lady Gaga enjoys with them as well as with other members of her multiple audiences should not be misunderstood. On the basis of the constructionist perspective, this discussion section will clarify some of the sociologically relevant aspects of Lady Gaga's publics.

By definition, the relationship between an audience and a person of fame is marked by an asymmetry inasmuch as the intimacy that is created in interactions with the audience's object of attention is objectively one-sided (Ferris 2001, 2010). The fans and other members of the many publics of Lady Gaga know much more about her (virtually everything) than she knows about them (just about nothing). However, sociologically it is more important to observe that audience interactions in the pop culture of fame are inter-subjectively rarely recognized in these terms, especially not in the context of a modern culture marked by a high degree of individualism. This characteristic of assumed reciprocal intimacy applies to the super fan who dreams of having conversations with Lady Gaga as much as it does to the person who deliberately walks out of a Lady Gaga concert and, indeed, those who proclaim, loudly and proudly, not to care about the singer at all.

It is also more true of the days of old rather than today that the icons of fame and celebrity do not mix with ordinary persons, as Jeffery Alexander (2010:329) claims. Although there are still many aspects of interpersonal privilege attached to fame, there is also an illusion at work that it is possible to cross over from the obscurity of the mundane everyday into the world of celebrity stardom, at least by interacting with those who inhabit that world. For especially in the current age of expanded technological opportunities to engage with a person of fame, the possibility of two-way communication is realized more than before. To be sure, many of these interactions remain objectively unreciprocated. Many more tweets are sent to Lady Gaga than she can ever hope to respond to. But any tweet sent to the star by one of her followers, whether they be super fans or "haters," can and might be responded to by her. Even when Lady Gaga has posted a message on one of her fan sites only once or has sent just one tweet to a fan she recognizes from attending many of her shows from the front row, such communications effectively establish symmetry by creating the consequential idea that the singer has a personal connection with all of her fans and speaks with them. The objective truth of this idea (as a remote possibility) is sociologically insignificant to the fact that is (inter-)subjectively believed to be true by many (as an accepted reality) and hence is real in its consequences (Merton 1995). As a result, also, many of Lady Gaga's most dedicated fans think they are genuinely changing the world to be a better place (Billboard 2015). Likewise, anyone who does not like the music or persona of Lady Gaga, for whatever reason, will find elements in her work and presentation that confirm that dismissive attitude, as much as any fan or Little Monster will find something to support their admiration. Lady Gaga discusses this very idea when she presents her work, herself, and the bond she establishes with her fans as a lie for which she would "kill to make it true" (in Sturges 2009).

The consequential idea of the symmetry that is assumed in the world of Lady Gaga is perhaps nowhere demonstrated better than among her dedicated fan base of the Little Monsters. With its own unique designation, its own universal gesture of greeting, and its many other tangible symbols, the Little Monsters can be said to form a veritable subculture of fans, with their own values and the structural position they correspondingly take up in the wider community of popular music and fame. Supported by the Lady Gaga website littlemonsters.com and the fans' own multiple modes of interaction online and at live shows, the Little Monsters are in that sense structurally and culturally similar to other fan communities known for their strong sense of identity and their unique names, such as "Deadheads" and the "Kiss Army." There has been a trend, at least since the popularity of Lady Gaga's Little Monsters, for such terms to become more common, also involving a noted shift from rock to pop music, as the super fans of many a contemporary pop star (among them, Justin Bieber's "Beliebers," Katy Perry's "KatyCats," the boy band One Direction's "Directioners," and Taylor Swift's "Swifties") are more likely to have their own unique name. Though possibly introduced as mere promotional devices, the very success of the adoption of such terms may indication the formation of a greater plurality of fan subcultures.

From the viewpoint of the popularity of Lady Gaga's career, the Little Monsters fulfill both symbolic and instrumental functions. In their various interactions and modes of participation in the world of Lady Gaga, the fans create a common identity and culture, united by gestures and words, leading to a formation of self that leads to identify the whole of one's existence in terms connected to the devotion for Lady Gaga. This understanding of self (of individual fans) also connects with the bond they experience with one another (as a collectivity of fans). The content of these communications includes both matters of substance and of style. From the viewpoint of the fans, the center of attraction consists of Lady Gaga's music and other artistic expressions as well as the related, implicit or explicit messages, on acceptance, tolerance, difference, and freedom, which she intends to communicate and practice in concrete acts of activism, as explained in the next chapter. The style aspects relate primarily to the wider Lady Gaga audience of fame, including the onlookers who stare not only at the star herself but also at her devoted following of Little Monsters, who thereby function as part of the fascination that draws attention and thus help to maintain the fame of Lady Gaga. In addition, the fans have also instrumentally been involved in helping Lady Gaga's professional career, such as by advertising her music, voting for her in award contests, speaking in her favor, and generally keeping her name and music alive. These forms of fan participation have also been actively encouraged by Lady Gaga and her team, for instance by offering support to the fans who run their own fan sites, recruiting fans to join the so-called Lady Gaga Street Team to promote her work in return for rewards, and using pictures, videos, and artwork made by fans for official promotional purposes.

Despite its possible exploitation for career purposes on the part of Lady Gaga and her team, the symbiotic relationship that is maintained between Lady Gaga and her Little Monsters sustains the idea that the promotion of her work needs no outside marketing strategies, but is fully organic and authentic. The bond Lady Gaga enjoys with her most dedicated followers, as shown above, is framed in distinctly emotional terms by both her and her fans, leading to both strong demonstrations of loyalty and love as well as of hostility and conflict. Some of these negative aspects stem from the usual conflicts that can be expected under certain social circumstances, such as the structural conditions that relate to the anonymity on the internet or the relatively high concentration of people in a concert environment. Yet, other dimensions of the peculiar negativity and hostility in the Lady Gaga community can be attributed to certain characteristics of its specific cultural location. Especially because of the positivity of Lady Gaga's messages surrounding tolerance and respect for others, members of her fan community may feel protected from any accusations over improper behavior or even entitled to speak ill of others. In fact, within the Lady Gaga fan community it has sometimes been acknowledged that the negativity that some of her fans display is more pronounced than among the fans of other artists. On at least one occasion, Lady Gaga herself demonstrated the irony of her own community's culture, when she blocked a fan on Twitter precisely when she was promoting an online kindness campaign (Wass 2013). And because of their dedication, of course, Lady Gaga's devoted following of Little Monsters will excuse, condone, and even justify each and every move made by Lady Gaga, even and particularly when others judge it to be problematic.

From a constructionist viewpoint, the observable consequences of the emotional bond between Lady Gaga and the Little Monsters, expressed both in terms of love and sympathy as well as hostility and aggression, makes sense from the viewpoint of an inter-subjective recognition of strong feelings between Lady Gaga and her fans. Much of the fan-related behavior both by Lady Gaga and her Little Monsters may be labeled as outlandish or downright crazy outside its own community where it will typically be greeted with appreciation and respect. What is important from the viewpoint of the constitution of fame is that such appraisals inevitably contribute to the attention Lady Gaga receives by virtue of her most dedicated followers.

Lady Gaga's association with the gay community has also contributed to her fame, especially because of the essential role fans from the gay community played in supporting the beginning of the singer's career. From the viewpoint of building her career, the early favorable response in the gay club scene was deliberately sought out as part of a grassroots approach to construct a platform from which to launch a broader strategy to gain popularity (Suster 2016). Historically, moreover, the special relationship Lady Gaga enjoys with the gay community finds its roots in the relatively unique place of popular music, particularly when it is performed by female singers, in the gay culture (Smith 1995). Especially in a society in which being gay is not, or was not yet, readily accepted, gays need a separate space to live out their identity in the company of other gays, leading to the establishment of gay bars and gay dance clubs and the adoption of some forms of music as especially fitting in those spaces. Moreover, female singers are more likely to be favorably accepted as icons of diva worship in the gay community inasmuch as (male) gays associate with their femininity and their flamboyance and style (Jennex 2013). What is interesting in the case of the reception of Lady Gaga in the gay scene is that it enabled the singer to gain more and more exposure, and by word of mouth, online and elsewhere, to eventually penetrate radio and other media and greatly expand her fan base and reach larger audiences by means of ever-expanding concert tours.

As much as Lady Gaga's fame gradually involved everybody over time, it also spread geographically, both through the exposure in various media and via live concert tours. In the geographical and social growth of her touring, varying functions of Lady Gaga's live shows are revealed, from getting exposure to reach a fan base toward expanding her audience, thereby extending the space of her popularity and her fame from being nowhere (before the fame) to being somewhere (in the dance clubs and the gay scene) to being everywhere (across the media and at concert all over the world). Eventually, Lady Gaga was able to present her own headlining shows as an artistic and commercial end in itself. Needless to say, as a site for witnessing Lady Gaga perform her craft live, concerts form an important moment of close encounter and celebration between Lady

Gaga and her fans as well as among the fans and all attending audience members.

From the viewpoint of the presentation of Lady Gaga's music, live shows to some degree involve a two-way relationship between the singer and her fans, concerning more than music alone, as fans can engage with her—by singing along, clapping, and screaming—and with one another, such as by discussing their fandom and engaging in a common celebration in the context of a physical setting. Live shows also serve as a prime expression for Lady Gaga to show her commitment to her music as well as her devotion to her fans, making sure to clarify, as she often does, that she does not lip-sync and puts all her money in the production of her shows. The objective fact that some of her music and background vocals are pre-taped (though most of her concerts' music and other show elements are indeed performed live) or that it is not her but her fans' money (in addition to that of her sponsors) that she is spending, the inter-subjective recognition of her dedication as a live performer contributes to the authenticity of Lady Gaga.

Conclusion

It is not true, this chapter has shown, that the so-called Little Monsters form the primary constituents of the audience of Lady Gaga's fame. Instead, what is most special about the singer's fame, in view of its reliance on a wide variety of audiences, is that Lady Gaga has creatively exploited the advantages of having her own loyal fan base to be part of her attention-grabbing spectacle, while at the same time also successfully engaging with multiple and diverse audiences to establish her fame on a global scale. The fame of Lady Gaga exists not merely in relation with those who like her, but also with all those who do not know much about her, and even those who proclaim not to like her but who cannot stop talking about her and watch her each and every move.

Several studies have been devoted to the sociological and economic aspects of the phenomenon of Lady Gaga's Little Monsters (Bennett 2014; Click et al. 2013; Huba 2013), but, not recognizing the proper role of Lady Gaga's most devoted fan base, they not only often miss the mark but also overlook the possibility that their scholarly attention is part of the fame they study. Congruent with what was said in Chap. 6 concerning the role of media, it matters most for the constitution of Lady Gaga's fame that a large and diverse number of publics knows Lady Gaga and speaks of her, in whatever way, rather than that she is liked and admired by her most dedicated and loyal fans. The true fame of Lady Gaga exists in the attention she gains, not from her hardcore devotees, but from a much wider mass of fans and semi-fans, non-fans, and anti-fans, who bestow attention to the performer in various forms, whether it be in the form of appreciation, indifference, or dislike. Thus, the positive response Lady Gaga receives from across multiple demographic categories geographically extending across the globe is functionally equivalent to the accusations of inauthenticity, censorship efforts, boycotts, and other negative feedback she occasionally receives as well. What may be lost on Lady Gaga's critics is that any controversy surrounding the singer will get her attention and thus contribute to her fame.

Live concert performances play a special role in connecting Lady Gaga to her audiences in the physical setting of a live show, where the economic benefits of concert tickets, merchandise sales, meet and greets, and other revenue-generating ventures go hand in hand with the intimately experienced authenticity of the fan experience. Today more than ever before, an entire sociology of the body could be written about the role of live concerts in the world of popular music and the interactions that in that context can be practiced with Lady Gaga as well as with other fans. An entire psychology, maybe even psychiatry, of the audience could complement such an approach. While these intellectual efforts need not be accomplished in the context of this book, it is useful to bring out the peculiar emotional energy of the Lady Gaga fan base as one element of her attention-grabbing spectacle. Referring to the object of their devotion as Mother Monster or using similar affectionate terms like "our queen", the Little Monsters declare their love, not a mere liking, for Lady Gaga and all she stands for. Being a Little Monster involves more than an aesthetic disposition toward the art of Lady Gaga and is instead understood in existential terms as the expression of an all-encompassing identity and way of life. The Lady Gaga fandom in that sense also connects with the authenticity that is attributed to Lady Gaga in her work, including her advocacy and activism.

References

Alexander, Jeffrey C. 2010. The Celebrity-Icon. *Cultural Sociology* 4(3): 323–336.
Bennett, Andy. 2015. Identity: Music, Community and Self. In *The Routledge Reader on The Sociology of Music*, eds. John Shepherd and Kyle Devine, 143–152. London: Routledge.

Bennett, Lucy. 2014. Fan/Celebrity Interactions and Social Media: Connectivity and Engagement in Lady Gaga Fandom. In *The Ashgate Research Companion to Fan Cultures*, eds. Linda Duits, Koos Zwaan, and Stijn Reijnders, 109–120. Farnham, Surrey: Ashgate.

Billboard. 2015. Lady Gaga Fan on Being a Little Monster: 'We Are Genuinely Trying to Make the World a Better Place'. *Billboard*, August 18, 2015. http://www.billboard.com/articles/events/fan-army/6633505/lady-gaga-fan-little-monster-fan-essay-army

Bychawski, Adam. 2012. Lady Gaga Banned from Performing in Indonesia after Islamic Objection. *New Musical Express*, May 15, 2012. http://www.nme.com/news/lady-gaga/63797

Click, Melissa A., Hyunji Lee, and Holly W. Holladay. 2013. Making Monsters: Lady Gaga, Fan Identification, and Social Media. *Popular Music and Society* 36(3): 360–379.

CNN. 2010. CNN Larry King Live. *Transcripts*. Aired June 1, 2010. http://transcripts.cnn.com/TRANSCRIPTS/1006/01/lkl.01.html

Deflem, Mathieu. 2012. Black Day for Indonesian Police as Lady Gaga Show Cancelled. Op-ed. *The Bali Times*, May 28, 2012. http://www.thebalitimes.com/2012/05/28/black-day-for-indonesian-police-as-lady-gaga-show-cancelled/

Dilling-Hansen, Lise. 2015. Affective Fan Experiences of Lady Gaga. *Transformative Works and Cultures* 20, http://journal.transformativeworks.org/index.php/twc/article/view/662/543

Ferris, Kerry O. 2001. Through a Glass Darkly: The Dynamics of Fan-Celebrity Encounters. *Symbolic Interaction* 24(1): 25–47.

———. 2010. The Next Big Thing: Local Celebrity. *Society* 47: 392–295.

Gagapedia. Manifesto of Little Monsters. http://ladygaga.wikia.com/wiki/Manifesto_of_Little_Monsters

Goodman, William. 2009. Lady Gaga and Kanye West's 'Fame Kills' Tour Canceled. *Spin*, October 2, 2009. http://www.spin.com/2009/10/lady-gaga-and-kanye-wests-fame-kills-tour-canceled/

Horkheimer, Max, and Theodor W. Adorno. 1972 (1944). *Dialectic of Enlightenment*. New York: Herder and Herder.

Huba, Jackie. 2013. *Monster Loyalty: How Lady Gaga Turns Followers into Fanatics*. New York: Portfolio/Penguin.

Jennex, Craig. 2013. Diva Worship and the Sonic Search for Queer Utopia. *Popular Music and Society* 36(3): 343–359.

JezebelAgogo. Twitter post, October 19, 2011 (12:47 AM). https://twitter.com/jezebelAgogo/status/126700913736941568

Johnson, Ryan Lee. 2013. Fan Friday: How Lady Gaga and 'Born This Way' Changed My Life. *Pop Dust*, September 6, 2013. http://popdust.com/2013/09/06/lady-gaga-born-this-way-life-changing/

LeBlanc, Larry. 2010. Industry Profile: Troy Carter. *CelebrityAccess*, June 7, 2010. http://www.celebrityaccess.com/members/profile.html?id=515

Lewis, Lisa A. (ed). 1992. *Adoring Audience: Fan Culture and Popular Media*. London: Routledge.

Maher, Cristin. 2011. Lady Gaga Talks to 'Good Morning America' About Her MAC Campaign, 'Born This Way,' Her Grammy Entrance. *PopCrush*, February 17, 2011. http://popcrush.com/lady-gaga-good-morning-america-mac-campaign-born-this-way/

Marshall, P. David. 1997. *Celebrity and Power: Fame in Contemporary Culture*. Minneapolis, MN: University of Minnesota Press.

Merton, Robert K. 1995. The Thomas Theorem and the Matthew Effect. *Social Forces* 74(2): 379–424.

Mills, C. Wright. 1956. *The Power Elite*. New York: Oxford University Press.

———. 1959. *The Sociological Imagination*. New York: Oxford University Press.

Montgomery, James. 2009. Lady Gaga's Pop Revolution Continues With 'LoveGame'. *MTV.com*, March 13, 2009. http://www.mtv.com/news/1606964/lady-gagas-pop-revolution-continues-with-lovegame/

Out. 2009. The Lady is a Vamp. *Out*, August 9, 2009. http://www.out.com/entertainment/2009/08/09/lady-vamp

Owen, Pamela. 2011. 'I Was Born This Weight': Lady Gaga Fans Take to Twitter to Bully Hit Soul Singer Adele. *Daily Mail*, November 13, 2011. http://www.dailymail.co.uk/tvshowbiz/article-2060981/Lady-Gaga-fans-Twitter-bully--hit-soul-singer-Adele.html

Sacks, Danielle. 2014. Troy Carter: Fired by Lady Gaga and Loving It. *FastCompany*, January 13, 2014. http://www.fastcompany.com/3024171/step-up-troy-carter

Samson, Pete. 2011. Gaga Is Our Guru. *The Sun*, May 29, 2011. http://www.thesun.co.uk/sol/homepage/showbiz/music/3607863/Lady-GaGas-Little-Monsters-make-the-pilgrimage-to-her-New-York-concert.html

———. 2013. Crazy Gaga. *The Sun*, July 27, 2013. http://www.thesun.co.uk/sol/homepage/showbiz/5037528/Lady-Gaga-cannot-switch-off-stage-persona-even-during-SEX.html

Shadbolt, Peter. 2014. After Three Years on the Blacklist, China Lifts Gag on Lady Gaga. *CNN.com*, January 21, 2014. http://www.cnn.com/2014/01/21/world/asia/china-lady-gaga-ban/

Shmeeans. Twitter post, December 5, 2015 (5:19 PM). https://twitter.com/Shmeeans/status/673265560071700480

Skarda, Erin. 2011. Is Lady Gaga More Powerful Than Oprah? *Time*, August 26, 2011. http://newsfeed.time.com/2011/08/26/is-lady-gaga-more-powerful-than-oprah/

Smith, Richard. 1995. *Seduced And Abandoned: Essays on Gay Men and Popular Music*. London: Cassell.

Straw, Will. 2001. Consumption. In *The Cambridge Companion to Pop and Rock*, eds. Simon Frith, Will Straw, and John Street, 53–73. Cambridge, UK: Cambridge University Press.

Sturges, Fiona. 2009. Lady Gaga: How the World Went Crazy for the New Queen of Pop. *The Independent*, May 15, 2009. http://www.independent.co.uk/arts-entertainment/music/features/lady-gaga-how-the-world-went-crazy-for-the-new-queen-of-pop-1684375.html

Suster, Mark. 2016. Spotting, Nurturing and Mentoring Talent – The Power of Troy Carter. *Both Sides of the Table*, February 26, 2016. http://www.bothsidesofthetable.com/2016/02/26/spotting-nurturing-and-mentoring-talent-the-power-of-troy-carter/

Turner, Graeme. 2016. Celebrity, Participation, and the Public. In *A Companion to Celebrity*, eds. David P. Marshall and Sean Redmond, 83–97. Chichester, UK: Wiley Blackwell.

Van Meter, Jonathan. 2012. Dream Girl: Lady Gaga Graces the September Issue of *Vogue*. *Vogue*, August 21, 2012. http://www.vogue.com/865316/dream-girl-lady-gaga/

Vena, Jocelyn. 2009a. Lady Gaga on Success: 'The Turning Point for Me Was the Gay Community'. *MTV.com*, May 6, 2009. http://www.mtv.com/news/1610781/lady-gaga-on-success-the-turning-point-for-me-was-the-gay-community/

———. 2009b. Lady Gaga's Monster Ball Tour a 'Post-Apocalyptic House Party'. *MTV.com*, October 22, 2009. http://www.mtv.com/news/1624426/lady-gagas-monster-ball-tour-a-post-apocalyptic-house-party/

———. 2011. Lady Gaga Tears Up While Singing with Fan Maria Aragon. *MTV.com*, March 4, 2011. http://www.mtv.com/news/1659183/lady-gaga-toronto-maria-aragon/

Wass, Mike. 2013. Lady Gaga Criticizes a Katy Perry Fan's Twitter Handle in the Name of Online Kindness. *Idolator*, November 26, 2013. http://www.idolator.com/7495675/lady-gaga-criticizes-a-katy-perry-fans-twitter-handle-in-the-name-of-online-kindness

Watkins, Gwynne. 2012. Portrait of an Influential Fan: Marc Cohen, One of Lady Gaga's Little Monsters. *Vulture*, October 16, 2012. http://www.vulture.com/2012/10/influential-fan-little-monster-marc-cohen-lady-gaga.html

Williott, Carl. 2013. Lady Gaga Tells Her Fans that Sending Death Threats to People Maybe Isn't the Best Idea. *Idolator*, August 20, 2012. http://www.idolator.com/7478923/lady-gaga-fans-death-threats-monsters-open-letter

Wood, Beci. 2013. Lady Gaga Pays for Fan's Hip Surgery and Gives Her Gold-Plated Wheelchair. *The Sun*, April 13, 2013. http://www.thesun.co.uk/sol/homepage/showbiz/4886467/lady-gaga-pays-for-fans-hip-surgery-and-gives-her-gold-plated-wheelchair.html

CHAPTER 8

Gaga Activism: The New Ethics of Pop Culture

As shown in the previous chapter, Lady Gaga often professes how much she cares about her fans. The singer's devotion to her Little Monsters is so pronounced that the connection with her fans has also taken on the form of various activist causes and charitable activities. Related to the particular make-up of Lady Gaga's fan base, it is not surprising that the singer has shown particular empathy toward, and also actively engaged in various causes related to, gay rights and the general well-being of youth in today's technological age. By doing so, what has taken place, sociologically speaking, is an infiltration of the ethics of politics and activism into the aesthetics of pop, even when, and particularly under the circumstances that, these two aspects of culture are differentiated in modern society. In the case of Lady Gaga, questions on the ethics of pop culture are additionally amplified by the fact that the singer has also explicitly addressed her religiosity and other matters related to religion.

In this chapter, the activism of Lady Gaga will be explained and discussed on the basis of the sociological model of culture which, as explained in Chap. 2, the constructionist framework of this book is situated in. The problem of ethics in popular culture will specifically be clarified in terms of the different kinds of values that are represented in these differentiated realms of culture and how a particular recombination between them has taken place in the case of Lady Gaga. By enthusiastically claiming an advocacy role, it will be shown, Lady Gaga presents herself—and is also widely perceived—as something different and more than a mere pop star. The

© The Author(s) 2017
M. Deflem, *Lady Gaga and the Sociology of Fame*,
DOI 10.1057/978-1-137-58468-7_8

public status of Lady Gaga as an activist accordingly invokes a wide variety of sentiments, both supportive and disapproving. What is peculiar about Lady Gaga's embrace of various activist causes from the viewpoint of the present study is that it involves an intrusion of ethical values into the world of popular aesthetics, which effectively, if not by intent, has also served to advance the attention the singer has received and thus contributed to her rise to fame.

THE POLITICS OF POPULAR CULTURE

The infusion of politics, activism, religion, and other ethical issues into the aesthetical realm of culture and popular culture is only peculiar in modern societies because of their high degree of differentiation. In the historical context of an undifferentiated culture, the ideals and values of truth, justice, and beauty co-existed and were deliberately pursued in unison. But as differentiation has taken hold and specialized cultures of expertise developed, the politics of aesthetic culture, not least of all in the realm of popular culture, have come to be understood as problematic. It will cause no surprise to know that the reductionist scholars of old swiftly asserted that any politics or ethics that exists in the dominant cultural practices of a modern society could only but manifest that society's similarly dominant political ideas and ethical values (Horkheimer and Adorno 1944). Popular culture, therefore, is not only trivial at best, but bourgeois and conservative at worst. In the reductionist framework of the proponents of the culture industry, the conservatism of popular culture is always argued to be manifested, because it is said to be either implicitly present by virtue of the pop-cultural silence on political and weighty ethical matters or it is explicitly expressed by addressing such issues, especially in a purportedly critical manner, as a mere pop commodity.

In the sociology of music, Theodor Adorno formulated the sharpest expression of the reductionist perspective on the relationship between politics and music by conceiving of popular music as market commodity (1976). Although Adorno sought to establish a sociology of music, he actually formulated his ideas on the basis of a musicological perspective, one that is strikingly elitist as well. Indeed, in order to substantiate his perspective of the various forms of music and their social functions, Adorno relies on assumed inherent sound characteristics that would differentiate popular from serious music, arguing that popular music is by definition standardized in form and therefore exhausted with reference to its economic function of consumption. As a result, any political or ethical orientation that is injected into popular music is superficial and, to Adorno's ears, ultimately unbearable, for political and aesthetic reasons alike.

Despite its stated ambitions, Adorno's perspective is distinctly unsociological in neglecting the cultural meanings that are attributed to various kinds of musical sound. A constructionist perspective focused on music as it exists in various cultural settings, instead, allows to distinguish the manner and mechanisms in which various forms of music are, in more or less problematic ways, related to a variety of political and other ethical issues. The relationship between politics and popular music need not, of course, be readily inverted from trivial and conservative to significant and emancipatory, as some of the early practitioners of the modern sociology of music tended to do when, especially in the wake of the growing role of music in the social movements of the 1960s, new perspectives emerged under the heading of the supposed revolutionary politics of rock (Street 2001). Such a perspective is as reductionist as its purported intellectual counterpart. A more fruitful alternative is to examine the variable role of politics in music as well as of music in politics and to examine the conditions under which music can shape political and otherwise ethical discussions and bring out both the variable politics of music as well as the music of politics, both right and left (Street 2003).

Political and ethical cultural themes, including religion, have had a distinctly ambivalent place in the history of rock and pop music. Whereas popular music in twentieth-century Western society was by and large implicitly or explicitly promoting traditional values, the rebelliousness of rock was associated with counter-cultural protest and a general rejection of dominant culture, religion, and politics. Interestingly, as John Street (2001) argues, the strongest claims about the politically subversive role of popular music have tended to come, not from its proponents and practitioners, but from its critics, both formal government agencies as well as informal cultural groups, who allege that some forms of music, especially those enjoyed by young people, exert a perverting influence. Empirically, however, the relation between politics and popular music is not stable, and the effects of activism in popular music are ambiguous. In much the same way, the relationship between religion and popular music is also variable. Whereas traditionally, music was closely connected to religion, either by being performed on behalf of religious powers or by implicitly or explicitly reflecting and promoting the dominant religious virtues, the turn against religious values that has since marked some forms of music on their self-proclaimed "highway to hell" may well reflect nothing more, nor less, than an aesthetic attitude. The manner in which the ethics of politics and religion co-exist with the aesthetics of popular culture cannot be theoretically stated in an *a priori* manner, but must remain an empirical question.

THE ACTIVISM OF LADY GAGA

From early in her career, at least since the period of her developing success as a pop star throughout 2009, Lady Gaga has been very outspoken and has extensively engaged in a variety of activist causes. Inspired by the favorable reception her music received in the gay community, gay rights and LGBT issues were among the first causes the singer actively took on. Lady Gaga has since expanded the substantive range of her activist work into many other areas as well, especially focusing on several issues she considers important for young people. Alongside of these advocacy efforts, moreover, Lady Gaga has articulated, in rather unexpectedly forceful and explicit ways, her religiosity and position on related religious matters.

Lady Gay Gay

In her activism, Lady Gaga has been most outspoken about her support for gay rights, a cause the singer has been involved with since the early days of her commercial popularity. Among the earliest instances of expressing her support for gay rights, at an appearance on the Ellen DeGeneres Show in May 2009, Lady Gaga called the host "such an inspiration for women and for the gay community" (in Daily Mail 2009). In October 2009, the singer both walked and talked at the National Equality March in Washington, DC, which had been organized to promote the legal protection of LGBT people. Lady Gaga's speech at that event focused on the need for "full equality for all," demanding "actions NOW" (in Lybio 2009). As a musician, the singer added, she would also refuse to accept any misogynistic or homophobic behavior in the music industry. She ended her speech by reiterating, "Bless God and bless the gays!" (ibid.). When later that day Lady Gaga performed John Lennon's famous song "Imagine" at the Human Rights Campaign's National Dinner, she changed some of the lyrics ("And only Matthew in the sky") to voice her support for LGBT rights, invoking Matthew Shepard, the 21-year old student who was murdered in 1998 over motives that have been related to his sexual orientation (Gregory 2009).

The most concrete actions Lady Gaga undertook related to gay rights have been her opposition to the so-called Don't Ask Don't Tell (DADT) policy that was introduced in the United States military in 1993 during the administration of President Bill Clinton. Developed on the basis of ideas from military sociologist Charles Moskos, the policy was meant to protect discrimination and harassment of gays in the military while also barring openly gay people from serving in the military, which was judged to "create an unacceptable risk to the high standards of morale, good order and discipline, and unit cohesion that are the essence of military capability" (Effoduh 2012). As part of the law, also, any gay action or speech would not lead to dismissal if it was done "for the purpose of avoiding or terminating military service" (ibid.). At the time the policy was introduced, it was considered a compromise solution to either maintaining or overturning a complete ban against gays serving in the military. But the policy became the subject of increased criticism, especially following the election of U.S. President Obama. The policy has since been repealed, after Obama in 2010 signed into law the "Don't Ask, Don't Tell Repeal Act," which went into effect on September 20, 2011.

Before the repeal of DADT, Lady Gaga was very vocal in her opposition to the policy, and garnered a lot of publicity from her efforts. At the Video Music Awards on September 12, 2010, the singer walked the red carpet accompanied by four ex-service people discharged under the DADT policy (Swash 2010). Later that night, she wore the now famous meat dress, which she said was a comment on fighting for LGBT rights, arguing that not fighting for such rights would imply that "pretty soon we're going to have as much rights as the meat on our bones" (in Mapes 2010). A few days later, on September 14, 2010, Lady Gaga went on Twitter asking Senate Majority Leader Harry Reid to schedule a vote on the policy, and Reid tweeted back that a vote was scheduled (Associated Press 2010). Then, on September 16, 2010, the singer posted a black-and-white video on YouTube in which she called on members of the US Senate to repeal DADT (Lady Gaga YouTube video). On September 20, 2010, the singer again spoke about the matter at a rally against the policy in Portland, Maine (Zezima 2010). In a speech entitled "The Prime Rib of America," she spoke (using her legal birth name) that anybody who cannot fight without prejudice and accept equality among all who serve in the military should just "go home!" (in MTV 2010).

Lady Gaga's support for the acceptance of gays and members of the LGBT community has also influenced some of her artistic output, in both substantive and stylistic respects. Especially on her *Born This Way* album, the singer inserted gay-friendly themes in her music. Most distinctly, the production of the song "Born This Way," not merely its lyrical content ("no matter gay, straight, or bi, lesbian, transgendered life"), is intentionally modeled on the sound of the archetypical gay disco anthem. Likewise indicating a gay-friendly orientation, the video to the song "Alejandro," was conceived, in the words of Lady Gaga, as "a celebration and an admiration of gay love" (in Warner 2010). Another example is the song "Boys, Boys, Boys" of *The Fame*, which is written from the viewpoint of a straight female as a response to the song "Girls, Girls, Girls" by the heavy metal band Motley Crüe, but which Lady Gaga during live performances typically transforms into a tribute to young gay men. Other Lady Gaga songs that were not written as LGBT-related, such as "Poker Face" and "Hair," have since also acquired the status of gay anthems.

Since her earliest involvement in gay-rights advocacy, Lady Gaga has over the years continued to show her support to the LGBT community in several ways. By example, during the Monster Ball tour, she promoted a program from Virgin Mobile to help homeless youth from the LGBT community (Virgin Mobile 2012). Lady Gaga also served as a spokesperson for the "It Gets Better" campaign from Google Chrome meant to raise awareness for LGBT youth (Teicher 2011). The singer has also released music to benefit LGBT causes, specifically the Country Road version of her song "Born This Way," some of the proceeds of which went to the Gay Lesbian and Straight Education Network (Vena 2011a). On June 26, 2015, Lady Gaga joined many other pop culture stars and celebrities in showing her support and joy over the Supreme Court's decision in Obergefell v. Hodges to effectively legalize same-sex marriage across the United States, when she tweeted "#Lovewins over prejudice" (Lady Gaga Twitter post 2015). Following the tragic shooting of 49 people at gay nightclub Pulse in Orlando on June 12, 2016, Lady Gaga spoke at a rally in Los Angeles to express her grief and support for the LGBT community (Nolfi 2016a). Later that month, she also joined some 180 other celebrities in an open letter to US Congress seeking gun control measures (Deerwester 2016).

Born This Way Advocacy

Throughout her career since the beginning of her success in 2009, Lady Gaga has taken on many other causes besides LGBT rights as well, so many in fact that it is nearly impossible to detail and explain them all in the space of this chapter. Yet, certain trends can be detected that have emerged over the course of Lady Gaga's advocacy activities, involving both more organized as well as individual-level efforts and specific interventions. Most distinct on an organized level is the Born This Way Foundation, the non-profit organization the singer and her mother Cynthia Germanotta have jointly founded to focus on a variety of youth-empowerment issues, especially concerning bullying (Born This Way Foundation website). First announced in November 2011, the Foundation was officially launched on February 29, 2012, at an event at Harvard University that was hosted by Oprah Winfrey and featured several high-profile panelists, including alternative-medicine advocate Deepak Chopra and US Secretary of Health and Human Services Kathleen Sebelius. Supported by the California Endowment and Harvard's Berkman Center for Internet & Society, the Foundation was originally funded by Lady Gaga, the John D. and Catherine T. MacArthur Foundation, and retail store Barneys New York.

In its activism, the Born This Way Foundation is essentially oriented at reaching youth in order to empower them "to create a kinder and braver world" (Born This Way Foundation website). Among the Foundation's most concrete programs and activities to date, it partnered with Office Depot in 2012 to sell a line of "Be Brave" school products, launched a Body Revolution project in 2013 to create awareness about body disorder issues, set up a research and advisory board on youth empowerment and tolerance programs, organized a Born Brave Bus Tour alongside of the US leg of the Born This Way Ball tour in 2013 to provide fans advice on bullying, and partnered with a number of private companies such as Prizeo (to contribute money with a possible prize of a dinner with Lady Gaga), Doritos (to support funding the Foundation with the chance to attend a Lady Gaga live show), and Intel (to promote an online anti-harassment program). In 2015, the Foundation partnered with the Yale Center for Emotional Intelligence to organize an Emotion Revolution event to foster awareness about the role of emotions in young people's lives (Dodero 2015).

On an individual level and in terms of specific causes, Lady Gaga has voiced her support on many occasions on a large number of issues. Among the many examples of the singer reaching out to help individual fans, in April 2010 she tweeted high school student Cole Goforth who had been sent home from school for wearing a "Lady Gay Gay" T-shirt, and in September 2011 she dedicated a live performance of her song "Hair" at the iHeartRadio Music Festival in Las Vegas to teenager Jamey Rodemeyer who had committed suicide after having been bullied for being gay (Kaufman 2010, 2011). Jamey's last tweet was sent to Lady Gaga to thank her for all she had done (Hausofjamey Twitter post). In November 2011, she sent a Canadian teenager a video message to thank him for the anti-bullying initiatives he had organized in his school (Schreffler 2011). In April 2015, the singer devoted a video message to a fan who was reported to have had struggled with depression (Marco 67 YouTube video).

Among the specific causes Lady Gaga has embraced, in 2011, as mentioned in Chap. 5, she sought to assist in the recovery of Japan after the country had been hit by an earthquake and tsunami by selling a "Pray for Japan" bracelet (Harrison 2012). The singer has also protested Russia's so-called gay propaganda law by speaking out in support of the LGBT community during a live show in Moscow in December 2012 (Peeples 2013). In 2015, she joined several other female celebrities in writing an open letter to some of the world's leading politicians to focus on gender equality issues in the international fight against poverty and hunger (Denham 2015). Further indicating the breadth of her advocacy, in March 2016 Lady Gaga tweeted in support of World Water Day (Lady Gaga Twitter post 2016).

Many other examples of support efforts to charitable causes involving Lady Gaga could be mentioned. Most recently, Lady Gaga received considerable notice for her contributions to the discussion on contemporary rape culture on college campuses after she had recorded the song "Til It Happens to You" for the 2015 documentary *The Hunting Ground* (Martins 2015). In February 2016, Lady Gaga gave a very well-received rendition of the "Til It Happens to You" song at the Oscars, where she was accompanied on stage by some 50 survivors from sexual assault (Paquette 2016). The performance was introduced by Vice President Joe Biden, who later also attended an event addressing sexual assault issues with the singer (Back 2016; Martins 2015).

Other advocacy efforts by Lady Gaga have involved collaboration with other groups and people from the world of politics and entertainment as well as with private companies. Following her dedication at the iHeartRadio Festival to the teenager who had committed suicide over bullying, for example, Lady Gaga met with President Obama at an anti-bullying event (Grindley 2011). She also wrote an op-ed about the issue with New York Governor Andrew Cuomo (Martins 2015). In June 2016, she joined the Dalai Lama at the US Conference of Mayors in Indianapolis to promote the idea of compassionate cities (Nolfi 2016b). The charity organizations that have benefited from Lady Gaga financially and otherwise include the Lupus Foundation of America, Oxfam, the Robin Hood Foundation, and Stand Up To Cancer, among others. In cooperation with various business, finally, the singer has also contributed to several campaigns, such as with cosmetics company MAC to promote safe sex in the fight against AIDS (Massa 2011), with Virgin Mobile to fight homelessness among LGBT youth (Virgin Mobile 2012), and with Macy's to sell a line of "Love Bravery" clothes and accessories, 25 % of which will go to the Born This Way Foundation and the Elton John AIDS Foundation (Wahba 2016).

Catholic Gaga

Lady Gaga has only rarely expressed an explicit political stance, although she has generally been supportive of Democratic politicians and, during the primaries in New York in April 2016, tweeted in support of Hillary Clinton's run for the White House, an endorsement she repeated on the occasion of the Orlando gay nightclub shooting (Wass 2016). In matters of religion, however, the singer has been more outspoken and has on several instances voiced a religious orientation. In an interview with Larry King in 2010, Lady Gaga spoke about her religiosity most explicitly. Referencing her Catholic upbringing, she said, "I'm very religious, I believe in Jesus, I believe in God" (in CNN 2010). But she also expressed some doubts and a measure of confusion on religion, saying that she struggles with religious questions. Differentiating between religious belief and its institutional organization, she said that "religion and the church are two completely separate things" and that she sees herself as "a quite religious woman" who, at the same time, is "very confused about religion" (ibid.).

Lady Gaga has explicitly connected her religious orientation with her activism, especially with respect to her support for gay rights. At the VMAs in 2009, the singer thanked "God and the gays" during her acceptance speech (Peeples 2013). The singer also expresses the relationship she makes between religion and her advocacy in some of her artistry. At her live shows during the Monster Ball tour, for instance, she proclaimed, "Jesus loves everybody!" while discussing tolerance toward people of different sexual orientation. In her song "Born This Way," likewise, Lady Gaga promotes tolerance toward people of various sexual orientations while singing "God makes no mistakes."

THE ETHICS OF LADY GAGA

From a sociological viewpoint, what the elaborate involvement of Lady Gaga in various activist causes and her explicitly stated religiosity reveal is that ethics and aesthetics co-exist in the singer's world. Despite the high degree of differentiation of the cultural spheres of justice and beauty, there is in the history of popular culture, of course, as such nothing new or spectacular about the politics of music (Street 2001). The impact of celebrities' involvement in political and ethical causes, likewise, has also been studied for some time now (Meyer and Gamson 1995). What can be observed in recent years, however, is that celebrity advocacy has taken on a new dimension, especially since the arrival of the internet and the possibility for people of fame, especially in the popular world of music and entertainment, to reach very large numbers of people, renewing the need to examine the causes and effects of celebrity advocacy in the current age (Bennett 2014; Markham 2015; Tsaliki 2016). In this discussion section, I focus on the responses Lady Gaga's activism and religiosity have invoked in various relevant communities and contrast this reception by others with Lady Gaga's own presentation of self and the motives she has attributed to her advocacy. In the complex constellation of bridging pop culture with the ethics of Lady Gaga's activism, I argue, it is the very controversy that is created that has fueled the singer's fame, leading to a reconsideration of the place of activism in the totality of the Lady Gaga culture.

The question on the impact of Lady Gaga's activism and religiosity in terms of their perception by others is relatively straightforward to answer inasmuch as her relevant actions have gone anything but unnoticed. The amount of attention paid to Lady Gaga's activist involvements and statements on religion alone is a clear indication hereof. The sociologically relevant question on the impact of Lady Gaga ethics, however, should not just focus on the effectiveness of her advocacy programs in reaching relevant audiences and affecting behavior (Click et al. 2013; Jang and Lee 2014; Trier-Bieniek and Pullum 2014) nor concentrate on the positive or negative impact of her religiosity in inspiring others (Cohn 2011; Holdaway 2013). Instead, from a constructionist viewpoint, attention should go to the social perception of the meaning and significance of Lady Gaga's activist and religious conduct, especially relative to her standing as a pop star.

With respect to the perception of Lady Gaga's activism, it is telling that her advocacy has received favorable as well unfavorable responses from directions that cannot always be anticipated on the basis of the content of the issues involved. To a large extent, Lady Gaga has received very positive responses to her LGBT activism from within the gay community, such as the gay press which has typically been very appreciative of her (Peeples 2013). The singer has, accordingly, also received awards, such as the Randy Shilts Visibility Award from the Servicemembers Legal Defense Network for her work to repeal the DADT policy and the Trevor Project Award for her contribution to suicide prevention among LGBT youth (Hughes 2011). More broadly, when in 2015 Lady Gaga received the Billboard Woman of the Year Award, it was not only because of her artistic accomplishments, but also because of her work as a "crusader," especially her efforts by means of her participation on the "Til It Happens To You" song to foster awareness on the problem of sexual assault (Martins 2015).

However, there have been negative reactions expressed against Lady Gaga's activism as well. Needless to argue at any great length, some of these concerns have come from conservative groups and traditional family values organizations. The Florida Family Association, for example, asked Office Depot to end its partnership in the "Born Brave" school supplies campaign, claiming that Lady Gaga was sending the "inappropriate message ... that it's okay to be gay" (Creedon 2012). More puzzling is that the generally favorable reception the singer has received from the gay community has not always been shared by all of its members. The sharpest example perhaps is the group "Gays Against Gaga," which maintains a tumblr blog to offer a dissenting gay voice in opposition to what it assumes to be part of a Lady Gaga marketing machine (Gays Against Gaga Tumblr). Although Lady Gaga's early outreach to the gay community has generally been well received, other gays have voiced similar concerns, such as when somebody argued that "Gaga does not represent some overarching symbol of my life as a gay man" (Alexiou 2011). Lady Gaga's deliberate embrace of gay themes in her music has also not always been welcomed, to wit some of the mixed reactions in the gay community to the song "Born This Way," which the singer wrote as "a completely magical message song" (in Van Meter 2011). Some found the song too forced precisely because of the all too concrete and direct nature of its message as well as its alleged derivative style (Bernstein 2011). Concerns have at times even been raised that Lady Gaga would have exploited the gay community to advance her career, charges the singer has vehemently denied (Sciarretto 2011).

Lady Gaga's activist causes besides her work on LGBT issues have generally received little negative response. Some criticism, however, has been expressed over the workings of the Born This Way Foundation, specifically with respect to financial dealings. It has been charged that the Foundation has spent much of its capital on legal fees and publicity, not on programs related to any of its causes (Michaels 2014). Lady Gaga has, of course, denied these claims, and her mother Cynthia Germanotta has defended the Foundation's expenses in terms of the non-profit organization not being a "grant-maker" but actually carrying out programs which "are having a profound impact" (ibid.). While there are no concrete measures on what that impact could be, other perhaps than its revenue-generating capacities to attract donations, especially from Lady Gaga fans, it is clear that the Foundation as well as many of Lady Gaga's other causes have had an influence, at least by creating public awareness and contributing to debate on certain issues, arousing sentiments from multiple corners.

With respect to the public reception to Lady Gaga's professed religiosity and its relation to her work, reactions have likewise been divided. One the one hand, some have criticized Lady Gaga's actions and statements on religious grounds. At the extreme end, members of the so-called Westboro Baptist Church in Kansas, for example, have used "God Hates Lady Gaga" signs to picket Lady Gaga concerts. Much less extreme voices objecting to Lady Gaga's religious ethics have come from within the religious community (Masley 2010; Williams 2011). The Catholic League, in particular, has charged the singer with abusing Catholic symbols in her work, such as in the video to "Alejandro" where the singer is shown dressed as a nun and swallows a rosary. Arguing that Lady Gaga has now become "the new poster girl for American decadence and Catholic bashing," Catholic League President Bill Donohue has claimed that Lady Gaga "was raised Catholic and then morphed into something unrecognizable," much like Madonna had done before her (ibid.). Other Christian commentators have expressed similar concerns and suggested that Lady Gaga has no moral story to tell (Judge 2010) and that Katy Perry was right when she criticized Lady Gaga for using "blasphemy as entertainment" (Carter 2010). Lady Gaga's presentation of her live shows as a "religious experience" and her call for "people to worship themselves" have likewise been condemned as unchristian (Cohn 2011).

However, others within the Christian religious community have been more receptive and even laudatory of Lady Gaga's religiosity and its relevance for her music and her fans (Gellel 2013; Sweeney 2011). Specific mention is hereby made of how Lady Gaga's songs demonstrating her pursuit and embrace of weirdness reflect the "words of a religious sick soul—disturbingly Catholic in their sensibility" (Schmalz 2010). Even more positive in its reception, it has been argued that Lady Gaga, precisely by embracing what is ugly as beautiful and by reaching out those who are at society's margins, shows a "sensitivity and appreciation for inevitable human suffering" that reflects "the Christian theme of uniting your sufferings with Christ's suffering" (Lee 2011).

Turning to Lady Gaga's own subjective disposition on her role in advocacy and her position on religion, the singer has typically associated herself closely with the causes she has been propagating and has also spoken candidly about her religious beliefs. Most clearly, responding to the early support she received from the gay community, Lady Gaga has been vocal about her gratitude and recognition toward her gay fans and shown her support through her actions for the acceptance of gays and LGBT rights. Her activism also reveals a special focus on youth-oriented issues, especially bullying, both because younger fans make up a large section of her fan base and because she has said to identify with those struggles herself. It is the younger people from "my generation," the singer said, who "are the ones coming up in the world and we must continue to push this movement forward and close the gap" (in Lybio 2009). On issues related to body image and mental well-being, likewise, Lady Gaga has come out as a victim herself, saying, "I've suffered through depression and anxiety my entire life" (Dodero 2015). The singer has also publicly stated that she was bullied in high school (Hiatt 2011) and that she is a survivor of sexual assault (Back 2016).

Manifesting the inevitable interactions that exist between self and other in the construction of identity and perception, Lady Gaga's stated motives and beliefs have received various public responses. There has been some debate, in particular, not only on her right or ability to speak on LGBT issues, her identity as a self-proclaimed bisexual has been questioned as well (see Chap. 9). Some of the singer's experiences in high school have also been subject to scrutiny for not having been sufficiently problematic as to rise to the level of bullying (Smith 2012). Even Lady Gaga's revelation that she is a sexual assault victim has been questioned, because she evaded giving any clarification when she first discussed the matter in 2014 during an interview with Howard Stern and, not actually saying that she was raped, may have recounted an inappropriate romantic involvement with a 20-year older producer when she was 19 (Rutter 2014), or misspoke when she explained her song "Swine" as being "about rape" and then continued that the song is "about rage" (in Takeda 2014). In an earlier track-by-track explanation of the songs on *ARTPOP*, the singer had explained the song "Swine" as being a "very personal song" that dealt with "some of the more troubling and challenging sexual experiences" earlier in her life (ARTPOP Jesus YouTube video). After her performance at the Oscars in February 2016, Lady Gaga revealed that she had only then spoken out about being a survivor to some of her relatives (Dostis 2016).

In the confession of her own religiosity, moreover, the subjective disposition of Lady Gaga as "a religious and spiritual person who's obsessed with religious art" (in Vena 2011b) has been confronted with the claim that her actions should primarily be judged as therapeutic for her, rather than to entail a message for others (Holdaway 2013). When in May 2016 a blogger on a Catholic website questioned an assumed trend among celebrities to publicize their faith while leading immodest lifestyles (Taylor 2016), Lady Gaga responded with an Instagram post that stated that "God is never a trend" (Lady Gaga Instagram post). The exchange ignited the debate over Lady Gaga's and other entertainers' religiosity anew, testifying to the peculiarly controversial nature of religion in the world of pop culture (Noble 2016; O'Hare 2016; Roach 2016).

It would not only be immensely difficult, if not altogether impossible, to entertain the question whether Lady Gaga's subjective presentation of self with respect to her advocacy and religiosity is valid and sincere, it is also sociologically unnecessary to engage in any such speculation. For what matters from the viewpoint of Lady Gaga in her social role is that the singer's actions have minimally shown their influence by the effect they have had, at an inter-subjective level, in adding to debate and arousing sentiments from multiple sides. Whether the new forms of celebrity activism by Lady Gaga and other so-called celebvocates effectively extend political (and other forms of ethical) engagement also remains an open question (Tsaliki 2016). But what can be asserted without a doubt is that there exists a socially accepted recognition that Lady Gaga's actions and statements about advocacy and religion have had such consequences and have led to debate. From the viewpoint of the fame of Lady Gaga, moreover, what is most important is that it is the controversial nature of such debate that determines the amount of fame that is consequently generated, irrespective of whether or not the majority of the opinions side with Lady Gaga. This impact may be even more amplified in the case of Lady Gaga as the singer is primarily known as a pop star whose music and image are mostly thought of as outrageous entertainment.

Harmonizing with what was said in Chap. 7 about the role of Lady Gaga's diverse audiences, especially those that exist outside the community of her fans, it can be argued that it is especially the opposition which Lady Gaga's activism occasionally brings about that has most contributed to her fame. Corresponding to the finding that the idea of a consequential politics of popular music is mostly assumed by its critics (Street 2001), the influence of Lady Gaga's activism and religiosity is in effect most strongly the result of the criticisms they have provoked, such as the claims that her music should be censored because of its implied message, that her actions on behalf of LGBT rights might pervert young people, that her religiosity should be questioned, or that the whole of her work is nothing but a sham. Irrespective of the validity of such claims, the argument can be made that a pop artist's activist and religion-related activities will be beneficial to that artist's fame precisely because the differentiated cultural worlds of the aesthetics of popular music and the ethics of political and religious values inevitably exist in a relationship of tension. Whereas from an advocacy viewpoint this finding would lead to strengthen the notion that pop culture celebrities could make for some of the most influential and effective activists and religious crusaders, from a sociological viewpoint it shows the undeniable role activism and religiosity can have in influencing popularity and fame in pop culture. Ironically, however, such a celebrity advocacy role can only be effective as long as it is perceived to be genuine and has not, precisely by being widely embraced, become just another part of celebrity culture and pop star entertainment.

Conclusion

This chapter has shown the ways in which Lady Gaga is extensively involved in various activist causes, both on an individual level as well as through her Born This Way Foundation, and has additionally engaged in debates on religion. Against a reductionist perspective, I have defended the argument that such activities cannot readily be reduced to their purported economic or political functions, whether conservative or emancipatory, but should be framed sociologically in terms of the reception they receive (from others) relative to Lady Gaga's presentation (of self). In the case of Lady Gaga, her advocacy work on behalf of LGBT rights, youth empowerment, and other causes, as well as her stated religious orientation have garnered many conflicting responses. Regardless of whether the public reactions to Lady Gaga's activism and religiosity has been supportive or dismissive and irrespective of the singer's stated or implied motives, it is the controversial nature of this reception that has in and of itself contributed to the rise and development of the singer's fame. As such, by example, it matters much less if Lady Gaga's collaboration with the Dalai Lama in June 2016 produced any of its intended spread of kindness in cities as that the meeting led the singer to be banned in China, thereby once again keeping the spotlight firmly on her (Guarino 2016).

Lady Gaga's advocacy role creates a measure of discomfort in its public perception by virtue of its transcendence beyond the aesthetics and entertainment associated with popular music. Corresponding to what was said about Lady Gaga as a versatile product (Chap. 4) and the role of the Little Monsters as an aspect of the singer's fascination-arousing spectacle (Chap. 7), her activism is part of what Lady Gaga is and does and a source of the recognition she receives to further her fame. As such, Lady Gaga's activism functions as both a medium to connect with a wide number of audiences as well as part of what they can connect with. As both a vehicle and an object of her fame, Lady Gaga's elaborate activist activities may indicate how a new ethics of pop culture is developing whereby the politics and economics of art co-exist, redefining the role of authenticity in fame (Varriale 2012). Lady Gaga manager Bobby Campbell recently expressed this idea when he argued that it makes sense, both economically as well as from the viewpoint of charitable activism, that an "authentic connection" is established between "the artist, the brand, and the charity" because, he continued, "it really makes a difference when it comes from the heart" (in Rys 2016). To the extent that such a co-existence of business and activism is accepted as legitimate, contemporary popular culture may be moving toward the development of a new economics of sincerity.

Among the qualitative characteristics the case of Lady Gaga reveals, the breadth and intensity of the singer's activism have brought about public reactions that were so strongly felt that it has reinforced an increasingly growing popularity of similar efforts by other stars in popular music and by celebrities of all kinds. It has today become rare to hear of a celebrity who does not advocate some kind of activism or is not somehow outspoken about political, religious, or other controversial topics. To the extent that such celebrity advocacy will (and already has) become normalized to turn into another part of entertainment, it will have obvious ironic consequences, both in terms of the effectiveness of the activism involved as well as with respect to its role in building a career and its resulting fame.

In the world of popular music, activism has traditionally been mostly associated with the masculine world of rock, not with pop and dance. Yet, precisely because Lady Gaga has adopted such a rock attitude from within the world of pop, her actions can be said to have been more noticeable and, for that reason, may have been more effective as well, if not in actually bringing about change then at least in affecting her popularity and fame. In any case, the antagonism Lady Gaga at times provokes is neither traditionally feminine nor traditionally pop, issues the next two chapters will explore.

References

Adorno, Theodor W. 1976. *Introduction to the Sociology of Music*. New York: Continuum.

Alexiou, Joseph. 2011. Bad Romance! The Gays Have Had Enough of Lady Gaga. *Business Insider*, February 16, 2011. http://www.businessinsider.com/lady-gaga-born-this-way-reviews-gays-1-2011-2

ARTPOP Jesus. Track-By-Track ARTPOP Commentary by Lady Gaga. *YouTube video*, uploaded November 30, 2013. https://www.youtube.com/watch?v=E7Voaj0xzpc

Associated Press. 2010. Lady Gaga, Senator Reid Discuss 'Don't Ask, Don't Tell' on Twitter. *Billboard*, September 15, 2010. http://www.billboard.com/articles/news/956310/lady-gaga-senator-reid-discuss-dont-ask-dont-tell-on-twitter

Back, Ellen. 2016. Joe Biden, Lady Gaga Reunite to Fight Sexual Violence. *USA Today*, April 8, 2016. http://www.usatoday.com/story/life/people/2016/04/08/joe-biden-lady-gaga-reunite-fight-sexual-violence/82792134/

Bennett, Lucy. 2014. 'If We Stick Together We Can Do Anything': Lady Gaga Fandom, Philanthropy and Activism Through Social Media. *Celebrity Studies* 5(1–2): 138–152.

Bernstein, Jacob. 2011. Gays Turn on Lady Gaga. *The Daily Beast*, February 14, 2011. http://www.thedailybeast.com/articles/2011/02/14/lady-gagas-new-single-born-this-way-makes-gays-turn-on-her.html

Born This Way Foundation. Website. https://bornthisway.foundation/

Carter, Kelley L. 2010. Did Katy Perry Dis Lady Gaga's 'Alejandro' Video? *MTV.com*, June 8, 2010. http://www.mtv.com/news/1641113/did-katy-perry-dis-lady-gagas-alejandro-video/

Click, Melissa A., Hyunji Lee, and Holly W. Holladay. 2013. Making Monsters: Lady Gaga, Fan Identification, and Social Media. *Popular Music and Society* 36(3): 360–379.

CNN. 2010. CNN Larry King Live. *Transcripts.* Aired June 1, 2010. http://transcripts.cnn.com/TRANSCRIPTS/1006/01/lkl.01.html

Cohn, Alicia. 2011. Lady Gaga: Where's the Outrage? *Christianity Today*, May 2011. http://www.christianitytoday.com/women/2011/may/lady-gaga-wheres-outrage.html

Creedon, Aine. 2012. Office Depot Asked to Sever Ties with Lady Gaga Charity. *Nonprofit Quarterly*, July 24, 2012. https://nonprofitquarterly.org/2012/07/24/office-depot-asked-to-sever-ties-with-lady-gaga-charity/

Daily Mail. 2009. Lady GaGa's Wacky Headgear Almost Knocks Out Chat Show Host Ellen DeGeneres. *Daily Mail*, May 13, 2009. http://www.dailymail.co.uk/tvshowbiz/article-1181210/Lady-GaGas-wacky-headgear-knocks--chat-host-Ellen-DeGeneres.html

Deerwester, Jayme. 2016. Lady Gaga, Miranda, Britney Spears Sign Open Letter on Gun Control. *USA Today*, June 23, 2016. http://www.usatoday.com/story/life/people/2016/06/23/lady-gaga-lin-manuelo-miranda-britney-spears-sign-open-letter-on-gun-control/86279230/

Denham, Jess. 2015. Beyonce, Lady Gaga and Meryl Streep Among High-Profile Women to Sign Open Letter Calling for Female Empowerment in Global Poverty Battle. *The Independent*, March 8, 2015. http://www.independent.co.uk/news/people/beyonce-lady-gaga-and-meryl-streep-among-high-profile-women-to-sign-open-letter-calling-for-female-10093889.html

Dodero, Camille. 2015. Lady Gaga Gets Personal About Saving Troubled Teens – 'I've Suffered Through Depression and Anxiety My Whole Life'. *Billboard*, October 15, 2015. http://www.billboard.com/articles/news/magazine-feature/6730027/lady-gaga-billboard-cover-born-this-way-foundation-depression-philanthropy

Dostis, Melanie. 2016. Lady Gaga Confessed She Is a Survivor of Sexual Violence to Grandmother and Aunt after Oscars Performance. *New York Daily News*, March 1, 2016. http://www.nydailynews.com/entertainment/gossip/lady-gaga-reveals-rape-grandmother-aunt-article-1.2549668

Effoduh, Okechukwu. 2012. The Demise of the "Don't Ask, Don't Tell" Policy from the U.S Military. *Daily Post*, August 21, 2012. http://dailypost.ng/2012/08/21/okechukwu-effoduh-the-demise-dont-ask-dont-tell-policy-u-s-military/

Gays Against Gaga. Tumblr. http://gaysagainstgaga.tumblr.com

Gellel, Adrian-Mario. 2013. Traces of Spirituality in the Lady Gaga Phenomenon. *International Journal of Children's Spirituality* 18(2): 214–226.

Gregory, Jason. 2009. Yoko Ono Praises Lady Gaga for Covering John Lennon's 'Imagine'. *MTV.com*, October 14, 2009. http://www.gigwise.com/

news/52969/Yoko-Ono-Praises-Lady-GaGa-For-Covering-John-Lennons-Imagine

Grindley, Lucas. 2011. Lady Gaga Talks to President Obama About Bullying'. *The Advocate*, September 26, 2011. http://www.advocate.com/news/daily-news/2011/09/26/lady-gaga-talks-president-obama-about-bullying

Guarino, Ben. 2016. China Bans Lady Gaga After the Pop Superstar Meets with the Dalai Lama. *The Washington Post*, June 29, 2016. https://www.washingtonpost.com/news/morning-mix/wp/2016/06/29/china-bans-lady-gaga-after-the-pop-superstar-meets-with-the-dalai-lama/

Harrison, Lily. 2012. Judge Orders Lady Gaga to Pay Over $100,000 to Settle Japan Bracelet Lawsuit. *Celebuzz*, October 25, 2012. http://www.celebuzz.com/2012-10-25/judge-orders-lady-gaga-to-pay-over-100000-to-settle-japan-bracelet-lawsuit-exclusive/

Hausofjamey. Twitter post, September 18, 2011 (1:27 AM). https://twitter.com/hausofjamey/status/115295838594535424

Hiatt, Brian. 2011. Deep Inside the Unreal World of Lady Gaga. *Rolling Stone*, June 9, 2011. http://www.rollingstone.com/music/news/deep-inside-the-unreal-world-of-lady-gaga-20110609

Holdaway, Xarissa. 2013. Idol Worship: The Beatitudes of Lady Gaga. *Religion & Politics*, February 19, 2013. http://religionandpolitics.org/2013/02/19/idol-worship-the-beatitudes-of-lady-gaga/

Horkheimer, Max, and Theodor W. Adorno. 1972 (1944). *Dialectic of Enlightenment*. New York: Herder and Herder.

Hughes, Sarah Anne. 2011. Lady Gaga Accepts Trevor Project Award: 'This Means More to Me Than Any Grammy I Could Ever Win'. *The Washington Post*, December 5, 2011. https://www.washingtonpost.com/blogs/celebritology/post/lady-gaga-accepts-trevor-project-award--this-means-more-to-me--than-any-grammy-i-could-ever-win/2011/12/05/gIQA9keJWO_blog.html

Jang, S. Mo, and Hoon Lee. 2014. When Pop Music Meets a Political Issue: Examining How 'Born This Way' Influences Attitudes Toward Gays and Gay Rights Policies. *Journal of Broadcasting & Electronic Media* 58(1): 114–130.

Judge, Mark. 2010. Lady Gaga Is No Madonna. *OnFaith*, June 19, 2010. http://www.faithstreet.com/onfaith/2010/06/19/lady-gaga-is-no-madonna/7242

Kaufman, Gil. 2010. Lady Gaga Supports Teen Sent Home for 'Lady Gay Gay' T-Shirt. *MTV.com*, April 8, 2010. http://www.mtv.com/news/1635666/lady-gaga-supports-teen-sent-home-for-lady-gay-gay-t-shirt/

———. 2011. Lady Gaga Questions President Obama on Bullying. *MTV.com*, September 27, 2011. http://www.mtv.com/news/1671571/lady-gaga-president-obama-bullying/

Lady Gaga. A Message from Lady Gaga to the Senate Sept 16 2010. YouTube video, uploaded September 17, 2010. https://www.youtube.com/watch?v=GG5VK2lquEc

Lady Gaga. Instagram post, May 10, 2016. https://www.instagram.com/p/BFO1b9rpFFC/
Lady Gaga. Twitter post, June 26, 2015 (2:15 PM). https://twitter.com/ladygaga/status/614497319589945344
Lady Gaga. Twitter post, March 22, 2016 (6:00 PM). https://twitter.com/ladygaga/status/712398555604910080
Lee, Helen. 2011. God in Gaga. *Busted Halo*, February 11, 2011. http://bustedhalo.com/features/god-in-gaga
Lybio. 2009. Lady Gaga – At The National Equality March – Oct. 11, 2009. *Transcript*. Lybio.net. http://lybio.net/lady-gaga-at-the-national-equality-march-oct-11-2009/speeches/
Mapes, Jillian. 2010. Lady Gaga Explains Her Meat Dress: 'It's No Disrespect'. *Billboard*, September 13, 2010. http://www.billboard.com/articles/news/956399/lady-gaga-explains-her-meat-dress-its-no-disrespect
Marco 67. To: Ryan-Lee Johnson. *YouTube video*, uploaded April 1, 2015. https://www.youtube.com/watch?v=zF3c0KqMExw
Markham, Tim. 2015. Celebrity Advocacy and Public Engagement: The Divergent Uses of Celebrity. *International Journal of Cultural Studies* 18(4): 467–480.
Martins, Chris. 2015. Woman of the Year Lady Gaga's Raw, Revealing Interview. *Billboard*, December 3, 2015. http://www.billboard.com/articles/events/women-in-music/6784920/lady-gaga-billboard-woman-of-the-year-2015-cover-story
Masley, Ed. 2010. Lady Gaga Video 'Alejandro' Outrages Catholics, Katy Perry. *AZCentral.com*, June 9, 2010. http://archive.azcentral.com/thingstodo/music/articles/20100609lady-gaga-video-alejandro-outrages-catholics-katy-perry.html
Massa, Amanda. 2011. Lady Gaga, MAC's Fundraising Miracle Worker. *Forbes*, February 17, 2011. http://www.forbes.com/sites/amandamassa/2011/02/17/lady-gaga-macs-fundraising-miracle-worker/
Meyer, David S., and Joshua Gamson. 1995. The Challenge of Cultural Elites: Celebrities and Social Movements. *Sociological Inquiry* 65(2): 181–206.
Michaels, Sean. 2014. Lady Gaga Denies Claims Regarding Born This Way Foundation Funds. *The Guardian*, March 14, 2014. http://www.theguardian.com/music/2014/mar/14/lady-gaga-denies-born-this-way-foundation-funds
MTV. 2010. Lady Gaga's 'Don't Ask, Don't Tell' Speech: The Full Transcript. *MTV.com*, September 20, 2010. http://www.mtv.com/news/1648304/lady-gagas-dont-ask-dont-tell-speech-the-full-transcript/
Noble, Sr. Theresa Aletheia. 2016. Lady Gaga and the Online Eucharist Police. *Aleteia*, May 17, 2016. http://aleteia.org/2016/05/17/lady-gaga-and-the-online-eucharist-police/

Nolfi, Joey. 2016a. Lady Gaga Breaks Down During Emotional Orlando Vigil: 'So Many Are Your Allies'. *Entertainment Weekly*, June 14, 2016. http://www.ew.com/article/2016/06/14/lady-gaga-orlando-shooting-vigil
———. 2016b. Lady Gaga, Dalai Lama to Address U.S. Conference of Mayors Together. *Entertainment Weekly*, June 22, 2016. http://www.ew.com/article/2016/06/22/lady-gaga-dalai-lama-us-conference-mayors
O'Hare, Kate. 2016. Sinead O'Connor, Abortion, Lady Gaga and Catholicism — It's Complicated. *Patheos*, May 17, 2016. http://www.patheos.com/blogs/kateohare/2016/05/sinead-oconnor-abortion-lady-gaga-and-catholicism-its-complicated/
Paquette, Danielle. 2016. How Lady Gaga and Hollywood Unexpectedly Tackled Rape at the Oscars. *The Washington Post*, February 29, 2016. https://www.washingtonpost.com/news/wonk/wp/2016/02/29/how-lady-gaga-and-hollywood-unexpectedly-tackled-rape-at-the-oscars/
Peeples, Jase. 2013. 12 Reasons Lady Gaga Deserves Our 'Applause'. *The Advocate*, August 20, 2013. http://www.advocate.com/arts-entertainment/music/2013/08/20/12-reasons-lady-gaga-deserves-applause
Roach, Becky. 2016. From Lady Gaga to Steph Curry: 5 Things to Remember When Celebrities Share Their Faith. *Catholic Link*, May 10, 2016. http://catholic-link.org/2016/05/10/celebrities-and-faith/
Rutter, Claire. 2014. Howard Stern Questions Lady Gaga over Rape and She Reveals Terrible Abuse as a Teen. *The Daily Mirror*, December 2, 2014. http://www.mirror.co.uk/3am/celebrity-news/howard-stern-questions-lady-gaga-4735299
Rys, Dan. 2016. 'What Can We Help You Achieve?' Lady Gaga's Manager and Branding Experts Mull the New Normal. *Billboard*, March 17, 2016. http://www.billboard.com/articles/business/7263735/sxsw-2016-branding-lady-gaga-mac-presents
Schmalz, Mathew N. 2010. Defending Lady Gaga. *OnFaith*, June 16, 2010. http://www.faithstreet.com/onfaith/2010/06/16/mark-judge-deserves-credit-for/8595
Schreffler, Laura. 2011. Lady Gaga Gives a Canadian Teen the Thrill of His Life by Sending a Personalised Video of Thanks For His Anti-Bullying Efforts. *Daily Mail*, November 26, 2011. http://www.dailymail.co.uk/tvshowbiz/article-2066434/Lady-Gaga-thanks-Jacques-St-Pierre-anti-bullying-efforts-personalised-video.html
Sciarretto, Amy. 2011. Lady Gaga Addresses Claims of Using the 'Gay Community' to Sell Records. *PopCrush*, July 5, 2011. http://popcrush.com/lady-gaga-advocate-magazine-gay-community-sell-records/
Smith, Emily Esfahani. 2012. The Anti-Bullying Moral Vogue. *Acculturated*, December 26, 2012. http://acculturated.com/two-views-lady-gagas-anti-bullying-campaign-2/

Street, John. 2001. Rock, Pop, and Politics. In *The Cambridge Companion to Pop and Rock*, eds. S. Frith, W. Straw, and J. Street, 243–255. Cambridge, UK: Cambridge University Press.

———. 2003. 'Fight the Power': The Politics of Music and the Music of Politics. *Government and Opposition* 38(1): 113–130.

Swash, Rosie. 2010. Lady Gaga Triumphs at the MTV VMAs. *The Guardian*, September 13, 2010. http://www.theguardian.com/music/2010/sep/13/lady-gaga-triumphs-mtv-vmas

Sweeney, Jon M. 2011. Is Lady Gaga Catholic? *The Huffington Post*, August 18, 2011. http://www.huffingtonpost.com/jon-m-sweeney/lady-gaga-catholic_b_926420.html

Takeda, Allison. 2014. Lady Gaga Opens Up About 'Horrific' Past Sexual Encounter in Discussion About Rape. *US Weekly*, December 2, 2014. http://www.usmagazine.com/celebrity-news/news/lady-gaga-reveals-horrific-sexual-encounter-in-discussion-about-rape-2014212

Taylor, Florence. 2016. Lady Gaga to Catholic Critic: 'We're Not Just Celebrities, We're Humans'. *Christian Today*, May 11, 2016. http://www.christiantoday.com/article/lady.gaga.to.catholic.critic.were.not.just.celebrities.were.humans/85832.htm

Teicher, David. 2011. Love of Google Trumps Cash for Will.i.am and Lady Gaga. *AdvertisingAge*, October 4, 2011. http://adage.com/article/digitalnext/love-google-trumps-cash-i-lady-gaga/230185/

Trier-Bieniek, Adrienne, and Amanda Pullum. 2014. From Lady Gaga to Consciousness Rap: The Impact of Music on Gender and Social Activism. In *Gender & Pop Culture: A Text-Reader*, eds. Adrienne Trier-Bieniek and Patricia Leavy, 81–102. Rotterdam: SensePublishers.

Tsaliki, Liza. 2016. 'Tweeting the Good Causes': Social Networking and Celebrity Activism. In *A Companion to Celebrity*, eds. David P. Marshall and Sean Redmond, 235–257. Chichester, UK: Wiley Blackwell.

Van Meter, Jonathan. 2011. Lady Gaga: Our Lady of Pop. *Vogue*, February 10. http://www.vogue.com/865458/lady-gaga-our-lady-of-pop/

Varriale, Simone. 2012. Is That Girl a Monster? Some Notes on Authenticity and Artistic Value in Lady Gaga. *Celebrity Studies* 3(2): 256–258.

Vena, Jocelyn. 2011a. Lady Gaga To Donate 'Born This Way' Country Remix Proceeds To Charity. *MTV.com*, April 5, 2011. http://www.mtv.com/news/1661315/lady-gaga-born-this-way-country-road-version/

———. 2011b. Lady Gaga Says 'Judas' Video Isn't 'an Attack on Religion'. *MTV.com*, May 5, 2011. http://www.mtv.com/news/1663387/lady-gaga-judas-video/

Virgin Mobile. 2012. Virgin Mobile Partners with Lady Gaga's 'Born This Way' Ball Tour to Empower Fans Through Social Outreach. *News release*, December 20, 2012. http://newsroom.virginmobileusa.com/press-release/general/virgin-mobile-partners-lady-gagas-born-way-ball-tour-empower-fans-through-soci

Wahba, Phil. 2016. Lady Gaga and Elton John Are Teaming Up for a New Line at Macy's. *Fortune*, April 27, 2016. http://fortune.com/2016/04/27/macys-lady-gaga-elton-john-love-bravery/

Warner, Kara. 2010. Lady Gaga Offers 'Alejandro' Video Sneak Peek on 'Larry King Live'. *MTV.com*, June 1, 2010. http://www.mtv.com/news/1640536/lady-gaga-offers-alejandro-video-sneak-peek-on-larry-king-live/

Wass, Mike. 2016. Lady Gaga Throws Her Support Behind Hillary Clinton. Again. *Idolator*, April 7, 2016. http://www.idolator.com/7629308/lady-gaga-support-hillary-clinton-jamie-lee-curtis

Williams, Mary E. 2011. Lady Gaga's Religion-Baiting Controversy. *Salon.com*, April 12, 2011. http://www.salon.com/2011/04/12/lady_gaga_judas_video_controversy/

Zezima, Katie. 2010. Lady Gaga Goes Political in Maine. *The New York Times*, September 20, 2010. http://www.nytimes.com/2010/09/21/us/politics/21gaga.html

CHAPTER 9

The Sex of Lady Gaga

As with many cultural issues in modern society, the degree of fame attained and maintained by an artist in the world of popular culture can rationally be expected to be influenced by various factors related to sex, gender, and sexuality. This chapter examines issues of sex, gender, and sexuality in the world of Lady Gaga, with special attention to the role they have played in the singer's rise to fame. Relying on the conceptual understanding of sex as a biological category and gender as the social use and cultural meanings associated therewith, there are many good reasons to explore the significance of these issues in the case of Lady Gaga. For, in the world of entertainment and popular music, gender can be even more readily than usual acknowledged to be relevant as singers and performers show themselves to display their physical being, often in striking and revealing ways. At a minimum, an analysis of the conditions of Lady Gaga's fame as a pop star must explore matters of sex, sexuality, and gender, not only in terms of social relations involving men and women but, additionally, with respect to the cultural expectations that exist on masculinity and femininity (Cohen 2001).[1]

Betraying the contemporary popularity of the study of sex, sexuality, and gender, these issues have in the case of Lady Gaga received considerable scrutiny, including several media reports (Aronowitz 2011; Camp 2010; Hoby 2010; Keller 2010; Teal 2010), scholarly analyses (Brooks 2015; O'Brien 2014; Williams 2014; Woolston 2012), and writings from students graduating from universities (Clark Mane 2012) and even high school (Madden 2011). Although these accounts can be informative on relevant facts, they mostly adopt interpretive modes of analysis and engage in much evaluative speculation and normative judgment. In this chapter, I will first instead focus on examining relevant issues that have been raised regarding the sexuality of the person of Lady Gaga as well as aspects of gender stratification and sexism that are manifested in the community that surrounds her. Based on these examinations, I will subsequently discuss the singer's stated positions on feminism as well as the perceptions that exist thereon. Fitting the theme and approach of this book, these issues will be explored as cultural constructions that have contributed to Lady Gaga's rise to fame.

Gaga Sexuality

Sexuality sociologically refers to the cultural construction of the sexual identity and conduct attributed to and perceived by the sexes. From the viewpoint of the cultural meanings and implications of the sexuality of Lady Gaga, at least four issues have received public scrutiny and debate: (1) the degree and ways in which aspects of sexuality are exhibited in Lady Gaga's work; (2) the perceived sexiness of Lady Gaga as a female performer; (3) the rumors that have been spread over the biological sex of Lady Gaga; and (4) the singer's stated and assumed sexual orientation. Some of these topics have received more popular attention than others, but all have been addressed to some extent or another in the public sphere, thereby contributing to cultivate the public's fascination with Lady Gaga.

Is Lady Gaga Sexual?

The question of the sexual nature of Lady Gaga pertains to whether or not and to what extent the singer's persona and her artistic endeavors are perceived to contain allusions to sexually charged themes. The answer is an unequivocal "yes," because there is widely acknowledged to be quite a bit of sexuality displayed in Lady Gaga's music. This observation should not come as a huge surprise, of course, not only because the display of sexuality has especially taken advantage of the visualization of musical sound since the rise of the music video (Andsager and Roe 2003), but also because of the historical fact that many forms of popular music are by their historical nature deeply imbedded in sexuality. The very term "rock 'n' roll" refers to intercourse. It is therefore also not surprising that

Lady Gaga has at times described her work in highly sexual terms. "When you make music or write or create," she once said, "it's really your job to have mind-blowing, irresponsible, condomless sex with whatever idea it is you're writing about at the time" (in Pop Dirt 2009). The singer also connects her sense of sexuality with a resolute commitment to lock herself in the culture of popular music. From early on in her career, the performer has said, she deliberately used her sexuality to get attention by performing in revealing clothing. Speaking about playing in the New York clubs as an unknown around 2006 and 2007, Lady Gaga recalls, "I didn't want to start singing while they were talking, so I got undressed. There I was, sitting at the piano in my underwear. So they shut up" (in Sturges 2009).

The most striking examples of sexuality in Lady Gaga's work are obviously found in some of her songs and videos. Her global smash hit "Poker Face," for example, deals autobiographically with her fantasies about sexually being with a woman while a man is having oral sex with her. The song "LoveGame" is, again autobiographically, based on a casual sexual encounter Lady Gaga had with a man whom she asked to ride his "disco stick." Although in her live shows, the disco stick appears as a sort of glowing magic wand held by Lady Gaga, the reference in the song is clearly to a penis. The video to the song "LoveGame" is also strikingly sexual in nature, containing lurid dance moves and a semi-naked Lady Gaga kissing both a man and a woman, leading the video to be censored in some countries. Several other Lady Gaga songs likewise explicitly deal with sex, such as: "Monster" and "G.U.Y." (an acronym for girl under you) about sexual desires involving dominance and submission; "Alejandro" about casual sex; "Teeth" about the joys of pain and sex; "Sexxx Dreams" about sexual attraction toward men; and the thematically obvious, but musically oddly romantic sounding "I Like It Rough."

Several videos to Lady Gaga songs, even when the song lyrics are not of a sexual nature, feature ample displays of sexuality as well. By example, the video to the song "Yoü and I," which thematically deals with romantic love (specifically about her ex-boyfriend Lüc Carl), shows Lady Gaga as a mermaid having sex with a man (played by Taylor Kinney, who would go on to become her boyfriend and later fiancé). Similarly, the track "Do What U Want" of the 2013 album *ARTPOP* is a biting critique against Lady Gaga's music critics but is strikingly sexual in its visual appeal and suggestive title. The video to the song was to feature rather provocative sexual scenes and nudity, but its release was canceled, presumably for it being too risqué and involving participation from R. Kelly and Terry Richardson (TMZ 2014).

In live performances for radio and television as well as during Lady Gaga's live shows, sexuality is likewise displayed freely. By example, during her performance of the song "LoveGame" on the arena version of the Monster Ball Tour, Lady Gaga encouraged the audience to "get your dicks out … and dance, you mother fuckers!" The dancers accompanying Lady Gaga at her shows also add to the sexual portrayal. When she began her career in 2008, the singer typically performed with two female dancers in an asexual artsy style invoking Warhol. But toward the end of 2008, she was joined on stage by three male dancers, who interacted with her to visualize choreographically the sexual meanings associated with the likes of "Poker Face" and "LoveGame." On her global world tours, the dance group consists of about a dozen men and women, further enabling choreographic representations of sex, including gay sex. The wardrobe used by Lady Gaga and her dancers additionally often amplifies sexuality by means of displaying nudity, glitter bras, codpieces, SM-styled clothing, and the likes. Even in the old-fashioned setting of the *Cheek To Cheek* live concert series with Tony Bennett, Lady Gaga at times resorted to explicit sexual appeal, such as by telling the audience how many of her touring musicians of the Brian Newman Quintet she had slept with in her pre-fame days.

Devoted fans of Lady Gaga respond to her sexuality in kind by a liberal display of (semi-)nudity at her shows, typically mimicking some of the singer's revealing outfits such as sequined glitter bras, bikini tops made of seashells, and see-through clothes. Likewise telling is the strongly sexualized talk of many of her most devoted fans in their communications on Twitter, Facebook, and Lady Gaga-related music forums. Strikingly, much of the sex talk directed at the person of Lady Gaga especially seems to come from non-gay female fans and gay males. Equally striking is that the singer firmly embraces the sexuality she receives from her fans, to wit her self-reference as a "hooker" or a "bitch" and her posing with fans for pictures in at times suggestive positions, at least once even allowing a fan to grab her behind.

As is not unusual for any popular music performers displaying a more or less explicit sexual style, some opposition to Lady Gaga has revolved around the sexual content of her work, such as the double entendre and occasionally suggestive language involved in some of her lyrics (Burke 2015). Despite its at times rather distinct sexual orientation, however, it is nonetheless to be noted that the majority of Lady Gaga's recorded songs are thematically not about sex. Of the 57 songs included on her first four major releases, the album *The Fame* of 2008 (containing 17 songs including bonus tracks), the 8-song EP *The Fame Monster* of 2009, the 2011 album *Born This Way* (containing 17 original songs on the expanded edition), and the 2013 album *ARTPOP* (15 songs), only 14 deal with sex in more or less explicit ways. The majority of Gaga's songs instead are about romantic love (15 songs), fun and friendship in her native New York (11 songs), and a variety of other themes, including gay rights, immigration, fashion, freedom, and her fans.

Is Lady Gaga Sexy?

The notion of being sexy or having sex appeal relates to the extent and manner in which Lady Gaga presents herself, as a woman, by standards of feminine sexiness. Needless to say, as such perceptions reside in the eye of the beholder, sexiness can sociologically be articulated on the basis of the cultural values that are relatively dominant in a community at any given time and place. By the cultural standard of a conventionally understood sexiness, the answer to the question of Lady Gaga's sexiness is a qualified "no." Lady Gaga is not, or at least not unequivocally, sexy by conventional standards and also does not wish to be a classic beauty, especially not in the sense traditionally associated with the world of pop music. The singer has said that she does not want to be "a sexy pop star writhing in the sand, covered in grease, touching herself" (in Elle 2009). "I am not sexy in the way that Britney Spears is sexy," she once claimed, "which is a compliment to her because she's deliciously good-looking. I just don't have the same ideas about sexuality that I want to portray. I have a very specific aesthetic—androgyny" (in The Sun 2009). At the VMAs in August 2011, Lady Gaga took this aspiration to the next level by appearing as the male alter ego of Jo Calderone (Perpetua 2011), a performance that has been interpreted as part of a gender-challenging dialogue (Kumari 2016).

In much of her conduct and her physical appearance, indeed, Lady Gaga does not present herself as a sexy female and is also not typically, or at least not always, perceived as such. Discussing her sense of fashion and style, she comments: "I just don't feel that it's all that sexy. It's weird … It's not what is sexy. It's graphic and it's art" (in Barthel 2009). Instead of wearing short skirts and tight pants, Lady Gaga prefers to be skirtless and pantless. And instead of wearing shoes with high heels along with a fancy skirt or dress, she is often seen to wear excessively high heels or leather boots with spikes along with shorts and leather pants or no pants at all. Few will associate sexiness with a meat dress and other such outlandish outfits Lady Gaga has been seen to wear. The theme of monstrosity that is often displayed by Lady Gaga is culturally by and large not perceived as sexy.

Lady Gaga's refusal to be conventionally sexy implies a statement about what is and what should be considered beautiful. At some of her Monster Ball shows, the performer would bite the head off from Barbie dolls thrown on stage to protest what she considers to be unrealistic standards of beauty. As she argues to be fighting preconceptions of what female performers have to be and do in order to be successful in popular music, it can be said that Lady Gaga deliberately "toys with conventional rules of attractiveness" (Williams 2010). On the covers of her music releases, also, Lady Gaga appears often only by face, not her entire body, with additional artwork involving the use of artificial facial protrusions, and slime. Even most times when Lady Gaga is seen wearing clothing or adopts a stylistic choice that might otherwise have been sexy, she does it in a way that is meant to be grotesque, even repulsive (Cochrane 2010), and deliberately gender-bending to display her LGBT activism (Hancock 2013). As such, as rock star Alice Cooper once observed, Lady Gaga intends to be a spectacle, not a sex symbol (CNN 2011).

By avoiding conventional portrayals of sex appeal, Lady Gaga and the members of her fan community seek to embrace a new and unique kind of sexiness. In a very distinct sense as it is understood by Lady Gaga and her fans alike, everybody who is part of the Lady Gaga world is considered sexy, even and especially when they are unlikely to be perceived as such outside of the fan community. Of course, this ideal cannot always be attained, and conventional standards of beauty and sex appeal will always be replicated in more or less overt ways. Tying in with Lady Gaga's acceptance and embrace of freakishness and monstrosity (Corona 2013; Macfarlane 2012; Rossolatos 2015), everybody who is part of her world is meant to be accepted for who they are and who they wish to be, even and especially when they by the conventions of mainstream society judged not to be sexy or even thought to be unattractive. As discussed in Chap. 7, the limits of this ideal are most strikingly revealed when some of Lady Gaga's Little Monsters turn against fellow fans, by calling them ugly, fat, and old.

What Is Lady Gaga's Sex?

Despite her explicitly gendered stage name and the obvious fact of her biological nature as a female, Lady Gaga has, especially early on during her rise to fame, been confronted with the rumor that she might be a so-called hermaphrodite. It is perhaps most striking to note, as an indication of the occasionally irrational nature of the obsession with Lady Gaga, that this rumor has not always met with the obviously ridicule it deserves and has instead at times been taken seriously. As always, the origins of the rumor are not clear. The allegation might date back to an interview with Christina Aguilera, who, when asked about Lady Gaga after she had only just begun to make some waves in the world of pop in 2008, said that she did not know who Lady Gaga was and did not even know "if it is a man or a woman" (in Amter 2008).

Some of Lady Gaga's initial reactions to the rumor, that spread virally on the internet, did little to quench the speculation, even though her conduct could rationally only be understood to be deliberately provocative. For example, when in August 2009 she voiced her happiness about the fact that her song "Poker Face" had gone to the top position on the charts in Japan, Lady Gaga tweeted, "I just had to go home and suck my own hermie dick, suckka" (Lady Gaga Twitter post). Right up until the Spring of 2011, she shouted out during her live performances of the song "LoveGame" at the Monster Ball that she had a "pretty tremendous dick!" On another occasion sometime in the Fall of 2009, Lady Gaga would have said, "I have both male and female genitalia, but I consider myself female. It's just a little bit of a penis, and it doesn't interfere much with my life … I have both a poon and a peener. Big fucking deal" (Lester 2010: 93–94). There is no independent source for the quote, but it circulated heavily on the internet at the time, which in itself indicates how much the story had gained traction and kept the focus on Lady Gaga.

Though mostly having fun with and deliberately sustaining the rumor, Lady Gaga has at other times refused to address the matter or denied the allegation. While promoting her tour in September 2009 she once responded, "My beautiful vagina is very offended by that question" (in FemaleFirst 2009). The interesting aspect of her answer is not the confirmation of her biology, but the affirmation of Lady Gaga's identity as a female whose strength is affirmed in opposition to the need to be a man. During an interview with Anderson Cooper for the television show "60 Minutes" that aired on the night of the Grammy Awards in February

2011, the singer showed herself even more decisive in reaffirming her female nature precisely by not answering the question. "Maybe," she said, she has a "male appendage," and added, "Why am I going to waste my time and give a press release about whether or not I have a penis? My fans don't care and neither do I" (in Sciarretto 2011). Despite its occasional re-appearance, by late 2011, the rumor had run its course as other issues about Lady Gaga started to take over the celebrity gossip columns.

What Is Lady Gaga's Sexual Orientation?

Like the hermaphrodite issue, the question of Lady Gaga's sexual orientation has been the subject of quite some speculation, especially on the internet, some of it sustained and nurtured by the singer herself. In interviews, Lady Gaga has most often flirted with the question of her sexual orientation and left some uncertainty on the matter. This ambiguity may relate to her feelings about romantic love, both as it exists in her life and how she has accordingly addressed love in her music. Most Lady Gaga's songs dealing with romantic love are decidedly conflicted, ambivalent, or even negative in tone, for instance by singing about bad (not good) romance and the possessiveness of her experiencing love for a man as a stalking paparazzi. Before her relationship with Taylor Kinney, the singer would in interviews typically deny having a boyfriend, despite her romantic involvement with Lüc Carl and others, and claim that her commitment to her work prevented her from having a steady romantic partner. "I make love to my music every day," she said in 2009, "I'm just not focused on having a boyfriend" (in Nissim 2009). In more recent years, however, especially after her engagement to Taylor Kinney on Valentine's Day 2015, the performer has regularly stated she is looking forward to one day, possibly sooner than later, being married with children.

Yet, at once as Lady Gaga proclaims conventional and heteronormative attitudes about love, marriage, and family, she is also deliberately provocative about her sex life and sexuality. Invoking the theme in her song "Poker Face" of dreaming about being with a woman while she is having sex with a man, she has said to have had sex with women but only to have been in love with men. In an interview with Barbara Walters in December 2009, she said, "I've never been in love with a woman ... I've certainly had sexual relationships with women" (in Larosa 2010). More recently, Lady Gaga has gone further and proclaimed that she is bisexual and considers herself a member of the LGBT community because of "The b letter," as she put it in a 2011 interview with the LGBT magazine *The Advocate* (Kinser 2011). In 2013, she repeated the claim, arguing in unequivocal terms, "I am bisexual and I like women" (in Panisch 2013).

Gaga Gender and Sexism

Understood as the differential treatment on the basis of sex and gender characteristics, it is difficult to imagine any aspect of social life, including the world of popular music, that would not be gendered to some degree and in some form or another. The gendered nature of culture can be of multiple kinds, either involving mere differences between the sexes or, indicating sexism, inequality on the basis of sexual identity, possibly as the result of oppression. In the case of Lady Gaga, the framework of the constructionist perspective of culture and the social-rationalist theory of meaning used in this book can immediately bring out an element pertinent to the present analysis, specifically the transformation of the rock-oriented style of Stefani Germanotta to the electro-pop sounds and performance art of Lady Gaga. Though not absolute in any way, as I will show in Chap. 10, the predominant cultural understanding is such that pop is of a more feminine nature as opposed to the masculine world of rock.

Gender differences between the worlds of rock and pop need not necessarily imply sexism, but there are at least some indications that certain gendered pressures were at work in Lady Gaga's initial decision to transform stylistically. According to producer Rob Fusari, the singer was, upon his insistence, ultimately persuaded to change her musical style because of a news article that discussed the gender aspects of singer Nelly Furtado's successful transition to dance-oriented pop music (Marks 2010). Whatever other personal and artistic reasons may have swayed her, anticipating success and fame to be more likely in the world of pop, Lady Gaga began her journey toward global stardom on the basis of her understanding of a distinctly gendered reality. The singer's ascent to fame thereafter contributed to, and was in turn positively affected by, an ever-growing and vibrant pop world that was dominated by a large number of highly successful women. From about 2010 until today, indeed, female pop stars ranging from Beyoncé, Taylor Swift, Katy Perry, Rihanna, and Nicki Minaj to Lana Del Rey, Adele, and Lorde, among many others, have ruled the world of popular music. These favorable conditions would eventually also allow Lady Gaga to explore artistic directions outside the realm of pop and dance. By the Spring of 2011, she released her *Born This Way* album as a deliberate effort to bring a rock sensibility to her music, and thereafter she even branched out to the world of jazz.

There are indications that the gendered structure of the Lady Gaga world has at times implied outright sexism. By Lady Gaga's own perception, the singer has, as a female artist operating in the world of popular music, been confronted with sexism, especially in connection with her liberal use of sexual themes, which, she argues, is much more discussed and criticized than equally sexually explicit material by male artists. "You see, if I was a guy," the singer said in a 2009 interview, "and I was sitting here with a cigarette in my hand, grabbing my crotch and talking about how I make music because I love fast cars and fucking girls, you'd call me a rock star. But when I do it in my music and in my videos—because I'm a female, because I make pop music—you're judgmental and you say that it is distracting" (in Gharnit 2015).

In response to the sexism Lady Gaga perceives, she will typically reaffirm her strength as a woman. This attitude is manifest in some of her music, such as when she sings "I'm a free bitch, baby!" (on her song "Dance in the Dark" of *The Fame Monster*) and expresses her desire as a woman to be "strong without permission" (on "Scheiße" of *Born This Way*). In interviews, likewise, Lady Gaga will fight sexism, especially in the world of pop music, by addressing it candidly. As early as 2009, the singer stated that "men get away with saying a lot in this business, and that women get away with saying very little" (in Powers 2009). Such proclamations have become more explicit in recent years since Lady Gaga's fame has been more established. During her artRAVE tour in 2014, for instance, the singer revealed that she "had really awful experiences with men in the studio" (in Fletcher 2014). In December 2015, on the occasion of her acceptance of Billboard's Woman of the Year award, Lady Gaga addressed sexism in the music industry head on, arguing that "it is really hard sometimes for women in music," a culture she described as "a f—ing boys club" (in Karlin 2015). She addressed the same issue again in the Spring of 2016 when she, along with other female pop stars, came out in support of singer Kesha, who had raised sexual assault allegations against one of her producers (Billboard 2016).

The Feminism of Lady Gaga

The question of Lady Gaga's feminism relates to the singer's conception of her cultural standing as a woman and its relation to the perceptions that exist thereon. Harboring a multitude of perspectives on women in society (valuing women as unique, unequal, or oppressed), feminism can be understood both as theory, referring to a perspective of study and/or a corresponding outlook on life, as well as to praxis, implying an activist attitude oriented at working toward the betterment of women in society and/or a corresponding mode of personal conduct. In other words, from a constructionist perspective, cultural issues of the feminism of Lady Gaga refer both to her subjective perspective on such matters and how her perspective is perceived by others. The question is not whether Lady Gaga can merely be used as a metaphor to describe a new kind of feminism (Halberstam 2012), but whether the singer in her attitude and conduct as well as the perception thereof represents feminism in whichever form it can be manifested.

Some ambiguity has existed over Lady Gaga's feminism because of the confusion that resulted from some of her own evolving statements on the matter. Over the course of several interviews, the singer adopted different conceptions of what feminism is, fueling considerable debate and speculation about the issue, especially online (Aronowitz 2011; Camp 2010; Seltzer 2010). Early on in her rise to fame, Lady Gaga claimed not to be a feminist, much to the discontent of feminists (Williams 2010). In a videotaped interview in the Summer of 2009, specifically, she said, "I'm not a feminist. I hail men, I love men. I celebrate American male culture, beer, and bars, and muscle cars" (in Sevilla 2009).

In later statements, however, Lady Gaga began to conceive of feminism differently and understood that the term need not imply an anti-male attitude (Feministcupcake 2011). In an interview with the *Los Angeles Times* in December 2009, she said she was "a little bit feminist" (Powers 2009). Finally, as her understanding of feminism had changed to encompass a sense of female empowerment, Lady Gaga affirmed herself explicitly as a feminist. In an in-depth article for *Rolling Stone* magazine in 2010, she proclaimed unequivocally, "I'm a feminist" (in Strauss 2010:71). Later in her career, alongside of her speaking out against sexism in the music industry, she reaffirmed her stance and proclaimed, "I'm certainly a feminist … A feminist to me is somebody that wishes to protect the integrity of women who are ambitious" (in Fletcher 2014).

From the viewpoint of both her perspective and its cultural reception, Lady Gaga can be said to practice a role congruent with a general philosophy of feminism. Although primarily working in the world of pop music, Lady Gaga typically does not seek to exemplify those roles and styles associated with female pop artists which are more conventionally associated with inequality and patriarchy. Instead, although she is not a feminist activist *per se*, Lady Gaga can be seen as a practicing critic of how women are and should be viewed and valued. By being independent, Lady Gaga factually portrays ideals of feminism, especially the notion that women can be free to explore their own ways and follow their own path of creativity. "I hope to be an inspiration that if you're talented enough," she said in a 2014 interview, "you can work hard and achieve your dreams" (in Fletcher 2014). By and large, also, Lady Gaga's vision and practice of feminism has not been subjected to the criticisms of white feminism which have befallen some other contemporary female pop stars, such as Taylor Swift (Filipovic 2015; Fabello 2015).

Much of Lady Gaga's feminism is distinctly associated with, rather than contradicted by, her sense of sexuality, which seeks to embrace sex without necessarily giving in to conventional standards of sex appeal and sexuality. Invoking images of monstrosity and lurid tales of sexual exploits of many kinds, Lady Gaga is said to expose conventional femininity "as a sham" (Cochrane 2010). Through her "blending of the beautiful with the monstrous," as sociologist Victor Corona (2013:11) puts it, Lady Gaga criticizes the role of the traditional female in society by showing that conventional "feminine sexuality is a social construct" (Bauer 2010). The video to the 2009 song "Bad Romance," for example, visually presents a story of Lady Gaga being sold into sex slavery only to eventually kill the man she was sold to by means of a pyro bra that shoots out sparkles, ostensibly after, or instead of, having had sex with him in bed. The pyro bra itself, which she also wore on the cover of *Rolling Stone* magazine in July 2010 and during her concerts on the Monster Ball tour, Lady Gaga has interpreted as a commentary on the fact that female breasts are culturally typically conceived of as weapons ("guns"), when they are merely a part of her and other women's bodies (Lester 2010:91).

Conceiving of feminist freedom as "allowing women to express their sexuality" in ways they themselves see fit (Aronowitz 2011), Lady Gaga practices feminism by being free-spirited and in charge of her career. For that reason, also, Lady Gaga can at the same time claim that she likes men and combine her career with traditional gender roles, even and especially when her embrace of convention (for instance, in terms of her relationship with her fiancé) is attacked by others for being non-feminist (Langsam Braunstein 2014). It can be argued, also, that the singer adopting the term "Lady" as part of her moniker as a performer precisely shows that the term is today no longer considered taboo in the feminist world (Reid

Boyd 2012). Throughout her work, likewise, Lady Gaga acts like a diva who transcends traditional feminine roles to display female empowerment (Kerr 2015).

As a *de facto* feminist, Lady Gaga has been said to have taken ownership of her body and her work (Cochrane 2010; Emitt 2013). Even when in the earlier period of her career she felt the need to take her clothes off to get attention, she did not see it as giving in to an oppressive masculine world, but as a moment of liberation. Against a perspective that views the sexuality of female pop stars as part of their successful "branding" in an ever-more crowded popular music market (Lieb 2013), Lady Gaga counteracts the conventional response to female sexuality that "she took her clothes off, so sex sells, right?" by arguing that "in the context of that moment ... I was doing something radical" (in Sturges 2009). As such, Lady Gaga's sense of sexuality, femininity, and sex appeal can be argued to constitute at least an attempt at critique of the masculine dominance and traditional conventions of the popular music world, a world in which the singer is at the same time firmly rooted. The domination in the world of pop music by female artists in the years since Lady Gaga rose to fame is something the singer accordingly welcomes with wide-open arms. "I'm pleased to see," she stated, "that it's mostly women who are dominating the charts" (in Daily Star 2009).

Conclusion

This chapter has discussed issues of sex, sexuality, and gender in the career of Lady Gaga and examined how they impacted her reception as a pop star and played a role in the singer's rise to fame. Especially during the years leading to the height of Lady Gaga's standing as a global pop star that was reached by 2010, it is revealed that debates on various gender issues in the world of Lady Gaga were at the foreground of popular discussions, particularly on the internet. A peculiar upswing in these discussions, especially concerning the feminism of Lady Gaga, occurred after cultural critic Camille Paglia published a condemnation of the new pop sensation, wherein she wrote, that Lady Gaga "isn't sexy at all. She's like a gangly marionette or plasticised android" (Paglia 2010). Not surprisingly, the provocative piece was quickly followed by a multitude of alternate perspectives on Lady Gaga's feminism and position as a female (Daily Mail 2010; Gliatto 2010; Hunt 2010; Needham 2010; Zanin 2010). Paglia was thereby critiqued for being "marooned in the past" (Needham 2010), unable to analyze relevant dimensions of a contemporary artist who was not even physically born at the time when the pop stars of old, adored by Paglia (1990), were all the rage (Deflem 2015). As such, Paglia was said to stand far from alone in writing about the cultural import of Lady Gaga in terms that betray a lack of the most basic descriptive information, at best being able to reference the "Gaga-savvy daughter" they have at home for the Summer (Bauer 2010).

Issues surrounding sex, sexuality, and gender in the world of Lady Gaga reveal a complex condition whereby the performer is seen to embrace some, but fight other aspects of the dominant cultural standards of femininity. Liberally relying on sexual themes in her music and videos, Lady Gaga mostly rejects a conventional notion of sex appeal. Toying with rumors about her biological sex and being ambiguous about her sexual orientation, she can be seen to at once understand, and use to the advantage of her career, the gendered dynamics of her society and the world of popular music. In seeking to practice her art as an independent female who wants to challenge sexist obstacles, Lady Gaga presents herself, and is mostly, though not always, also recognized, as a practicing feminist. Regardless, harmonizing with what was said in the previous chapter about the impact of the controversial nature of Lady Gaga's activism and religiosity, what the popular debate and at times divisive speculations about the singer's sexuality, sex, feminism, and other gender issues bring out is that they nourish a considerable measure of interest in the singer. As such, it is again controversy that can be observed to fuel fame. While Lady Gaga's self-identification as a bisexual woman, for instance, may not be accurate, the validity of Lady Gaga's (subjective) presentations of self is, as shown throughout this book, not relevant to its (inter-subjective) public reception and the attention it receives.

Questions of gender and sexism in the world of popular music can also throw a useful light on the puzzling fact that Lady Gaga and other female artists are often compared with one another. When Lady Gaga was still a relatively unknown, she would often be asked in the media how she differed from or compared herself to the likes of Christina Aguilera and Britney Spears. Once her style and visibility were more developed and she came to be successful, it was Madonna who was used as a yardstick for comparison, especially by older members of the public and the journalistic profession. And as Lady Gaga had become a global sensation, other young female aspiring pop singers were asked to clarify their relation to Lady Gaga. There are, no doubt, elements of an artistic and aesthetic nature that can be articulated to justify such comparison questions. However, there are also indications that similar such questions are less often asked about male performers, especially those who perform in the world of rock. Being a woman and having blond hair alone can culturally suffice to justify a comparison among several female pop singers, while being male and having long hair and tattoos are often overlooked as equally shallow similarities among a considerable number of rock stars. It is telling that Lady Gaga has not been able to avoid this fundamental gender dichotomy in popular music and that she has, for these and other reasons with distinct gender consequences, also embraced aspects of the attitude and style commonly associated with the masculine world of rock, as the next chapter will explain.

Note

1. This chapter is revised and updated from a chapter published in a book edited by Richard J. Gray II that was published by McFarland (Deflem 2012).

References

Amter, Charlie. 2008. Five Minutes with Xtina: Christina Aguilera Takes a Look Back at a Decade on Top. *Los Angeles Times Blog*, November 11, 2008. http://latimesblogs.latimes.com/music_blog/2008/11/five-minutes-wi.html

Andsager, Julie, and Kimberly Roe. 2003. 'What's Your Definition of Dirty, Baby?' Sex in Music Video. *Sexuality & Culture* 7(3): 79–97.

Aronowitz, Nona W. 2011. Lady Gaga: Celebrity Feminist? *On the Issues*, Winter 2011, http://www.ontheissuesmagazine.com/2011winter/2011_winter_Aronowitz.php

Barthel, Mike. 2009. A Child's Treasury of Lady GaGa Quotes about not Wearing Pants. *Idolator*, March 23, 2009. http://www.idolator.com/5262222/a-childs-treasury-of-lady-gaga-quotes-about-not-wearing-pants

Bauer, Nancy. 2010. Lady Power. *The New York Times*, June 20, 2010. http://opinionator.blogs.nytimes.com/2010/06/20/lady-power/

Billboard. 2016. Lady Gaga: Kesha Is 'Being Publicly Shamed for Something That Happens in the Music Industry All the Time'. *Billboard*, March 7, 2016. http://www.billboard.com/articles/columns/pop/6898402/lady-gaga-kesha-case-dr-luke-interview

Brooks, Oliver. 2015. 'I'm a Free Bitch Baby', a 'Material Girl': Interrogating Audience Interpretations of the Postfeminist Performances of Lady Gaga and

Madonna. In *The Politics of Being a Woman: Feminism, Media and 21st Century Popular Culture*, eds. Heather Savigny and Helen Warner, 67–90. New York: Palgrave Macmillan.

Burke, Jill. 2015. Burke's Law: Don't let Lady Gaga Teach Your Kids About Sex. *Alaska Dispatch News*, October 28, 2015.

Camp, Kevin. 2010. Lady Gaga and Emergent Feminism. *Examiner.com*, March 14, 2010. http://www.examiner.com/democrat-in-washington-dc/lady-gaga-and-emergent-feminism

Clark Mane, Rebecca Lynne. 2012. *Using Female Empowerment as a Cover Story for Whiteness and Racial Hierarchy in Pop Culture: Interrogating the Intersections of Racial Appropriation and Feminist Discourse in the Performances of Fergie, Gwen Stefani, and Lady Gaga*. Doctoral dissertation, University of Washington.

CNN. 2011. Joy Behar Show. *Transcripts*. Aired May 6, 2011. http://transcripts.cnn.com/TRANSCRIPTS/1105/06/joy.01.html

Cochrane, Kira. 2010. Lady Gaga Exposes Femininity as a Sham. *The Guardian*, September 16, 2010. http://www.guardian.co.uk/music/2010/sep/17/lady-gaga-feminist-icon

Cohen, Sara. 2001. Popular Music, Gender and Sexuality. In *The Cambridge Companion to Pop and Rock*, eds. S. Frith, W. Straw, and J. Street, 226–242. Cambridge, UK: Cambridge University Press.

Corona, Victor P. 2013. Memory, Monsters, and Lady Gaga. *The Journal of Popular Culture* 46(4): 725–744.

Daily Mail. 2010. Has Lady Gaga Killed Off Sex? Top Feminist Claims Biggest Pop Star on the Planet is All Style and No Substance. *The Daily Mail*, September 14, 2010. http://www.dailymail.co.uk/tvshowbiz/article-1311874/Has-Lady-GaGa-killed-sex-Feminist-Camille-Paglia-claims-star-substance.html

Daily Star. 2009. Going GaGa, Gone! *Daily Star*, February 9, 2009. http://www.dailystar.co.uk/showbiz/playlist/68976/Going-GaGa-gone

Deflem, Mathieu. 2012. The Sex of Lady Gaga. In *The Performance Identities of Lady Gaga: Critical Essays*, eds. Richard J. Gray II, 19–32. Jefferson, NC: McFarland.

———. 2015. Die Pop-Revolutionärin. *Melodie und Rhythmus* 20, March/April 2015, p. 64.

Elle. 2009. Lady Gaga: The Singing Sensation on Stress, Sexuality, and Her Romantic Future. *Elle*, December 1, 2009. http://www.elle.com/culture/celebrities/a10701/lady-gaga-386961/

Emitt, Andrew. 2013. Dismissed Feminist Revision or: How I Learned to Stop Trolling and Love Lady Gaga's 'Applause'. *The Feminist Wire*, October 25, 2013. http://www.thefeministwire.com/2013/10/17833/

Fabello, Melissa A. 2015. 5 Ways Taylor Swift Exemplifies White Feminism—And Why That's a Problem. *Everyday Feminism*, September 8, 2015. http://everydayfeminism.com/2015/09/taylor-swift-white-feminism/

FemaleFirst. 2009. Lady GaGa: 'My Beautiful Vagina Is Very Offended'. *FemaleFirst*, September 4, 2009. http://www.femalefirst.co.uk/music/music-news/Lady+GaGa+My+beautiful+vagina+is+very+offended-71054.html

Feministcupcake. 2011. The Age Old Question: Is Lady Gaga a Feminist? *Feministing*, July 7, 2011. http://community.feministing.com/2011/07/07/the-age-old-question-is-lady-gaga-a-feminist

Filipovic, Jill. 2015. Sorry, Taylor Swift: Being a Feminist Is About More Than Just Supporting Your Girlfriends. *The Washington Post*, July 23, 2015. https://www.washingtonpost.com/posteverything/wp/2015/07/23/sorry-taylor-swift-being-a-feminist-is-about-more-than-just-supporting-your-girlfriends/

Fletcher, Harry. 2014. Lady Gaga: 'Men Took Advantage of Me Early in My Career'. *Digital Spy*, October 15, 2014. http://www.digitalspy.com/music/news/a603755/lady-gaga-men-took-advantage-of-me-early-in-my-career/

Gharnit, Yasmeen. 2015. Watch Lady Gaga Shut Down a Sexist Reporter. *Nylon*, June 15, 2015. http://www.nylon.com/articles/lady-gaga-shuts-down-sexist-reporter

Gliatto, Tom. 2010. Lady Gaga and Camille Paglia. *The Huffington Post*, September 24, 2010. http://www.huffingtonpost.com/tom-gliatto/lady-gaga-and-camille-pag_b_716994.html

Halberstam, J. Jack. 2012. *Gaga Feminism*. Boston: Beacon Press.

Hancock, Joseph H. II. 2013. Brand This Way: Lady Gaga's Fashion as Storytelling Context to the GLBT Community. In *Fashion in Popular Culture: Literature, Media and Contemporary Studies*, eds. Joseph H. Hancock II, Toni Johnson-Woods, and Vicki Karaminas, 1–22. Bristol, UK: Intellect.

Hoby, Hermione. 2010. So Much for Lady Gaga's Feminist Credentials. *The Guardian*, February 27, 2010. http://www.guardian.co.uk/music/musicblog/2010/feb/28/lady-gaga-feminist-credentials

Hunt, Carol. 2010. This Lady Will Never Be a Tramp. *The Independent*, September 26, 2011. http://www.independent.ie/opinion/analysis/this-lady-will-never-be-a-tramp-2353323.html

Karlin, Lily. 2015. Lady Gaga Slams Music Industry Sexism. *The Huffington Post*, December 12, 2015. http://www.huffingtonpost.com/entry/lady-gaga-boys-club_us_566c440ee4b011b83a6b79fe

Keller, Jessalynn. 2010. 'I'm Not a Feminist… I Love Men': Rethinking Lady Gaga's Postfeminist Rhetoric and Its Potential for Social Change. *In Media Res*, August 2, 2010. http://mediacommons.futureofthebook.org/imr/2010/08/01/im-not-feminist-i-love-men-rethinking-lady-gaga-s-postfeminist-rhetoric-and-its-potential

Kerr, Rosalind. 2015. The Fame Monster: Diva Worship from Isabella Andreini to Lady Gaga. *Italian Studies* 70(3): 402–415.

Kinser, Jeremy. 2011. Portrait of a Lady. *The Advocate*, July 5, 2011. http://www.advocate.com/arts-entertainment/music/2011/07/05/portrait-lady

Kumari, Ashanka. 2016. 'Yoü and I': Identity and the Performance of Self in Lady Gaga and Beyoncé. *Journal of Popular Culture* 49(2): 403–416.
Lady Gaga. Twitter post, August 7, 2009 (8:42 PM). https://twitter.com/ladygaga/status/3186200513
Langsam Braunstein, Melissa. 2014. Who Should Feminists Really Hate: Kirsten Dunst or Lady Gaga? *Acculturated*, April 11, 2014. http://acculturated.com/who-should-feminists-really-hate-kirsten-dunst-or-lady-gaga/
Larosa, Brad. 2010. How Stefani Germanotta Became Lady Gaga. *ABC News*, January 21, 2010. http://abcnews.go.com/2020/lady-gaga-tells-barbara-walters-felt-freak/story?id=9612835#.TrBA-GCEYps
Lester, Paul. 2010. *Lady Gaga: Looking for Fame. The Life of a Pop Princess.* London: Omnibus Press.
Lieb, Kristin J. 2013. *Gender, Branding, and the Modern Music Industry: The Social Construction of Female Poplar Music Stars.* New York: Routledge.
Macfarlane, Karen E. 2012. The Monstrous House of Gaga. In *The Gothic in Contemporary Literature and Popular Culture: Pop Goth*, eds. Justin D. Edwards and Agnieszka Soltysik Monnet, 114–134. New York: Routledge.
Madden, Kelley. 2011. *Lady Gaga: A Modern Feminist Debate.* Unpublished Senior Exhibition of Mastery Thesis, Heathwood Hall Episcopal School, Columbia, South Carolina, April 15, 2011.
Marks, Craid. 2010. Producer Rob Fusari Dishes on Lady Gaga, Beyoncé. *Billboard.com*, February 24, 2010. http://www.billboard.com/news/producer-rob-fusari-dishes-on-lady-gaga-1004070301.story#/features/producer-rob-fusari-dishes-on-lady-gaga-1004070301.story
Needham, Alex. 2010. Camille Paglia's Attack on Lady Gaga is Way Off the Mark. *The Guardian*, September 13, 2010. http://www.guardian.co.uk/commentisfree/2010/sep/13/camille-paglia-lady-gaga
Nissim, Mayer. 2009. Lady GaGa: 'I'm Not Promiscuous'. *Digital Spy*, May 29, 2009. http://www.digitalspy.com/showbiz/news/a157078/lady-gaga-im-not-promiscuous/
O'Brien, Lucy. 2014. Not a Piece of Meat: Lady Gaga and that Dress. Has Radical Feminism Survived the Journey? In *Lady Gaga and Popular Music*, eds. Martin Iddon and Melanie L. Marshall, 27–43. London: Routledge.
Paglia, Camille. 1990. Madonna: Finally, a Real Feminist. *The New York Times*, December 14, 1990. http://www.nytimes.com/1990/12/14/opinion/madonna-finally-a-real-feminist.html
———. 2010. Lady Gaga and the Death of Sex. *The Sunday Times*, September 12, 2010. http://www.thesundaytimes.co.uk/sto/public/magazine/article389697.ece
Panisch, Alex. 2013. Lady Gaga to Fans: 'I Am Bisexual'. *Out*, November 1, 2013. http://www.out.com/entertainment/popnography/2013/11/01/lady-gaga-fans-i-am-bisexual

Perpetua, Matthew. 2011. Lady Gaga as Jo Calderone: 'Britney Spears Is Hot'. *Rolling Stone*, August 29, 2011. http://www.rollingstone.com/music/news/lady-gaga-as-jo-calderone-britney-spears-is-hot-20110829

Pop Dirt. 2009. Lady Gaga: Making Music Is Like Irresponsible, Condomless Sex. *Pop Dirt*, March 9, 2009. http://popdirt.com/lady-gaga-making-music-is-like-irresponsible-condomless-sex/72248/

Powers, Ann. 2009. Frank Talk with Lady Gaga. *Los Angeles Times*, December 13, 2009. http://articles.latimes.com/2009/dec/13/entertainment/la-ca-ladygaga13-2009dec13

Reid Boyd, Elizabeth. 2012. Lady: Still a Feminist Four-Letter Word? *Women and Language* 352: 35–52.

Rossolatos, George. 2015. Lady Gaga as (Dis)simulacrum of Monstrosity. *Celebrity Studies* 6(2): 231–246.

Sciarretto, Amy. 2011. Lady Gaga Addresses Hermaphrodite Rumors, Says She Gets Bravery From Dressing Up. *PopCrush*, February 16, 2011. http://popcrush.com/lady-gaga-hermaphrodite-rumors-bravery-dressing-up/

Seltzer, Sarah. 2010. Lady Gaga, Grrrl Power, and Rock 'n' Roll Feminism. *RH Reality Check*, March 22, 2010. http://www.rhrealitycheck.org/blog/2010/03/22/lady-gaga-grrrl-power-rocknroll-feminism

Sevilla, Cate. 2009. Lady Gaga: 'My Sexuality Is Not Distracting, I'm a Rock Star'. *bitchbuzz*, August 3, 2009. http://bitchbuzz.com/news/lady-gaga-my-sexuality-is-not-distracting-im-a.html

Strauss, Neil. 2010. The Broken Heart and Violent Fantasies of Lady Gaga. *Rolling Stone*, July 8, 2010. http://www.rollingstone.com/music/news/the-broken-heart-and-violent-fantasies-of-lady-gaga-20100708

Sturges, Fiona. 2009. Lady Gaga: How the World Went Crazy for the New Queen of Pop. *The Independent*, May 15, 2009. http://www.independent.co.uk/arts-entertainment/music/features/lady-gaga-how-the-world-went-crazy-for-the-new-queen-of-pop-1684375.html

Teal, Whitney. 2010. Young Women and Feminism in the Lady Gaga Age. *Change.org*, February 23, 2010. http://news.change.org/stories/young-women-and-feminism-in-the-lady-gaga-age

The Sun. 2009. Gaga Thinks She Looks Manly. *The Sun*, March 6, 2009. http://www.thesun.co.uk/sol/homepage/showbiz/music/2296562/Gaga-thinks-she-looks-manly.html

TMZ. 2014. Lady Gaga Music Video Pulled Reportedly Because of Sexual Assault Claims. *TMZ*, June 19, 2014. http://www.tmz.com/2014/06/19/lady-gaga-music-video-sexual-assault-do-what-u-want/

Williams, Juliet. 2014. 'Same DNA, but Born this Way': Lady Gaga and the Possibilities of Postessentialist Feminisms. *Journal of Popular Music Studies* 26(1): 28–46.

Williams, Noelle. 2010. Is Lady Gaga a Feminist or Isn't She? *MS blog*, March 11, 2010. http://msmagazine.com/blog/blog/2010/03/11/is-lady-gaga-a-feminist-or-isnt-she/

Woolston, Jennifer M. 2012. Lady Gaga and the Wolf: 'Little Red Riding Hood,' The Fame Monster and Female Sexuality. In *The Performance Identities of Lady Gaga: Critical Essays*, ed. Richard J. Gray II, 107–121. Jefferson, NC: McFarland.

Zanin, Katie. 2010. Not Even Camille Paglia Understands the Phenomenon That Is Lady Gaga. *Bust Magazine*, September 14, 2010. http://bust.com/feminism/5590-not-even-camille-paglia-understands-the-phenomenon-that-is-lady-gaga.html

CHAPTER 10

Art Pop: The Styles of Lady Gaga

Lady Gaga is most commonly referred to as a pop singer and is placed in the company of other, oftentimes female, singers. This characterization accurately reflects a major aspect of the style of Lady Gaga as well as its cultural reception, but it should not lead to overlook the extent to which the singer's aesthetic crosses the conventional boundaries of pop. Of course, it is commonly known that Lady Gaga is more than a pop singer inasmuch as she is also a pianist, a songwriter, and a record producer, for which reason also the designation of her as a singer in this book should only be understood as a practical shorthand description. But what is more important to note is that her music and public persona are not restricted to pop but are also connected with other musical and artistic forms. Mostly neglected, studies that have been devoted to Lady Gaga's music and artistry (Auslander 2016; Dionne and Hatfield 2016) have not been sufficiently connected to the reception of her work and its role in her rise to fame.

In this chapter, I will unravel the main aspects of the various styles Lady Gaga has engaged with—understood both in terms of her music and other artistic products as well as with respect to the relevant self-presentation by Lady Gaga and the reception thereof by others—and examine how this mixture of styles has contributed to her fame. Because the focus of this book is on the origins of Lady Gaga's fame, my main emphasis will be on the singer's fusion of rock and pop as this aspect of her work was already present at the beginning of her career and has remained among its charac-

© The Author(s) 2017
M. Deflem, *Lady Gaga and the Sociology of Fame*,
DOI 10.1057/978-1-137-58468-7_10

teristics since. Additional attention will be devoted to Lady Gaga's forays into jazz and other musical and artistic genres, including acting, which she has begun to explore in more recent years in a manner not (yet) as developed as her orientation to rock.[1]

The underlying idea of this analysis is that the artistic expressions of Lady Gaga derive part of their unique appeal from a mixing of various artistic styles. From a constructionist viewpoint, no value statements can be made on the relative merit of Lady Gaga's various musical styles and artistic forms from an aesthetic point of view. Instead, the sociological claim I will defend is that Lady Gaga's use of multiple styles of music and her presentation as a multi-talented artist have had distinct consequences relating to her success and fame. In the following pages, I will specifically unravel Lady Gaga's multiple styles in terms of their respective musical cultures, the singer's related presentation of self, and perceptions by others of Lady Gaga as a genre-crossing artist. As mentioned, the emphasis will be on rock and, to a lesser extent, jazz as the two dominant styles Lady Gaga has embraced, harmonizing with the relative importance of these genres over the course of Lady Gaga's career.

THE ART OF LADY GAGA

In terms of her artistic and musical styles, it is most conspicuous that Lady Gaga combines a variety of elements from a range of sounds and genres. In much of her music, Lady Gaga has particularly incorporated elements of rock into her pop and dance music, thereby seeking to merge the implied authenticity of rock with the entertainment and aesthetics of pop. Early on in her career, Lady Gaga transitioned from indie rock to pop and dance, but she has since continued to work toward an understanding of pop as rock and has at several times brought rock music styles deliberately into her music. In more recent years, moreover, she has branched out into the world of jazz and other non-pop musical genres and additionally, albeit minimally, involved herself with acting. Because the adoption of pop and rock is central in Lady Gaga's work, a few words are first in order about the sociological understanding of these musical styles.

The Cultures of Pop and Rock

In earlier parts of this book, I already discussed aspects of the place of pop and rock in popular music (Chap. 2) and its implications for issues of sex and gender in the career of Lady Gaga (Chap. 9). Applying the constructionist understanding of music, the styles of pop and rock can be conceived of as two forms of popular music which, over time, have differentiated to become relatively autonomous, with occasional bridge-building attempts and various forms of separation, co-existence, and (re-) combination between them. Based on a musicological and reductionist understanding, pop and rock are differentiated on the basis of their respective sound characteristics and their differing commercial appeal and implications (Frith 2001). Such perspectives overlook the relevance of the meanings associated with the sounds of musical styles as well as the qualities that are assigned thereto in a given social setting. From a constructionist perspective, instead, pop music is not music that is simple from a musicological viewpoint or profitable from an economic standpoint, but music that is culturally associated with having those qualities. Similarly, rock music is sociologically not understood as music that is more authentic, rebellious, or marginal but music that understands itself, and will variably be perceived by others, as being associated with authenticity, rebellion, and marginality (Keightley 2001).

Up until at least the earlier half of the 1970s, the expression "pop and rock (music)" was commonly used to refer to a relatively broad range of popular music forms that had emerged in the wake of the rock 'n' roll era of 1950s and the development of popular music during the 1960s. The terms rock and pop were initially used together or interchangeably, but this broad understanding capturing a variety of popular music styles gradually dissolved. Especially during the latter half of the 1970s, a multitude of new terms were coined to designate various popular music forms (hard rock, disco, soul, funk, punk, heavy metal, etc.), involving a separation between pop and rock. The very demarcation between rock and pop betrays a constructed hierarchy. Whereas pop music is culturally perceived as simple, commercial, superficial, conformist, and safe, rock is typically defined as complex, artistic, profound, rebellious, and dangerous. Whereas pop is primarily delivered in the form of hit singles by male and female singers who seek to entertain, rock music is more typically expressed in the form of long-play albums on which guitarists and other predominantly male musicians display the presumed dangerous qualities of their self-professed authentic existence. Against the ambition of pop music to be enjoyable or functional (for dancing and for romancing), rock music associates itself with an assumed authenticity that mixes the aesthetics of music with the ethics of politics, protest, and rebellion. This cultural understanding is at times also endeavored to be transcended, however, as the case of Lady Gaga indeed will show.

From Pop to Rock

As explained in Chap. 3, the artist known today as Lady Gaga emerged from the person of Stefani Germanotta who sought to establish herself as a professional musician, a transition that also entailed a transformation in style and sound. When the singer began to perform her music at open-mic nights and small clubs, her music was broadly situated in the realm of indie rock with occasional excursions into classic rock. From the start of Stefani Germanotta's music career, there was a considerable measure of confusion over the direction her music should take. While her musical talent was never questioned, the proper expression thereof in a suitable format underwent a gradual transformation. Among the reasons the singer decided to leave NYU, she has said that she grew restless and found herself out of place and attacked for being "too pop," "too rock," "too brunette," "a character," and "not an artist" (in Perry 2008). When the singer was first brought in touch with producer Rob Fusari following her performance at The Cutting Room on March 23, 2006, it was explicitly in terms of her potential as a prospective rock vocalist styled after the sound of The Strokes. But after Fusari and Germanotta began working together, the singer's music soon changed toward a pop and dance sound.

Besides the advice of producer Fusari, Lady Gaga also independently moved toward a change in style through the exposure she enjoyed to various rock music styles via some of her friends in the Lower East Side in New York, where she had moved after dropping out of college. Especially performance artist and heavy metal DJ Lady Starlight introduced the aspiring artist to the world of go-go dancing, glam rock, and the heavy metal sounds of bands like Black Sabbath, Metallica, and Iron Maiden. From April 2007 onward, the two friends performed together on about a dozen occasions in New York City as well as at the Lollapalooza festival in Chicago, where Lady Gaga was seen dancing to "Forever My Queen," a classic song by the cult US heavy metal band Pentagram. On pictures that have since surfaced on the internet, Lady Gaga is shown with Lady Starlight dressed in a denim jacket emblazoned with an Iron Maiden patch. At the same Chicago show, also, the singer is arrested for walking around in her panties. As the collaboration with Lady Starlight indicates, even in the early presentation of her pop and dance music, Lady Gaga has sought to maintain a distinct rock appeal, one which she will never abandon and which she at times will deliberately exhibit in manifest ways.

Pop as Rock (and Art)

Re-styled as a pop and glam performance artist, Lady Gaga sought to bring pop back into the mainstream of popular culture, which she in part pursued by infusing her pop music with aspects of the attitude, styles, and aesthetics of rock. This ambition also relied on some of her personal background and musical roots. As mentioned in Chap. 3, via her father Joe, the singer was exposed to the major sounds of classic rock. Among her acknowledged influences, she has mentioned David Bowie, Queen, The Beatles, Pink Floyd, and Bruce Springsteen (Stryker 2013). Through this infusion of rock Lady Gaga sought to make pop popular once again, precisely by practicing as well as transcending it. As an interesting side note related to the singer's upbringing, the Pythian Temple building in which the Germanotta family has resided since the early 1990s is a remodeled residential apartment complex that originally housed a recording studio. On April 12, 1954, Bill Haley and His Comets there recorded the groundbreaking rock 'n' roll classic "Rock Around the Clock" (Gray 2009).

Lady Gaga's ambition to present pop as rock also ties in with her New York City background, in particular her merging of some of the many different cultural traditions the city has to offer. The singer was favorably exposed to the unique cultural mix the city has to offer by having been brought up near the Theater District in the Upper West Side and then, when she was 19, moving to the Lower East Side and its rock 'n' roll scene. The essential aspect of the resulting blend that emerged from what Lady Gaga herself has called her "transition from New York uptown to New York downtown" was that Lady Gaga could present her pop as the new rock, as "the new underground" (Daily Motion 2008b). She thereby sought to overcome the dominant understanding of the hierarchies of musical genres, proclaiming that "pop music will never be low brow," as she would chant during early live performances of "Just Dance" (Juzwiak 2010). In her own words, the singer's ambition was to "re-invent pop music in a fresh way" and present a new form of "future pop" (Daily Motion 2008a).

The fact that Lady Gaga's music developed in the vibrant and diverse setting of New York also brought about that she came under the influence of the artistry of Andy Warhol. The exposure to Warhol enabled the singer to transform herself into a performance artist and set up her own creative team, the Haus of Gaga, in the image of the so-called superstars Warhol had assembled in The Factory. A Warhol-influenced style is also apparent in some aspects of Lady Gaga's live performances, such as by her use of interlude videos on the Fame Ball tour concerts in which she appears as the fictional character Candy Warhol. The successful Monster Ball tour, likewise, featured similarly surreal videos, including one in which Lady Gaga was vomited on by puke artist Millie Brown, a feat she would later perform live at the 2014 South by Southwest (SXSW) festival in Austin, Texas (Edwards 2014). The Austin show took place in the buildup toward the artRAVE tour of 2013's *ARTPOP*, an album that was explicitly conceived as an attempt to bring (high) art into pop culture in terms of a reversal of Warhol's pop art (Strang 2013). Whereas Warhol established the idea of pop art to invalidate the existing hierarchies of high and low art (an idea adopted by Lady Gaga in her notion of pop as rock), Lady Gaga's inverted Warholian ambitions of *ARTPOP* were particularly revealed visually, for instance, by including images of historical works of art, such as the Sandro Botticelli painting "The Birth of Venus," on the album cover, presenting herself as a canvas on the cover of the "Applause" single, and having contemporary artist Jeff Koons design the album artwork and build various installations at the album's release party (Brito 2013).

Rock in Pop

Besides conceiving of pop as rock, there are various audio-musical elements of rock present in Lady Gaga's work, both early on after her transformation from Stefani to Lady Gaga as well as more recently. Thematically, rock is referenced several times in Lady Gaga's music. Her earliest recorded songs are heavily inspired by her life at that time in the rock 'n' roll scene of New York's Lower East Side scene, personal experiences that are directly reflected in her songs, specifically in the form of lyrical references to rock and metal. Many of her love songs, then and later, dealt with her ex-boyfriend Lüc Carl, whom she dated off and on for several years, both before and after her rise to fame. Onetime an aspiring rock drummer, Carl is a self-proclaimed heavy metal aficionado who currently hosts a metal radio show (Kurutz 2012). Lady Gaga's songs about Carl reference the world of rock and metal several times, such as in the unreleased song "Shake Ur Kitty," recorded in 2006, where she sings "I met a drummer last week … We hit the floor … with your Van Halen pin." References to rock are also present on Lady Gaga's first two major releases from 2008 to 2009, *The Fame* and *The Fame Monster*. By example, the song "Boys, Boys, Boys" was written as a direct response to the song "Girls, Girls, Girls" by glam metal band Motley Crüe. It also contains the lyric, "Let's go see the Killers," about a concert by that band which the singer attended at Madison Square Garden in 2006. The hit song "Paparazzi" again displays Lady Gaga's obsession with Lüc Carl in the context of the world of rock when she sings, "Leather and jeans, garage glamorous ... Yeah cause you're my rock star in between the sets." The hit song "Bad Romance" once again references Carl's heavy metal style when Lady Gaga sings, "I want your leather-studded kiss in the sand."

On Lady Gaga's 2011 album *Born This Way*, references to rock and metal take center stage. Showing the singer's body on the cover morphing into a motorcycle, the album features several songs that explicitly deal with rock, such as "Heavy Metal Lover" about Lüc Carl and his heavy metal friends (the so-called Rivington Rebels), "Electric Chapel" about rock bar St. Jerome's where Carl used to work, and the ballad "Yoü and I" about Lady Gaga reconnecting with Carl while visiting him at St. Jerome's during a break on her Monster Ball world tour in June 2010. The 2013 album, *ARTPOP*, released well after Lady Gaga's breakup with Carl, mostly lacks references to rock, with the possible exception of "Mary Jane Holland," a song about Lady Gaga smoking marijuana in Amsterdam.

Stylistically, some of Lady Gaga's music is also rock oriented. Lady Gaga's singing voice is at times raw and raspy, not soft and smooth, and incorporates the contrast of gentle and harsh vocal styles, alternating singing softly with screaming loudly. Examples can be heard on "Bad Romance" from the 2009 album *The Fame Monster* and on "MANiCURE" and "Swine" from the 2013 album *ARTPOP*. Rock vocal stylings are even more pronounced at Lady Gaga's live concerts. During one of her raps at the Monster Ball, for instance, she would often yell and growl, and scream her name loudly: "My name is ... LADY GAGA!" At her artRAVE concerts in 2014, the singer could similarly be heard to scream, for instance, during the song "Swine," in a manner much more evocative of a heavy metal singer rather than a female pop star.

The instrumentation and production of some of Lady Gaga's songs are at times delivered in a rock style as well. Her earliest rock collaborators include guitarist Nico Constantine on her unreleased album for Island Def Jam as well as Tommy Kafafian, the former Fusari collaborator who plays guitar on several songs on *The Fame*. In the Summer of 2009, both Constantine and Kafafian, who had then just come from the disbanded rock band Program The Dead, joined Lady Gaga as members of her first live band, along with metal drummer Andreas Brobjer (and R&B keyboard player Brian London), on her first headlining world tour. The tour also featured rock arrangements to many of her songs, as first seen and heard at the Glastonbury festival in England in June 2009. On all of her concert tours since 2009, Lady Gaga has relied on rock guitarists, giving her songs an extra edge beyond the sounds that can be heard on her recordings. On the Monster Ball tour, featured guitarists were Ricky Tillo and Kareem "Jesus" Devlin, both players with a background in rock music. On the Born This Way Ball and artRAVE tours, Ricky Tillo was joined by Tim Stewart, a guitarist experienced in both heavy metal and pop, to add to the R&B sounds from the other band members, drummer George "Spanky" McCurdy, keyboardist Brockett Parsons, and bassist/bandleader Lanar "Kern" Brantley. Guitarists have also been instrumental in bringing a rock sound to some of Lady Gaga's recordings. Examples include "Heavy Metal Lover" on *Born This Way* and "MANiCURE" on *ARTPOP*. The singer's piano-driven ballads, moreover, are produced as rock songs. Examples include "Speechless" on *The Fame Monster*, "Dope" on *ARTPOP*, and most famously, *Born This Way*'s "Yoü and I," which was produced by Mutt Lang, the producer famous for his work with AC/DC and Def Leppard.

At her live shows, Lady Gaga additionally brings in a distinct rock and metal element by inviting along some of her rock 'n' roll friends from her days in New York City's Lower East Side. During the Monster Ball tour, for instance, one of the support acts was glam rock band Semi Precious Weapons, whom the singer knew from her early days in New York when she would perform as support act to the band. The arena version of that tour also featured Lady Starlight spinning heavy metal records before the show. More generally, Lady Gaga associates herself with rock acts, such as by having British hard rock band The Darkness as opening act on her Born This Way Ball tour, and by decorating her dressing room with pictures of the likes of The Sex Pistols, Motley Crüe, Poison, and Jimmy Page of Led Zeppelin.

The musical implications of Lady Gaga's ambition to transcend pop are most explicit on her 2011 album *Born This Way*, several of the songs of which are performed and produced in a rock style. For example, the song "Electric Chapel" opens with a heavy metal guitar riff, and Lady Gaga herself played electric guitar during the live version of this song on the

Born This Way Ball. The song "Yoü and I" features former Queen guitarist Brian May and contains drum samples from the Queen song "We Will Rock You." The track "The Edge of Glory" is stylistically influenced by the sound of Bruce Springsteen and features Clarence Clemmons, the late saxophonist of the E. Street Band. Although the 2013 album *ARTPOP* was primarily produced as a dance album in the style of contemporary EDM (Electronic Dance Music), there are nonetheless some excursions into rock, such as the piano ballad "Dope," the classic-rock-influenced "Gypsy," and the song "MANiCURE," which features the rock guitar sounds of Tim Stewart, who played with funk metal band Infectious Grooves, and Doug Aldrich, who is well-known for his work with heavy metal bands Dio and Whitesnake.

Classical Music, Jazz, and Beyond

Besides Lady Gaga's infusion of rock in the world of pop, there are other genre-crossing aspects in the singer's music, such as by bringing in elements of her classical music background. By example, Lady Gaga's hugely successful live concert tour The Monster Ball featured classically trained Judy Kang on violin and Rashida Jolley on harp playing in the context of a pop and rock oriented band. Lady Gaga's ambition to bring in elements of classical music is even better demonstrated in some of the singer's piano performances, especially in the acoustic renditions of some of her dance songs, such as "Poker Face" and "Born This Way." These acoustic renditions have classical music stylings, transforming Lady Gaga's pop songs into singer-songwriter's ballads, and as such are popularly often perceived as more serious musical performances. At Lady Gaga's headlining shows since the Fame Ball of 2009 right up until her artRAVE tour that began in May 2014, a section of Lady Gaga's live concerts is always reserved for several all-acoustic piano songs. The fact alone that some music journalists and critics have expressed to only like this part of the show testifies to the non-pop, "serious" artistic qualities that are assigned to this component of Lady Gaga's work.

The genre-crossing ambition of Lady Gaga to transcend pop music beyond rock has to date been most clearly revealed in her work with Tony Bennett. In 2014, the two singers released the album *Cheek To Cheek*, containing a collection of jazz standards. The critically acclaimed album was supported by several television appearances and a relatively short but highly successful series of concerts that began in Las Vegas on December

30, 2014, with most shows being held from April through May 2015 in theaters in the United States and at European jazz festivals. Further extending her musical reach in recent years, Lady Gaga sang a medley of songs from the musical "The Sound of Music" at the 2015 Academy Awards. The singer's excursions into musical ventures outside the boundaries of pop and dance have continued thereafter, particularly in February 2016 when she sang the National Anthem at the Super Bowl, gave a live piano performance of the ballad "Til It happens To You" at the Academy Awards, and performed a medley of songs of the late rock icon David Bowie at the Grammy Awards (Hendicott 2016). Thus, in the period leading up to her next major music releases, Lady Gaga generally took on a broad range of musical styles besides the electronic sounds of contemporary pop and dance music. At the time of this writing in 2016, a new jazz album with Tony Bennett was planned to follow her solo album *Joanne* which producer Mark Ronson described as "very honest, authentic, kind of analog" (in Spanos 2016b).

THE CULTURE OF LADY GAGA

As explained in Chap. 2, culture is sociologically not primarily understood in terms of its material products, such as sound recordings, paintings, and writings, but is conceived of as the meanings associated with such symbolic expressions in any given social context. In the case of music and other art forms, the inter-subjective nature of culture implies that meaningful symbols are transmitted in the relation between the producer and the recipient thereof. A sociological perspective of music—as of fame and other aspects of culture—must therefore also consider the respective perceptions of the artists and the various members of their audience. In terms of the styles of Lady Gaga, it therefore makes sense to investigate how Lady Gaga presents herself in musical and other artistic terms and how, in turn, she is perceived by others, including fellow musicians as well as fans and other members of the public.

Gaga Chameleon

Lady Gaga has often shied away from presenting herself in the vein of a typical female pop star. By her own saying, as explained in Chap. 9, Lady Gaga does not want to be a sexy pop singer and instead presents herself in terms of an identity connected with freakishness and monstrosity. The monster theme in Lady Gaga's presentation of self is revealed in multiple ways. Her 2009 album is called *The Fame Monster*, which also contains a song called "Monster." At her now famous performance of "Paparazzi" at the Video Music Awards in September 2009, Lady Gaga staged her own demise, walking on a medical cane with her clothes covered in blood and eventually dying, thereby even using disability to portray monstrosity (Apolloni 2014). These portrayals of decay and death are alien to the safe and clean world of pop and instead resonate with the horror and shock themes that are portrayed by rock artists such as Alice Cooper, Rob Zombie, and Marilyn Manson.

In her presentation of self, Lady Gaga regularly indeed invokes a rock attitude. She connects her sexual identity explicitly with being, in her own words, "a rock star" (in Gharnit 2015). Unamused by the constant comparisons others make of her with other female singers who have come long before her, the singer once proclaimed that she was "the next Iron Maiden" (in Vkanty 2015). Likewise, the singer's fashion styles include sometimes risky, unsafe elements that are more rock than pop, such as by using S&M references, leather, rubber, metal, and studs in her clothes. Reinforcing the rock style of the *Born This Way* album, for example, Lady Gaga held an in-store appearance at Best Buy in New York to promote the record, dressed in leather and sitting in front of a motorcycle (Schoonmaker 2011). When she is not dressed in one of her outlandish outfits, she is oftentimes seen, typically when she is at work in a recording studio, wearing rock and metal T-shirts, displaying the name and imagery of bands such as Megadeth, Iron Maiden, Motley Crüe, and Slipknot.

The reach of Lady Gaga's self-presentation of her work beyond pop broadened most distinctly when she began working with Tony Bennett in the world of jazz. Coming shortly after the relatively disappointing response to *ARTPOP* and the artRAVE tour, it was no coincidence, no doubt, that the collaboration with Bennett was taken very seriously and heavily promoted on television and in the form of its own concert series. In interviews, Lady Gaga expressed how much the collaboration with Tony Bennett meant to her, at some point even saying that the career move had saved her life by having her be able to finally be true to herself as an artist (Rader 2014). The singer also explained how her turn to jazz was a revisiting of her past as she had been singing jazz for several years before her rise to fame when she had, as a young teenager, been taking voice lessons that had exposed her to jazz and musical theater (Myers 2014). During the years of her rise as a pop star, moreover, Lady Gaga had off and on also been performing jazz in live settings, especially with trumpeter Brian Newman, one of her friends from the Lower East Side, and his jazz band featuring drummer Paul Francis, saxophonist Steve Kortyka, and pianist Alex Smith, musicians who also performed with the singer during her concert series with Tony Bennett.

Indicating the relevance Lady Gaga herself attributed to the diversity of her musical experiences, in December 2014, the singer's Twitter description read that she was "not just a chameleon in person, but a chameleon in music" as well (Gagamonster96 Twitter post). Additionally based on her acting role in the fifth season of the television series *American Horror Story* during the Fall of 2015 and her work as editor for *V* magazine in January 2016 (Sowray 2016), by the Spring of 2016 Lady Gaga presented herself artistically even more broad and wide-ranging, with her Twitter bio reading, "jazz art pop punk actress fashion magazine editor and columnist!" (LadyGagaNowNet Twitter post).

From Musicians to Fans and the General Public

Turning to the perceptions others have expressed of the various styles of Lady Gaga, there can be no doubt, of course, that the singer's worldwide acclaim has primarily rested on the favorable response to her commercially successful ventures in the world of pop and dance music. Yet, the singer's excursions into rock, jazz, and other musical and artistic exploits have also been recognized, as such also contributed to her fame. This reception by others of the styles of Lady Gaga pertains to other musicians as well as to the singer's fans and other members of her fame audience more broadly.

With respect to Lady Gaga's embrace of rock, her pop-transcending orientation has often been recognized and embraced by (other) rock musicians as they want to meet the singer, be seen with her in public, and collaborate with her on concerts and recordings. Examples of rockers meeting Lady Gaga and being photographed in her company are too numerous to mention. They include Paul McCartney, Alice Cooper, the band Kiss, Sting, Biff Byford of metal band Saxon, members of Iron Maiden, and singer Rob Halford of heavy metal band Judas Priest, among many others (BlabberMouth 2010, 2015). Many well-known rock stars have also been very positive about Lady Gaga and her standing as an innovative artist. Alice Cooper, for example, has praised Lady Gaga as a performer who "totally gets it," particularly commending her for bringing a sense of theatricality to her shows (in Sciarretto 2011). Bassist Gene

Simmons of the rock group Kiss has called Lady Gaga "the only rock star out there" to emerge over the past decade (in Titus 2012). And punk icon John Lydon (aka Johnny Rotten of the Sex Pistols) has dubbed Lady Gaga fantastic and called her music witty and clever (Jones 2013).

Lady Gaga's meetings with rock musicians have on some occasions enabled collaboration in musical respects as well. Examples include Marilyn Manson, who is featured on a remix of her song "LoveGame," and Elton John, with whom Lady Gaga recorded a song for the movie *Gnomeo and Juliette* and who has also participated on recordings for her upcoming album. Collaborations with rock musicians have also taken place at live shows. With Elton John, for instance, Lady Gaga performed live at the Grammy Awards of 2010 (Spanos 2016a) and at a promotional concert in Los Angeles in February 2016 (Kreps 2016). Sting, Bruce Springsteen, and Debbie Harry performed with Lady Gaga at a live concert charity event at Carnegie Hall in New York in 2010, and she joined the Rolling Stones on the song "Gimme Shelter" during the legendary band's show in Newark, New Jersey, in 2012 (Pareles 2010; Billboard 2012). Other such rock collaborations with Lady Gaga were planned but did not take place, such as a performance of the Queen song "Radio Ga Ga" by Lady Gaga and surviving members of Queen during the singer's 2009 summer tour.

As another sign of appreciation from the rock community, Lady Gaga songs have also been covered and performed by rock musicians. By example, Alice Cooper performed "Born This Way" at the Bonnaroo Festival in Tennessee in 2012 (The Week 2012). Guitar legend Jeff Beck regularly performed an instrumental version of "Bad Romance" during his 2011 tour (Frith 2011). And Faith No More covered "Poker Face" at live shows in 2009 during the band's Second Coming reunion tour, much to delight of Lady Gaga herself (Lady Gaga Twitter post). Showing her own appreciation for her colleagues in the world of rock, Lady Gaga has been seen attending rock and metal shows since her rise to fame, including concerts by heavy metal legends Iron Maiden in 2011 and British contemporary punk band Fat White Family in 2016 (BlabberMouth 2011; Renshaw 2016). In March 2014, when she performed at the South by Southwest (SXSW) festival in Austin, Texas, Lady Gaga was seen in an Iron Maiden T-shirt attending the show by thrash rockers Lazer/Wulf (Teitelman 2014). Lady Gaga's occasional appearances at music festivals tie in with her often commenting on having attended festivals as a teenager, such as when she and her friend Lady Starlight took their tops off when they saw Iggy Pop perform at a festival (Malec 2014).

Collaborations with Lady Gaga, and favorable receptions from, artists in musical genres besides rock, especially in jazz, classical music, and musical theater, have also taken place, especially in more recent years after the singer's fame was more established. The jazz collaboration with Tony Bennett is most outstanding in this respect, not only because the legendary singer called Lady Gaga's approach to jazz "very authentic," but also because it was Bennett who first suggested the collaboration after he had heard Lady Gaga sing a jazz classic at a charity event (Marie 2014). Likewise showing the esteem the singer has been able to receive from some of the world's most revered performers, Lady Gaga has been congratulated by Julie Andrews for her medley of songs from *The Sound of Music* at the 2015 Oscars and received generous cooperation and feedback from former David Bowie producer Nile Rodgers for her Bowie tribute at the 2016 Grammy Awards (Strecker 2015; Aswad 2016).

Turning to the fan base and broader audience responding to Lady Gaga's artistic expressions, the singer's fans have at times explicitly acknowledged and favorably responded to her status as a rock star and genre-crossing artist. Some of her fans at her concerts can be seen to have adopted rock and heavy metal stylings in their dress and appearance, for instance by using spikes and studs in their clothing and showing their tattoos and piercings. Some fans also refer to Lady Gaga as a rock star and have encouraged her to adopt rock music more explicitly in her work, echoing the sentiments of Kiss bassist Gene Simmons who has encouraged Lady Gaga to make a rock album (Kielty 2016). Among the rock fans of Lady Gaga are especially noteworthy those who are primarily at home in the worlds of rock, metal, and punk, and who otherwise do not associate much, if at all, with pop music (Ford 2011). Although they may not form a sizeable minority in Lady Gaga's fan base, it is all the more striking that they explicitly identify as fans of the singer even when their devotion is not always well-received in their respective non-pop communities. Conforming to her own admiration of rock music, Lady Gaga has generally embraced the fans at her concerts who adopt metal and rock stylings, such as when she did a shoot-out to a fan at one of her Monster Ball concerts when she saw him wearing a Kiss T-shirt. The same fan would later successfully persuade Alice Cooper to pose for a picture doing the monster claw gesture (Gagafrontrow 2013).

Whereas the positive reception of Lady Gaga's rock orientation has primarily taken place on the part of her fan community of the Little Monsters, the favorable response the singer has received for her work in jazz and other non-pop and non-rock genres, especially in more recent years, has mostly come from a broader audience, including some who are not very familiar with Lady Gaga's exploits in pop and dance music. Especially the jazz album *Cheek To Cheek* with Tony Bennett has been extraordinarily well-received, both among critics and by the general public (Duren 2014). This positive reception has typically focused on the artistic merit that the music is said to display, arguing that the songs are "great artistic works" that imply strong musicianship and showcase Lady Gaga as "an authentic jazz vocalist" (McDonald 2015).

Likewise, some of Lady Gaga's televised live performances in 2015 and 2016, especially her *Sound of Music* medley at the 2015 Oscars, her rendition of the National Anthem at the 2016 Super Bowl, and her piano performance of "Til It Happens To You" at the 2016 Oscars, have generally received a lot of positive feedback (Benjamin 2016). For her starring performance in *American Horror Story*, Lady Gaga has also received praise, and the role even garnered her Golden Globe Award (D'Addario 2015; Wagmeister 2016). Reflecting the success of Lady Gaga's broader directions in most recent years, the singer won multiple awards of various kinds in 2015 and 2016, such as the 2015 Woman of the Year Award from Billboard Women in Music, the Young Artist Award from Americans for the Arts, the inaugural Contemporary Icon Award from the Songwriters Hall of Fame, and the Jane Ortner Artist Award from the Grammy Museum, along with a nomination for the Oscar for best original song. At the same time as she has received recognition and praise, however, Lady Gaga's recent artistic accomplishments have at times also been less generously received, specifically critiquing her performance and vocal abilities in her medley from *The Sound of Music* and her chaotic David Bowie tribute (Takeda 2015; Beaumont 2016). Whatever the relative merits of such criticisms, the occasionally controversial nature of Lady Gaga's excursions in musical and artistic ventures beyond pop once again contributed to keep the public's attention firmly on her.

Conclusion

In this chapter, I have analyzed the multiple styles and aesthetic components of the art of Lady Gaga that she has engaged in beyond her work in pop and dance. I specifically showed that the singer's position in the world of pop is complemented with elements of rock and jazz in the themes and style of her work, her self-presentation as a multi-talented performer, and the corresponding reception by others, including both rock musicians and fans, of her chameleon-like status. Based on a constructionist sociological perspective, this analysis was meant to be instructive to illuminate a factor in the singer's rise to fame, but additionally also sought to offer some sense and sensibility relative to many of the distorted interpretations of meaning concerning Lady Gaga's work, of which there are alas all too many.

Indeed, the number of misrepresentations and unfounded interpretations of the music and style of Lady Gaga may well exceed the number of wardrobes the singer has been seen wearing over the years. This observation is sadly not a joke, for interpretive analyses of Lady Gaga's music routinely suffer from a lack of appropriate contextualization or mere relevant factual knowledge. Humorous references to sexuality in Lady Gaga's music (for instance, in the song "LoveGame" where she sings about a "disco stick") are interpreted as dangerous signs of a hyper-sexualized world or are otherwise dismissed as manufactured gimmicks (Paglia 2010). Aspects of Lady Gaga's aesthetic style and presentation, ranging from the color of the singer's hair to the words and chords used in her songs, are interpreted on the basis of shallow similarities with other performers. By example, because Lady Gaga's 2009 song "Alejandro" contains the word "Fernando," the track has been dismissed as an ABBA rip-off, when the insertion of the name actually resulted from her producer RedOne's deliberate reference, by word and in tone, to a song by the famous group from his adopted country of Sweden.

This chapter has uncovered various ways in which Lady Gaga merges, bridges, and fuses pop with rock, jazz, and other musical styles. However, although Lady Gaga can be considered a rock star, a jazz singer, and, more broadly, a multi-dimensional artist, there is at the same time no doubt that she is primarily located in the world of pop music and branches out to other genres from within pop. It is precisely also because she is primarily known as a pop star that Lady Gaga receives special accolades when she practices rock, jazz, and other non-pop music and art. The more recent years during which Lady Gaga has broadened her artistic reach, also, came after there had taken place a turn toward more organic forms of acoustic music (especially under influence of such successful singers as Adele and Lorde), which took place after many other female singers (such as Taylor Swift, Miley Cyrus, and Katy Perry) had adopted a more extravagant pop style following Lady Gaga's early success. Besides the changing musical landscape, the reasons for Lady Gaga's preference to work in multiple musical worlds no doubt relate to personal choices of an aesthetic nature. But subjective motives aside, Lady Gaga's broad artistic reach is also related to the hierarchical and gendered nature of music and the consequences it can be anticipated to have for her fame. As rock music is conceived to be more masculine, a female performer can, all other conditions being equal, expect to become more successful in pop, especially when one of her instruments is voice. In that sense, Lady Gaga's choice to associate with pop, especially after an earlier start in indie rock, may have been at least partly strategic. Yet, once she had attained a level of fame, Lady Gaga could go back to rock and indeed to the jazz and classical music of her days as a young student precisely to claim and attain the authenticity that is commonly associated with those musical styles.

Lady Gaga's turn toward jazz and other non-pop musical styles came after the relatively subdued reception to her pop album *ARTPOP* and its accompanying artRAVE tour. It makes sense, therefore, to assume that the decision to step outside the world of pop was deliberate as well, demonstrating once again that claims to authenticity and strategic planning can effectively co-exist, at least in their social reception. For whereas die-hard fans of Lady Gaga's music might view some of the singer's recent stylistic choices as mere stunts for her to be "rebranded" as a middle-of-the-road but "serious artist" (Deliz 2015; Reymann-Schneider 2016), the much larger audience of the general public can indeed be expected, and has, overwhelmingly responded very favorably and embraced a newly transformed Lady Gaga. As such, the singer's manager Bobby Campbell is entirely justified, and no doubt amused, to observe of his client that in most recent years the "world is celebrating her talent in a very mainstream way" (in Hampp 2015). The present challenge is for Lady Gaga to take this newly found popularity and apply it successfully toward the next phase of her music career and, without losing the devoted fan base that once contributed so effectively to create her spectacle, thereby also secure her fame into the future.

NOTE

1. The sections of this chapter that deal with the rock aspects of Lady Gaga's music have been revised from a book chapter published by transcript Verlag in Bielefeld, Germany (Deflem 2015). Revisions and updates on these sections and those that deal with other musical styles such as jazz are original to this book.

References

Apolloni, Alexandra. 2014. Starstruck: On Gaga, Voice, and Disability. In *Lady Gaga and Popular Music*, ed. Martin Iddon, and Melanie L. Marshall, 190–208. London: Routledge.

Aswad, Jem. 2016. Lady Gaga Dazzles with David Bowie Tribute at 2016 Grammys. *Billboard*, February 15, 2016. http://www.billboard.com/articles/news/grammys/6875281/lady-gaga-david-bowie-tribute-grammys-2016

Auslander, Philip. 2016. Twenty-First-Century Girl: Lady Gaga, Performance Art, and Glam. In *Global Glam and Popular Music: Style and Spectacle from the 1970s to the 2000s*, eds. Ian Chapman and Henry Johnson, 182–198. New York; London: Routledge.

Beaumont, Mark. 2016. Was Lady Gaga's Bowie Medley a Fitting Tribute? *New Musical Express*, February 16, 2016. http://www.nme.com/blogs/nme-blogs/was-lady-gaga-s-bowie-medley-a-fitting-tribute

Benjamin, Jeff. 2016. Lady Gaga Nails Career-Spanning David Bowie Tribute at Grammys 2016. *Fuse*, February 16, 2016. http://www.fuse.tv/2016/02/lady-gaga-david-bowie-tribute-performance-grammys-2016

Billboard. 2012. Rolling Stones' 'Gimme Shelter': Did Gaga, Mary J. or Florence Sing It Best? *Billboard*, December 16, 2012. http://www.billboard.com/articles/news/1481366/rolling-stones-gimme-shelter-did-gaga-mary-j-or-florence-sing-it-best

BlabberMouth. 2010. Saxon Frontman Hangs Out With Lady Gaga; Photo Available. *BlabberMouth*, December 19, 2010. http://www.blabbermouth.net/news/saxon-frontman-hangs-out-with-lady-gaga-photo-available/

———. 2011. Lady Gaga: 'Iron Maiden Changed My Life'. *BlabberMouth*, May 25, 2011. http://www.blabbermouth.net/news/lady-gaga-iron-maiden-changed-my-life/

———. 2015. Judas Priest's Rob Halford Was 'Really Happy' to See Lady Gaga Become Pop Superstar. *BlabberMouth*, November 18, 2015. http://www.blabbermouth.net/news/judas-priests-rob-halford-was-really-happy-to-see-lady-gaga-become-pop-superstar/

Brito, Maria Gabriela. 2013. Lady Gaga and Jeff Koons' ArtRave – What Does It Mean for the Art World? *Huffington Post*, November 13, 2013. http://www.huffingtonpost.com/maria-gabriela-brito/lady-gaga-and-jeff-koons-_b_4261154.html

D'Addario, Daniel. 2015. Lady Gaga's *American Horror Story* Performance Is Her Greatest Reinvention Yet. *Time*, October 7, 2015. http://time.com/4063969/lady-gaga-american-horror-story-2/

Daily Motion. 2008a. ManiaTV's All Access Host Samantha Maloney Interviews Lady G. *Daily Motion*, May 28, 2008. http://www.dailymotion.com/video/x5l1jh_maniatv-s-all-access-host-samantha_news#.UVomEFei_As

———. 2008b. Lady Gaga – Interview. *Daily Motion*, November 1, 2008. http://www.dailymotion.com/video/x79hia_lady-gaga-interview_music

Deflem, Mathieu. 2015. Lady Gaga – The Scream of a Rock Star. In *Pop-Frauen der Gegenwart: Körper – Stimme – Image*, ed. Christa Brüstle. Bielefeld, Germany: transcript Verlag.

Deliz, Jamie. 2015. Lady Gaga's Transformation in the Mainstream. *The Excelsior*, October 13, 2015. http://bcexcelsior.com/lady-gagas-transformation-in-the-mainstream/

Dionne, Jake, and Joe Hatfield. 2016. Life as Performance: Dramatism and the Music of Lady Gaga. In *Communication Theory and Millennial Popular Culture: Essays and Applications*, ed. Kathleen Glenister Roberts, 23–34. New York: Peter Lang.

Duren, Rand. 2014. What Critics Are Saying about Lady Gaga and Tony Bennett's New Jazz Album. *GuideLive*, September 22, 2014. http://www.guidelive.com/music/2014/09/22/critics-saying-lady-gaga-tony-bennetts-new-jazz-album

Edwards, Gavin. 2014. Lady Gaga Stages Dramatic Performance-Art Spectacle at SXSW. *Rolling Stone*, March 14, 2014. http://www.rollingstone.com/music/news/lady-gaga-stages-dramatic-performance-art-spectacle-at-sxsw-20140314

Ford, Leyla. 2011. 'Heavy Metal Lover': Lady Gaga Is One of Us. *MetalSucks*, May 24, 2011. http://www.metalsucks.net/2011/05/24/heavy-metal-lover-lady-gaga-is-one-of-us/

Frith, Simon. 2001. Pop Music. In *The Cambridge Companion to Pop and Rock*, eds. Simon Frith, Will Straw, and John Street, 93–108. Cambridge, UK: Cambridge University Press.

Frith, Holly. 2011. Jeff Beck Covers Lady Gaga's 'Bad Romance' at Classic Rock Awards. *Gigwise*, November 10, 2011. http://www.gigwise.com/news/68603/jeff-beck-covers-lady-gagas-bad-romance-at-classic-rock-awards

Gagafrontrow. 2013. Alice Cooper Monster Claw! *Gagafrontrow.blogspot*, July 2013. http://Gagafrontrow.blogspot.com/2013/07/coopermonsterclaw.html

Gagamonster96. Twitter post. December 9, 2014 (11:24 AM). https://twitter.com/gagamonster96/status/542354173099257856

Gharnit, Yasmeen. 2015. Watch Lady Gaga Shut Down a Sexist Reporter. *Nylon*, June 15, 2015. http://www.nylon.com/articles/lady-gaga-shuts-down-sexist-reporter

Gray, Christopher. 2009. An Improbable Cradle of Rock Music. *The New York Times*, June 18, 2009. http://www.nytimes.com/2009/06/21/realestate/21scapes.html

Hampp, Andrew. 2015. Inside Lady Gaga's Latest Reinvention (It's All Part of a Long-Term Plan). *Billboard*, March 6, 2015. http://www.billboard.com/articles/business/6494560/inside-lady-gaga-reinvention-long-term-plan

Hendicott, James. 2016. Lady Gaga to Become First Artist to Play the Grammys, Super Bowl and Oscars the Same Year. *New Musical Express*, February 7, 2016. http://www.nme.com/news/lady-gaga/91305

Jones, Josh. 2013. Sex Pistols Frontman Johnny Rotten Weighs In on Lady Gaga, Paul McCartney, Madonna & Katy Perry. *Open Culture*, April 6, 2013. http://www.openculture.com/2013/04/johnny_rotten_on_lady_gaga_paul_mccartney_madonna_katy_perry.html

Juzwiak, Rich. 2010. Lady Gaga Isn't So Much a Phenomenon as a Prophecy Fulfilled. *Phoenix New Times*, July 29, 2010. http://www.phoenixnewtimes.com/music/lady-gaga-isnt-so-much-a-phenomenon-as-a-prophecy-fulfilled-6433249

Keightley, Keir. 2001. Reconsidering Rock. In *The Cambridge Companion to Pop and Rock*, eds. Simon Frith, Will Straw, and John Street, 109–142. Cambridge, UK: Cambridge University Press.

Kielty, Martin. 2016. Gene Simmons: Lady Gaga Could Be Next Big Rock Star. *TeamRock*, March 18, 2016. http://teamrock.com/news/2016-03-18/kiss-gene-simmons-lady-gaga-next-big-rock-star

Kreps, Daniel. 2016. Watch Elton John and Lady Gaga Perform Together in Los Angeles. *Rolling Stone*, February 27, 2016. http://www.rollingstone.com/music/news/watch-elton-john-and-lady-gaga-perform-together-in-los-angeles-20160227

Kurutz, Steven. 2012. Lady Gaga's Muse Tests His Poker Face. *The New York Times*, March 7, 2012. http://www.nytimes.com/2012/03/08/fashion/rocking-on-his-own-lady-gagas-ex.html

Lady Gaga. Twitter post. June 13, 2009 (6:08 AM). https://twitter.com/ladygaga/status/2152456096

LadyGagaNowNet. Twitter post. January 4, 2016 (3:26 PM). https://twitter.com/ladygaganownet/status/684108711032414208

Malec, Brett. 2014. Lady Gaga Announces Debut SXSW Performance, Says She 'Can't Wait' to Rock Austin! *Eonline*, March 6, 2014. http://www.eonline.com/news/517951/lady-Lady%20Gaga-announces-debut-sxsw-performance-says-she-can-t-wait-to-rock-austin-all-the-details

Marie, Brownie. 2014. Lady Gaga Is a 'Very Authentic Jazz Singer,' Says Tony Bennett. *AXS*, September 21, 2014. http://www.axs.com/lady-gaga-is-a-very-authentic-jazz-singer-says-tony-bennett-20602

McDonald, Soraya Nadia. 2015. Why Do Pop Singers Like Lady Gaga Keep Releasing Jazz Albums? The Upsides Are Tremendous. *The Washington Post*, July 22, 2015. https://www.washingtonpost.com/news/arts-and-entertainment/wp/2015/07/22/why-do-pop-singers-keep-releasing-jazz-albums-the-upsides-are-tremendous/

Myers, Marc. 2014. Lady Gaga on Tony Bennett: 'He Thinks I'm Old School'. *The Wall Street Journal*, September 17, 2014. http://www.wsj.com/articles/lady-gaga-on-tony-bennett-he-thinks-im-old-school-1410961999

Paglia, Camille. 2010. Lady Gaga and the Death of Sex. *The Sunday Times*, September 12, 2010. http://www.thesundaytimes.co.uk/sto/public/magazine/article389697.ece

Pareles, Jon. 2010. Stars Sing to Save Rain Forests (and Maybe Redeem the '80s, Too). *The New York Times*, May 14, 2010. http://www.nytimes.com/2010/05/15/arts/music/15rainforest.html?_r=0

Perry, Clayton. 2008. Interview: Lady GaGa – Singer and Songwriter. *Blogcritics*, September 24, 2008. http://blogcritics.org/interview-lady-gaga-singer-and-songwriter/

Rader, Dodson. 2014. Tony Bennett and Lady Gaga Talk About Their New Album and Close Friendship: "He Saved My Life," She Says. *Parade*, September 10, 2014. http://parade.com/335908/dotsonrader/tony-bennett-and-lady-gaga-talk-about-their-new-album-and-close-friendship-he-saved-my-life-she-says/

Renshaw, David. 2016. Lady Gaga Hangs Out with Fat White Family after New York Gig. *NME*, May 4, 2016. http://www.nme.com/news/lady-gaga/93360

Reymann-Schneider, Kristina. 2016. Happy Birthday, Lady Gaga: From Provocative Performer to a Serious Artist. *Deutsche Welle*, March 28, 2016. http://www.dw.com/en/happy-birthday-lady-gaga-from-provocative-performer-to-a-serious-artist/a-19146107

Schoonmaker, Vaughn T. 2011. Lady Gaga Greets Fans at *Born This Way* Promo. *MTV.com*, May 24, 2011. http://www.mtv.com/news/1664475/lady-gaga-monsters-nyc-born-this-way/

Sciarretto, Amy. 2011. Alice Cooper: 'Lady Gaga Is the Female Me'. *Ultimate Classic Rock*, September 3, 2011. http://ultimateclassicrock.com/alice-cooper-lady-gaga-is-female-me/

Sowray, Bibby. 2016. Lady Gaga Turns Editor and Pays Tribute to Late, Great Fashion Friends. *The Telegraph*, January 5, 2016. http://www.telegraph.co.uk/fashion/people/lady-gaga-turns-editor-and-pays-tribute-to-late-great-fashion-fr/

Spanos, Brittany. 2016a. Flashback: Lady Gaga's First Grammy Performance. *Rolling Stone*, February 10, 2016. http://www.rollingstone.com/music/news/flashback-lady-gagas-first-grammy-performance-20160210

———. 2016b. Watch Mark Ronson Tease Lady Gaga's 'Analog' Album. *Rolling Stone*, May 12, 216. http://www.rollingstone.com/music/news/watch-mark-ronson-tease-lady-gagas-analog-album-20160512

Strang, Fay. 2013. 'My Intention Was to Put Art Culture into Pop Music': Lady Gaga Reveals She Aimed to 'Reverse Warhol' in New Record. *Daily Mail*, November 4, 2013. http://www.dailymail.co.uk/tvshowbiz/article-2486872/Lady-Gaga-reveals-aimed-reverse-Warhol-new-album-ARTPOP.html

Strecker, Erin. 2015. Oscars 2015: Lady Gaga Sings 'Sound of Music' Medley. *Billboard*, February 22, 2015. http://www.billboard.com/articles/events/oscars/6480254/lady-gaga-sings-sound-of-music-medley-oscars

Stryker, Sam. 2013. Lady Gaga and the Glam Rock Men Who Inspire Her. *Arts. Mic*, November 14, 2013. https://mic.com/articles/73263/lady-gaga-and-the-glam-rock-men-who-inspire-her

Takeda, Allison. 2015. Stephen Sondheim Belittles Lady Gaga's Sound of Music Tribute: 'She Was a Travesty'. *US Weekly*, March 16, 2015. http://www.usmagazine.com/entertainment/news/stephen-sondheim-slams-lady-gagas-sound-of-music-tribute-travesty-2015163

Teitelman, Bram. 2014. Lady Gaga Takes in Lazer/Wulf at SXSW. *Metal Insider*, March 12, 2014. http://www.metalinsider.net/secret-metalhead/lady-gaga-takes-in-lazerwulf-at-sxsw

The Week. 2012. Alice Cooper's 'Born This Way' and 6 other Unlikely Lady Gaga Covers. *The Week*, June 12, 202. http://theweek.com/articles/474737/alice-coopers-born-way-6-other-unlikely-lady-gaga-covers

Titus, Christa. 2012. Gene Simmons Q&A: On Kiss Empire, New Album and Advice for Lady Gaga. *Billboard*, October 5, 2012. http://www.billboard.com/articles/news/474778/gene-simmons-qa-on-kiss-empire-new-album-and-advice-for-lady-gaga

Vkanty, Edward. 2015. Lady Gaga Says 'I'm the Next Iron Maiden'. *Inquisitr*, August 21, 2015. http://www.inquisitr.com/2356170/lady-gaga-says-im-the-next-iron-maiden/

Wagmeister, Elizabeth. 2016. Lady Gaga Says Golden Globe Win for 'American Horror Story' is 'One of the Greatest Moments of My Life'. *Variety*, January 10, 2016. http://variety.com/2016/tv/news/lady-gaga-golden-globe-winner-american-horror-story-hotel-1201676564/

CHAPTER 11

Conclusion

It has been the central objective of this study to offer a sociological examination of the conditions of the fame of Lady Gaga. Adopting an analytical orientation rooted in the sociological specialty areas of popular culture and fame, the study specifically relied on a constructionist perspective to investigate the conditions of Lady Gaga's fame against the backdrop of today's celebrity culture and recent transformations of popular music culture. Focused on a variety of social conditions, the study unraveled the origins of lady Gaga's fame besides its foundations on a successful music career that, inevitably, must rely on a measure of talent and dedication on the part of the singer. That fact alone not only separates fame from celebrity but also makes the case of Lady Gaga all the more worthwhile to investigate as her fame took place precisely at a time when celebrity culture had already developed, in all its shallow splendor, as never before.

By virtue of its in-depth focus on one case, this study cannot pretend to be able to offer a general theory of fame (and celebrity). Yet, as this examination hopes to build fruitfully toward the development of such a theory, several broader lessons can be learned from the case of the fame of Lady Gaga, both in terms of the sociological potential of the suggested theoretical framework and its application as well as with respect to some of the dynamics and implications of fame in today's celebrity age. Thus, this Conclusion will offer some food for thought based on, yet thereby also extending beyond, the analysis offered in the previous chapters to suggest the contours of a more or less integrated model of the conditions of fame in the case of Lady Gaga. This model may also have consequences for other case studies in the world of popular music and beyond. In terms of the fame of Lady Gaga itself, furthermore, some observations on its course and direction can be made that are grounded in the here presented empirical analysis, for which reason alone they should not need to be misunderstood as unwarranted speculations but might reasonably reveal some of the continued dynamics of fame in society.

Rooted in a social-rationalist understanding of fame as a cultural phenomenon situated in a wider societal context, this investigation of the origins of the fame of Lady Gaga focused on various forms of privilege. Most obvious is the economic privilege that Lady Gaga rather swiftly attained as her fame rose on a global scale. Supported by an effective support team and the star treatment she received in an otherwise struggling music industry, Lady Gaga gained considerably in monetary respects from the exploitation of her many talents. Yet, such economics alone do not exhaust the singer's fame and cannot be used as an argument for a reductionist approach as similar gains can also be made in altogether different realms of culture or, indeed, may not be bestowed in cases where fame is nonetheless attained. While the basic logic of such empirical variations continues to baffle some scholars in the celebrity studies camp, it usefully drew the present study's attention to a number of other, non-economic factors. A brief review of the chapters' central findings may clarify the value of the constructionist model.

The legalities of fame that accompanied Lady Gaga's rise as a successful pop star have taken on proportions that already situated the singer in a multi-dimensional space, not exhausted with reference to its economic aspect. Even more clearly extending beyond any political economy of fame is the central relationship between Lady Gaga's presentation of self, both as a performer as well as a so-called practitioner of the fame, on the one hand, and its mediated reception by a multi-faceted audience, on the other. The focus in the sociological study of the conditions of fame thus shifts toward the centrality of the relationship between the subject of fame and its audience. Sociologically, fame exists inevitably in this relationship, and it cannot be assumed to be exhausted with reference to any sinister mechanisms of commercial exploitation on the part of the media, lest we would lose sight of an empirical study of relevant social facts. This study showed, indeed, that Lady Gaga and her team managed to infiltrate the media, and both use and disrupt them to the greatest advantage of the singer's career at a time when social-networking sites were still left unexplored by most music professionals. At the same time, the wider audience was also reached through the traditional avenues of the news media as well as radio and television. More effectively than other success stories in the popular music of that era, Lady Gaga managed to attract multiple publics as her demographic appeal and global reach could benefit from the fact that her artistry was able to cross conventional audience boundaries more readily than both the likes of Justin Bieber and Taylor Swift as well as Adele and Susan Boyle at the time of those stars' respective rise to fame.

While the perspective of this study does not allow to make any precise conclusions on the relative weight of the social conditions of Lady Gaga's rise to fame, it can be observed that the other conditions considered besides media and audience were not foundational to the singer's fame but functioned to facilitate it as additionally contributing factors. Of particular attention were Lady Gaga's activism and religiosity, the sex and gender aspects of her work and persona, and the multiple styles and artistic forms she has engaged in. Sociologically relevant hereby were not merely Lady Gaga's presentations and understandings of the role of these factors in furthering her career as were their reception on the part of the audience that bestows the attention on which fame is established. Lady Gaga may fancy herself a master in the art of fame and manipulate various aspects of the presentation of herself accordingly; it is always and necessarily the multiple constituents of her audience that will determine how such manipulations are perceived and accepted or rejected and how, consequently, fame is constructed. The centrality of the audience in the constitution of fame is thereby affirmed, and, as a result, it is also the audience that is responsible in maintaining fame into the future inasmuch as it is nurtured and steered in a particular direction on behalf of the subject of fame. As such, the fame of Lady Gaga is not a matter of Lady Gaga (alone) but (also) of the public at large and the extent to which it wants, or can be persuaded, to function as her attention-bestowing audience. The fame of Lady Gaga, as of anybody else, is essentially social. The societal context of the relationship between Lady Gaga and her audience, especially its cultural dynamic to value some things above others, will thereby play a great role that can never be predicted.

Turning to the direction and future of the fame of Lady Gaga itself, there is no doubt that the singer is not only famous, on a widely acknowledged scale, but has also become a celebrity, whether she wanted to attain that revered and dubious status or not. Fame in pop culture, especially when it is achieved on a career that is successful on a global level, comes with great rewards and many forms of privilege. On an interpersonal level, the privilege of celebrity brings about a high degree of closure to remove and safeguard oneself from the ordinary world of common folks. To some extent, the celebritization of Lady Gaga is inevitable as it, like fame, is established in interaction with other celebrities who want to be seen with the star and with whom the star cannot avoid being seen. There are also indications, moreover, not only that celebrity status has been unavoidable to Lady Gaga but also, despite some of her own statements on the matter, that she has fully embraced her attained celebrity position. While in 2010, at the height of her then newly acquired fame, the singer could still say, "I don't like celebrities; I don't hang out with them; I don't relate to that life" (in Silva 2010), in the following years such statements would have been rendered wholly without meaning as the singer had fully immersed herself into her own celebrity. Among its visible indications, Lady Gaga's celebrity status is revealed from her hanging out with other stars from the world of entertainment and beyond, from the likes of Karl Lagerfeld and Elton John to Joe Biden and Julian Assange. Lady Gaga may proclaim her fans are the center, but the symmetry of her social world is displayed more realistically than anywhere else in her many interactions with other celebrities.

As a peculiar sign of the estrangement that has come with her celebrity, Lady Gaga has also exploited her relative position of privilege as an influential artist who is willing to take on any cause, no matter whether it relates to anything she can claim to be knowledgeable about or even legitimately be interested in. Having successfully aligned herself with LGBT causes, in part because of an objectively dubious identification as a bisexual, her reception as an admired celebrity activist will especially have played a part in the singer extending, on an almost infinite scale, the number of causes she thinks she has to speak out on. The number of causes taken on, however, may be related negatively to the effectiveness with which each can be taken on, which in itself could be perceived to be problematic. Moreover, the singer's incessant self-presentation as a victim of all kinds of suffering, including her publicly shared sorrow over wanting to quit the music industry (Bailey 2015) and the supposed isolating effects of fame itself (Cavassuto 2016), may also have effects on the reception of her work and, as such, might ironically influence her fame adversely.

As noted before, the singer's career has already experienced some ebbs and flows since the years of her initial rise to fame. But the question who will be the next star after Lady Gaga cannot possibly be answered with "nobody," as it once was claimed (Parker 2010), because the singer herself has already presented another, post-pop Lady Gaga. The immediate result of Lady Gaga's relative disappearance from the pop limelight a few years ago, indeed, has been that the singer has since broadened her artistic appeal, especially as a jazz singer and an actor, in an effort that appears deliberately oriented at re-establishing her connection with the general public. It remains to be seen, of course, if this strategy to present Lady Gaga as a multi-dimensional and more broadly acceptable entertainer will be successful to continue her career in a more lasting way, for it cannot be predicted if the audience of the singer's fame will stay around and not be diverted to the next big thing, whatever or whoever it may be. The unpredictable nature of fame may be especially poignant in the case of an artist who was seen to so deliberately have pursued the fame and present herself in all the attention-grabbing guts and glory of a shocking spectacle. Although a refashioned Lady Gaga might garner renewed attention as the singer's artistic talents are better recognized by an audience extending well beyond her most devoted followers, it is also not outside the realm of possibilities that a safe and wholesome Lady Gaga is not what will continue to receive the public's attention as the necessary source of her fame.

References

Bailey, Alyssa. 2015. Lady Gaga: I Needed to Stop Being a Pop Star or I Was Going to Die. *Elle*, December 3, 2015. http://www.elle.com/culture/celebrities/news/a32304/lady-gaga-billboard-woman-of-the-year-interview/

Cavassuto, Maria. 2016. Lady Gaga: Fame Is the Most Isolating Thing in the World. *Variety*, June 3, 2016. http://variety.com/2016/tv/news/lady-gaga-fame-isolation-jamie-lee-curtis-1201787973/

Parker, James. 2010. The Last Pop Star. *The Atlantic*, June 2010. http://www.theatlantic.com/magazine/archive/2010/06/the-last-pop-star/308089/

Silva, Horacio. 2010. The World According to Gaga. *The New York Times Style Magazine*, March 4, 2010. http://tmagazine.blogs.nytimes.com/2010/03/04/the-world-according-to-gaga/

CHAPTER 12

Epilogue: Professor Goes Gaga—Teaching Lady Gaga and the Sociology of Fame

The rise of theoretical and empirical studies on fame and celebrity in the sociological community and elsewhere, which I reviewed in Chap. 2, has also been accompanied by relevant teaching efforts.[1] It is within the perspective of the sociology of fame and celebrity that I have since the Spring of 2011 organized a sociology course on the fame of Lady Gaga at the University of South Carolina. To date, the course has been taught on five occasions, including two Summer terms and an honors class. The idea for the course originated when, sometime in the Spring of 2010, I developed the idea to teach a course on the career of Lady Gaga as a case study in the sociology of fame. Having discussed the idea with a few students, who all responded favorably, I emailed my Department Chair on July 15 that I wanted to teach a new course, "Lady Gaga and the Sociology of the Fame." I mentioned that I was a fan of the singer's music, but that the course would focus sociologically on the social conditions of her fame. By noon, the Chair responded that she thought it was "a great, great idea for a class." In September 2010, the course was formally approved under the title "SOCY 398D: Lady Gaga and the Sociology of the Fame."

As soon as the course was publicly announced, it became the number-one Lady Gaga news story and was reported and discussed in a wide variety of internet sources and media outlets across the world. The unprecedented attention devoted to the course placed myself as instructor in an unexpected and unique position to experience various dimensions of contemporary fame and celebrity culture while teaching on that very subject matter. In this epilogue chapter, I will examine this experience to uncover the conditions and consequences of how my sociology course on fame itself became a subject of fame. This exposition may also clarify some of the circumstances of the study of Lady Gaga's rise to fame that is explored in the various chapters of this book as the course was organized on the same theme (Deflem 2012).

In the following pages, I will review the main aspects of the course's reception and discuss its dynamics in terms of the fame of Lady Gaga. My course was evidently not the first college course in the realm of pop music to have received popular attention (e.g., Adams 1998; The Seattle Times 1997). But the measure of fame that has been bestowed on my so-called Lady Gaga course has surely been unprecedented. To avoid any misconception from the start, this attention could not be the result of any accomplishment on the part of its instructor for it began to take shape well before the first class was even held.

THE FAME OF SOCIOLOGY

Even now some six years since the course was initially planned, it is difficult to fully comprehend the amount of attention and resulting fame which my course received. On the internet, reports and discussions on the course were most intense and extensive. At the time of this writing in the Spring of 2016, a Google search for references to the course generated almost 90,000 results. This number was much higher in the immediate years following the announcement of the course and its organization, because some of those online postings merely duplicated or linked to other reports. In the Spring of 2013, a Google search for references to the course generated 334,000 results, a number that stood at 477,000, including some 154,000 of which that also mentioned my name, in November 2012. During the height of reporting on the course in the Autumn of 2010, the total number of internet references exceeded 800,000. These variations notwithstanding the volume of attention devoted to the course can safely be concluded to be unprecedented in university teaching. The quantity in feedback to the course, moreover, was matched by some striking qualitative characteristics as well.

News Media

In September 2010, when the course was listed on the web pages of the USC Registrar in preparation of the Spring semester of 2011, I posted a web page with information about the course on my university website, to which a few days I added as separate blog (Gagacourse website). Within days after the course web page had been posted, I began to receive emails from students interested in the course. My first effort to communicate about the course to the media was made on October 1, 2010, when I emailed USC Media Relations and a journalist I had spoken to before who works for the *USC Times*, an internal publication at the University of South Carolina. While Media Relations was still considering my request, my email was already passed on to *The Daily Gamecock*, the student newspaper at the university. Later that day, I received the first email from a student asking permission to take the class.

On October 19, 2010, I conducted my first interview about the course with the *USC Times* journalist I had initially informed, which was published online on the University web pages a few days later (USC News 2010). The article focused appropriately on the fact that I organized the course at a time when the first part of my career was coming to a close and I sought to redirect my work. "New sociology course on Lady Gaga provides 'vacation' from terrorism" and "Mid-Career Renewal" were the appropriate taglines to the article. Later that week, I did my second interview about the course with the student reporter from *The Daily Gamecock* who had contacted before. Also that day, USC Media Relations decided to circulate the article as a formal University news release to the off-campus working press.

On October 28, 2010, the first published reports on my course began to appear, specifically an article in *The Daily Gamecock* (Fitzgerald 2010) and a blog posting by the *Washington Post* based on the USC press release (Johnson 2010). That same day, I accepted additional requests for interviews from journalists of a local TV station, a local newspaper, and a reporter of the *New York Times*. Later that day, the local television station aired a segment about my course featuring an interview with me and some students on campus, and the next day, *The State* (the main local paper in Columbia, South Carolina) and *The New York Times* published articles in print and online (Knich 2010; Seelye 2010).

Especially because of the USC press release being picked up by the *Washington Post* and the article that appeared in the *New York Times*, news about my course subsequently traveled like wildfire, far beyond any proportion I could have imagined. By October 31, I already emailed a colleague that the attention was "overwhelming." By November 2, I had a standardized email response prepared that mentioned that I was "swamped" with requests and that, in lieu of an interview, referred to information posted on the course blog. I selectively accepted requests for interviews, especially from media abroad, the first of which came from a reporter of the BBC, whose website featured a story about the course later that day (BBC News 2010).

The news stories that were featured by *The Washington Post*, *The New York Times*, and the BBC got picked up by all kinds of media outlets all over the world and were discussed or reprinted in a multitude of print publications, on radio and TV, and on the internet. Within days, hundreds of stories were published, and soon the total number of reports about my course ran into the thousands. After the initial wave of attention during the first few weeks when the course had been announced, a second surge in the news coverage took place mid-November when a story for the French news agency Agence France-Presse was distributed as a press release available to journalists across the world (Carli 2010).

Special mention must be made of the response to the media coverage which I received from within the University of South Carolina, because it shaped part of my own continued conduct toward the media. On October 29, 2010, the day after the course had received news coverage in the local media and from *The New York Times*, my Department Chair informed me that she had received a call from the Dean of Arts and Sciences to let me know that the University had received some phone calls about the course, apparently from members in the community who were challenging the validity of the course. The Chair told me that I was advised by the Dean to not speak about the course to the media so that news about it would die down. USC Media Relations likewise took efforts to silence news about the course. The online article posted on the University website was promoted via the University's Twitter account (UofSC Twitter post), but not included in the print edition of the *USC Times*. I also refused a planned interview with a local TV station, because I was told it could only take place with a USC Media Relations staff present. A few days later, the Department Chair called me to her office to tell me that I was now encouraged, at the recommendation of the Dean, to speak publicly about the course. Apparently, news coverage on the course had gotten to be so enormous that it was bringing worldwide publicity to the University. And in the judgment of the higher administration of the University, of course, nothing can be better than publicity, whatever it may be. At a university faculty senate meeting around that time, the President of the University commented favorably about my course along with flattering comments about the University's baseball team. The University Provost made an unconscionable disparaging and hostile remark at the same meeting, but later had no qualms about congratulating me in person for the course having been discussed in a newspaper from his native Greece.

As soon as the first reports on my course had appeared, I felt it best to reject several requests for interviews because there had been some sensationalist accounts written that focused unnecessarily on my fandom of Lady Gaga's music rather than the course's sociological perspective. Because my opinions had at times been misrepresented, I chose to selectively accept interview requests only by email. But in the latter half of November 2010, as I began to feel more comfortable about the media attention and trusted certain sources because of their standing as legitimate news media, I accepted additional interview requests, specifically to appear on the Gayle King Show, on NewsNation with Tamron Hall on MSNBC, on ABC News Now, as well as on several radio stations from my country of origin Belgium, where I received special attention when it was discovered that the Lady Gaga course in the United States was taught by a Belgian-born professor.

Taking a closer look at the media coverage about my course, a few notable highlights can be mentioned. Besides the *New York Times* and the BBC, other globally impactful news outlets discussing the course included CNN, MTV, *USA Today*, *Time* magazine, the popular British music publication *NME*, and the trade magazine *Billboard*, among many others. Print news stories were published in a wide variety of nations, such as Russia, Slovenia, India, Vietnam, Zambia, Senegal, Lebanon, and Oman, to name but a few. Multiple television and radio shows broadcast features about the course as well. Via an online search, I discovered at least 20 television shows from across the world that devoted a segment to the course, including programs in France, Italy, Germany, and China. Based on an online search of news stories discussing the course, it is safe to conclude that just about every newspaper, radio and TV station, and online media site, especially those with some interest in Lady Gaga, either by means of a focus on celebrity or on popular music, reported on the course. Needless to say, this extensive news coverage was a manifestation of the fame of Lady Gaga at that time in her career, from which my course benefited. For several days in the first week of November 2010, news about my course was the top-featured Lady Gaga story on Google News.

For more than a year since I first taught the course in the Spring of 2011, I continued to get media requests to discuss the course, including requests from national television stations ABC and NBC to have a class meeting televised. In March 2013, the course was used in a question on the popular television game show "Who Wants To Be a Millionaire." Ironically, the latest remarkable resurgence of media interest in the course took place after an earlier version of this epilogue chapter was published in the journal *The American Sociologist* in May 2013 (Deflem 2013a). Aided by a press release sent out by the publisher of the journal (Springer 2013), my initial article about the fame of teaching a course on fame itself regenerated that fame anew in the form of various news reports (Harris 2013; Low 2013). In most recent years, news stories specifically addressing my course have appeared only sporadically (Torres 2014), but just about every news item devoted to pop-culture college courses as well as several features on Lady Gaga continue to mention it (Before 2015; Gillis 2016).

Internet and Email

Within weeks after news about the course had appeared, I could barely keep up with the online sources I found about the course. At some point, there appeared more than 60 online media sources on the course over a time span of just 12 hours in the Russian language alone. Toward the end of November 2010, the volume of news reports on my course was so great that my name appeared as a trending term in Google Trends. The course blog I had set up mid-October 2010 received some 800 views that month, a number that had risen to 40,000 by November (and that since has fluctuated from about 500 to about 1500 visitors per month).

News about my course has been repeatedly discussed on social-networking sites, especially on Twitter and Facebook. Tweets about the course occurred multiple times per day in the initial weeks when the course had been announced and have continued until the present, albeit at a gradually much lower rate. At the time of this writing in 2016, almost six years after the course was announced and more than three years since it was last taught, news of the course is still being tweeted about once or twice a week. Internet users have also been eagerly looking for information about the course, as indicated by the fact that automatic completions of partial Google searches include references to the course. In the Spring of 2011, the Google search "Lady Gaga a__" found the name of my course competing with the popular Lady Gaga song "Alejandro." In November 2012, the search "Lady Gaga and the" found my course in the company of the "illuminati," the "devil," and the "pope." By 2016, "Lady

Gaga and the s__" mentioned my course alongside of references to Lady Gaga and "the sound of music" and "the super bowl."

Anonymous comments on various online forums and networking sites were manifold and mostly laudatory in the months following the course announcement. Negative online comments typically discussed my course as an example to lament the state of higher education, among them a YouTube clip under the title, "Univercity [sic] Teach Course on Illuminati Puppet Lady Gaga" (New Freedommkfl YouTube video). Most unanticipated on my part were the negative judgments that commented not on my teaching but on my fandom in music (Allen 2011). Explaining the course, I had in interviews revealed that I was indeed a fan of Lady Gaga's music (and of popular music in general) precisely because I was concerned that students might not accept my teaching of a Lady Gaga course unless I could claim expertise as a connoisseur of the singer's music and career as well as a sociologist. But the media response was at times much less articulate. In February 2012, in the midst of the Republican presidential primary, conservative commentator Ann Coulter (2012) lamented the state of higher education and mentioned my course as an example. A member of the Christian Parents Forum posted that my course indicated not only that "education in the States continues to plummet to new lows" but also that "Christ is coming soon" (Christian Parents Forum 2010). Another forum member agreed, "Yes he is sister!!! I can not wait!" (ibid.).

By November 16, 2010, I had received well over 800 emails about the course, the vast majority of which were positive and congratulatory. Just seven of these communications were viciously negative, vilifying me as a "monster" in a meaning of that term different than how it is used in the Lady Gaga fan community. One emailer said he was "embarrassed for America as a result of the absolutely ludicrous nonsense you are passing off as education," that I should undergo "psychological evaluation," and that "well educated Chinese, Indians, Europeans, etc.—and even the terrorists—are probably laughing their asses off." One email was passed on to police authorities for possibly involving a death threat, but no charges were filed.

Students

Most communications I received about the course, especially by email, have come from students. Some of them came from students at USC who asked for permission to register for the class even though they did not meet the course prerequisites. One student included a picture of himself dressed up at a Lady Gaga show. Other such requests came from students at other universities, several of them in foreign countries. Forming a special part of the student feedback are the responses the idea for the course received from students in the college press. Immediately upon the first report about the course in *The Daily Gamecock*, a student wrote a negative op-ed (Seidel 2010). A few students at other universities similarly condemned my teaching (Everett 2010; Torch 2010). However, the vast majority of student feedback was very positive, including editorial endorsements in the college press (Edwards 2010; The Harvard Crimson 2010).

Once student registration for the Spring 2011 term had begun in November 2010, the class filled up within a mere few hours. Limited to 50 students in its inaugural semester, some students dropped out before the first class was held, but their slots were immediately filled by others. On the first day of class, a few flyers with negative comments about the course had been posted in the building of the USC Sociology Department, and some were anonymously dropped in my inbox in the Department's mailroom. The Department Chair at some point raised the possibility of having campus police present at the first class, but, partly because a sudden snowstorm had led to a cancellation of classes on the first day of the semester, this drastic measure proved unnecessary. Shortly after the first class was held in the Spring of 2011, a report appeared in *The Huffington Post* written by one of the student participants (Griggs 2011). The article was used along with the feedback from another student in a story published in *The Daily Gamecock* under the headline, "Students Vouch for Gaga Class" (Quinn 2011).

In the physical world, too, I was sometimes confronted with student feedback relating to the course. As I walked on campus during the days after news about the course had first appeared, more students than usual were looking at me, presumably because they recognized me from a picture that was printed on the front page of *The Daily Gamecock* student paper. As I walked on campus one day on my way to lunch, a student recognized me while she was reading an article about the course. Sometime in October 2010, as I was walking home, a driver stopped his truck in the middle of the road and leaned out of the window to make a sign of a cross pointed in my direction. When I attended the inaugural concert of the Lady Gaga Born This Way Ball in Seoul, Korea, in April 2012, two traditionally dressed Korean fans came up to me, one holding in her hand a Samsung phone displaying a news report in Korean about my course, asking me if I was "Professor Mathieu."

With respect to the impact of the teaching of the Lady Gaga course, my attempt to have students learn about certain aspects of their society and, even more ambitiously so, to draw them into the discipline of sociology by means of the analysis of a popular theme cannot be said to have been greatly successful. Although explicitly framed in terms of the analytical aim to unravel a contemporary social issue, the objectives of the course were not always well understood by students who enrolled in the class. Despite my more than usual clarity in describing the course objectives in the syllabus and during the first class meeting, 10 out of the 50 enrolled students eventually dropped the course. When the class was again offered during in the Fall of 2011, it attracted about the same number of students as during the inaugural term despite the class being open to 120 students. Apparently, word had gotten out that the class was not an "easy A." Some exceptions notwithstanding, the interest level of university students today is such that not even the words "Lady" and "Gaga" can stimulate their weakly developed motivations for learning. Apart from whatever shortcomings might be attributed to the instructor, the impact of the course was also conditioned by some of the contemporary realities that characterize higher learning at a large state university, specially the marketization of higher education and the mass of students attending college as a result thereof. Much like my other classes, the anonymous comments received via the University evaluation forms were generally positive. A comment posted on a well-known privately maintained site of professor ratings was clear as well: "Stay away from the Lady Gaga class. You have to do the readings and work your butt off ..." (RateMyProfessors 2011).

Sociologists

In contrast to the attention the course was given in the popular media, it received virtually no response from sociologists (and other academics). The exceptions are few and telling. Several sociologists commented on my course on a blog where a post from Jeremy Freese, then the Chair of the Sociology Department at Northwestern University, generated a handful of comments (Scatterplot 2010). Among them is the remark by Professor of Sociology Andrew Perrin of the University of North Carolina at Chapel Hill that I would not have "any credentials whatsoever in the study of music or culture" (ibid.). The comment is obviously astounding because of its lack of professionalism, but even more so considering that cultural sociology was my initial specialty when I studied sociology before I continued on as a student in cultural anthropology and only subsequently turned to the sociology of law. An additional comment by Jay Livingston, Professor and Chair of Sociology at Montclair State University, references a definition of the word "gaga" that includes the adjectives "demented," "crazy," and "infatuated" (ibid.).

Following the blog post, Jeremy Freese continued his disturbed online ranting when he sub-tweeted me as "that guy" who would have abandoned sociology to "follow Lady Gaga" (Freese Twitter post). The presently at Stanford employed sociologist also blogged about having detected purported "Gaga references" after a pseudonymous blogger named "drektheuninteresting," a sociologist who maintains a blog called "Total Drek" that is filled with highly offensive content (Total Drek blog), had stated that he was "really Mathieu Deflem" (Scatterplot 2011). No matter how disgustingly unprofessional and potentially revealing of much deeper issues only psychiatrists might hope to comprehend, such conduct is perhaps less puzzling in the context of some of the effects of today's celebrity culture on academia and whatever psychology that goes along with it. The same might also be said about the editorial decision to deflect an earlier version of this epilogue chapter in its original article form from publication in a journal that is specifically devoted to celebrity studies.

Lady Gaga

As amusing as it is interesting is the fact that Lady Gaga has herself on a few occasions commented on my course. The first time the singer spoke about the course was during an interview with Anderson Cooper for the popular CBS television program "60 Minutes" (CBS News 2011). The singer claimed that she considered herself to be a student of the "sociology of fame." Using the expression "sociology of fame" a second time during the interview, she mentions that Mr. Cooper had asked her about the matter. The reference to my course—also alluded to in the title of the segment ("Lady Gaga and the Art of Fame")—made sense because the interview was originally conducted in November 2010 when news about the course had gone global. To the delight of myself and my students, the interview aired during the inaugural semester of the course on the night of the Grammy Awards in February 2011.

In July 2011, Lady Gaga again spoke about the course when she was a guest on an AMP Radio talk show hosted by Carson Daly. Incidentally contributing to the fame of my course, Mr. Daly asked about the course under the impression that it was organized at USC in Los Angeles, from where the show airs, rather than the other USC in Columbia, South Carolina. As before, the singer took the question as an opportunity to reflect on the meaning of fame. "Especially in today's media with social networking and cameras," she said, "everyone can take that same picture that the paparazzi used to take…It's not so much about doing it as it is about embracing the art of it. And I think that's what the course is about" (Costello 2011). In the spring of 2012, in one of the very few interviews Lady Gaga granted during her Born This Way Ball tour, she was asked about the course for Eesti Televisioon in Estonia in August 2012. The singer said that she would not take the class herself "because," she stated, "I would know everything that they were teaching," but she did add that "it's very nice of them that they have that class there" (Deflem YouTube video).

Finally, in May 2011, during a press conference in Mexico, Lady Gaga was again asked about the course, but the available online reports of that interview do not include her comments. A few weeks after the interview, on May 25, 2011, Lady Gaga appeared as a guest on an episode of Saturday Night Live (SNL) hosted by Justin Timberlake. In one of the sketches on the show, the two pop stars take part in a mock TV game quiz called "What's That Name" (NBC 2011). At some point during the sketch, the actor Fred Armisen appears on stage portraying the fictional character of "Alphonse," a fan of Lady Gaga. Much to my surprise and to the consternation of many of my friends, Alphonse was in appearance and dress modeled after me. Admittedly, although my teaching of the course had by then also come to the attention of various members of Lady Gaga's entourage, my inclusion as an SNL character may have been related more to my status as a fan rather than my academic position.

The Celebrity of Fame

In its wide and at times intense public reception, it is most striking to note how my course on fame became a manifestation of its very subject matter. Since the course was announced, media reports on Lady Gaga have often continued to mention that the fame of the singer has reached such proportions that she even has her own college course. For instance, when the French television station M6 aired an hour-long special on Lady Gaga on the occasion of her Born This Way Ball concert in Paris in September 2012, the course was discussed at some length, including video segments of some of my public lectures. On the occasion of the performer's 27th birthday in 2013, a popular astrology blog again included the course as proof of the performer's cultural relevance (Fox 2013). As late as February 2016, a post on the popular business-networking site LinkedIn discussed the marketing of Lady Gaga as a personal brand with reference to my teaching (Delia 2016).

No doubt a result of the fame of Lady Gaga but also aided by the fame of my course, it is striking to note that other scholars have been taking up Gaga-related efforts in their teaching and research. Several courses have been organized on various aspects of the phenomenon of Lady Gaga (Brackett 2012; Gonzalez 2012; Hollands 2012; Nobel 2011; Oo 2011; Tyson 2010). Some instructors, moreover, have placed the name of Lady Gaga in the title of their courses as a convenient and attractive shorthand descriptor to discuss other issues, such as gender, beauty, pop music history, and sociological theory (Colton and Muñoz 2016; Genco 2012; Rosenwald 2012). Besides the appearance of various Lady Gaga courses, there has also been a more general increase in various other pop-culture courses, a development that has at times been met with some consternation. My course on the fame Lady Gaga has in the media regularly been discussed in conjunction with other pop-culture courses on various themes (Conradt 2011; Khan 2012). The opinion is regularly voiced that such courses would indicate a disintegration of higher education, even though courses focused on pop stars already existed in the 1980s and 1990s (Strecker 2015). Additionally, it is telling that pop-culture courses are often considered to be part of a concerted effort, when, in truth, the perspectives and objectives of such courses vary widely across disciplines and educational settings.

Under circumstances of a celebrity culture it is to be expected that the sociologist of fame can share some of the subject matter's joys and tribulations. Since the course was announced, I have often been contacted by the media to address not only the course but also various other aspects of the fame of Lady Gaga as well as other, more or less closely related themes, such as interviews concerning Kim Kardashian, New Kids On The Block, the concept of the diva, and the passing of Whitney Houston. At some point in November 2010, I was contacted by a Swedish fashion magazine asking me about a photo shoot. When I responded that my interests concern the sociology of fame and that I know very little about the fashion of Lady Gaga, I was more than a little surprised to discover that the magazine wanted to do a photo shoot of me, not her. Of course, I was happy to accept the offer, but, alas, no shoot was eventually scheduled.

As the instructor of the course, I have also received recognition in unexpected places. At a conference on terrorism and security in Turkey in May 2011, a colleague from Israel stepped up to tell me I was famous in her country, not because of my elaborate scholarship on counterterrorism, but because of the Gaga course. While attending Lady Gaga concerts in Tokyo in May 2013, I was astonished to meet several Japanese fans who recognized me because they knew about my course and who, referring to me as *Gaga sensei* (Gaga professor), asked me to pose for pictures and give autographs. Throughout my travels in the Lady Gaga fan community, I have regularly continued to encounter such experiences. In large measure, of course, they are due to the fact that anyone associated with Lady Gaga functions in a hierarchy of fame concentrically revolving around the performer. As many fans, myself included, enjoy talking to Lady Gaga's touring musicians and members of her staff, others can likewise—absent the chance to talk to Lady Gaga herself—at least talk to the "Gaga professor." As such, Lady Gaga's notion of the fame as being shared in her community has indeed been realized.

Conclusion

This reflection has revealed how the mere planning of my course on the fame of Lady Gaga became itself a subject of fame through its discussion in multiple venues in the contemporary popular media landscape. To be sure, higher education courses about pop stars and various aspects of pop culture have existed for a while, but their conditions and impact are surely different today. In the case of my sociology course on the fame of Lady Gaga, the timing of the course will have been fortuitous for entirely accidental reasons, as a more serious social event would likely have prevented something as banal as a new college course from attaining such notoriety. Yet, as an aspect of, and not just a reflection on, the rise to fame of Lady Gaga, the course was also able to rely on a technologically accelerated and culturally propelled obsession with celebrity and fame that characterizes the present time. As the intensity of the fascination with Lady Gaga was sustained, so did the course remain a topic of popular media attention. The gradual decrease in interest over the past few years can likewise be attributed to a decline in the obsession that marked the public's fascination with the singer's rise to fame.

From the viewpoint of the sociology of fame and celebrity, the fame of the Lady Gaga course itself is one indication that the Warholian days of a 15-minute fame are a thing of the past. In our age of celebrity, a university course on Lady Gaga proposed at the height of the singer's rise to fame might well be argued to have been noteworthy had it remained unknown. As this book has shown in the case of Lady Gaga, indeed, the cultural world of fame and celebrity today is very different than ten years past, let alone two or three decades ago. The case of my course on the fame of Lady Gaga shows that there is no reason to assume that sociologists and other scholars of fame can manipulate news coverage in the direction of their scholarly interests. Instead, the norms of the discipline must remain guided by academic standards rather than any quest for publicity (Deflem 2013b). On the basis of my teaching experience, I therefore also question the value of a sociological specialty on fame and celebrity unless its research and teaching are firmly rooted in the theoretical traditions of the discipline. It would be an unfortunate byproduct of certain obsessions of our age were we to treat the culture of celebrity more seriously than to acknowledge that it moves a great many people and that, for that reason alone, fame and celebrity deserve to be analyzed sociologically.

Note

1. This chapter is revised from an article in *The American Sociologist*, a journal published by Springer (Deflem 2013a).

References

Adams, Rebecca G. 1998. Inciting Sociological Thought by Studying the Deadhead Community: Engaging Publics in Dialogue. *Social Forces* 77(1): 1–25.

Allen, Charlotte. 2011. Lady Gaga Makes it to Harvard. *Minding the Campus*, November 18, 2011. http://www.mindingthecampus.org/2011/11/lady_gaga_makes_it_to_harvard/

BBC News. 2010. University Offers Lady Gaga Course. *BBC News*, November 2, 2010. http://www.bbc.co.uk/news/education-11672679

Before, Lynda. 2015. Zombies in College: Is That Really What You Paid For? *The Huffington Post*, May 5, 2015. http://www.huffingtonpost.com/lynda-bekore/zombies-in-college-is-that-really-what-you-paid-for_b_7215488.html

Brackett, Charlotte. 2012. New Rhetoric Course Focuses on Lady Gaga. *The Collegian*, March 22, 2012.
Carli, Rob. 2010. Lady Gaga and the Sociology of Fame: College Course. *Agence France-Presse*, November 17, 2010.
CBS News. 2011. Lady Gaga on 'Mastering the Art of Fame'. Transcript. *CBS News*, February 14, 2011. http://www.cbsnews.com/8301-18560_162-7337078.html
Christian Parents Forum. 2010. US University Launches Lady Gaga Class. *Forum discussion*, November 5, 2010. http://www.christianparentsforum.com/forums/showthread.php?t=4436
Colton, Kenneth, and José A. Muñoz. 2016. Lady Gaga Meets Ritzer: Using Music to Teach Sociological Theory. *Dialogue: The Interdisciplinary Journal of Popular Culture and Pedagogy* 31: 35–43. http://journaldialogue.org/issues/lady-gaga-meets-ritzer-using-music-to-teach-sociological-theory/
Conradt, Stacy. 2011. 22 Fascinating and Bizarre College Classes Offered This Semester. *CNN.com*, August 29, 2011. http://www.cnn.com/2011/08/29/living/bizarre-college-courses-mf/index.html
Costello, Carly. 2011. Lady Gaga Addresses Embracing the Art of Fame. *ArtistDirect*, July 31, 2011. http://www.artistdirect.com/entertainment-news/article/lady-gaga-addresses-embracing-the-art-of-fame/9042065
Coulter, Ann. 2012. The Problem with Santorum. *Human Events*, February 29, 2012. http://www.humanevents.com/article.php?id=49879
Deflem, Mathieu. 2012. The Presentation of Fame in Everyday Life: The Case of Lady Gaga. *Margin*, 1(The Divas Issue): 58–68.
———. 2013a. Professor Goes Gaga: Teaching Lady Gaga and the Sociology of Fame. *The American Sociologist* 44(2): 117–131.
———. 2013b. The Structural Transformation of Sociology. *Society* 50(2): 156–166.
Deflem, Mathieu. Lady Gaga About Sociology of Fame Course (Estonian TV 2012). *YouTube video*, uploaded September 3, 2012. https://www.youtube.com/watch?v=Mxyn-C-HoCk
Delia, Colin. 2016. Lady Gaga and the Professor. *LinkedIn*, February 10, 2016. https://www.linkedin.com/pulse/lady-gaga-professor-colin-delia
Edwards, Adrienne. 2010. Lady Gaga Class Is No (Fame) Monster. *The Daily Pennsylvanian*, November 17, 2010. http://www.thedp.com/article/2010/11/adlibs_lady_gaga_class_is_no_fame_monster
Everett, Ian. 2010. Gaga's Class Leaves One Speechless. *The Daily Cougar*, November 12, 2010. http://thedailycougar.com/2010/11/12/gaga's-class-leaves-one-speechless
Fitzgerald, Jake. 2010. Professor Goes Gaga. *The Daily Gamecock*, October 26, 2010. http://scholarcommons.sc.edu/gamecock_2010_oct/3/

Fox, Kelli. 2013 Happy Birthday Lady Gaga. *OM Times*, March 28, 2013. http://astrology.omtimes.com/happy-birthday-lady-gaga/

Freese, Jeremy. Twitter post. July 9, 2013 (11:51 PM). https://twitter.com/jeremyfreese/status/354810002957008897

Gagacourse. Website. http://www.gagacourse.net

Genco, Emily. 2012. Music Icons Rock the "Ivory Tower" of Higher Education. *USA Today College*, February 10, 2012. http://college.usatoday.com/2012/02/10/music-icons-rock-the-ivory-tower-of-higher-ed/

Gillis, Avery. 2016. 16 Secrets About Lady Gaga That Even Her Little Monsters Might Not Know. *Diply*, May 6, 2016. http://diply.com/trendyjoe/article/lady-gaga-secrets/4

Gonzalez, Noemi. 2012. Lady Gaga 101. *The State Press*, March 6, 2012. http://www.statepress.com/article/2012/03/lady-gaga-101/

Griggs, Malia. 2011. Why I enrolled in 'Lady Gaga and the Sociology of Fame'. *The Huffington Post*, January 7, 2011. http://www.huffingtonpost.com/malia-griggs/insiders-perspective-of-l_b_805590.html

Harris, Paul. 2013. The Nature of Fame: The Lady Gaga Professor Who Became a Global Star. *The Guardian*, May 25, 2013. http://www.theguardian.com/music/2013/may/25/lady-gaga-celebrity-fame

The Harvard Crimson. 2010. Gaga for Gaga: USC's Upcoming Course Promises to Engage Students. Editorial. *The Harvard Crimson*, November 1, 2010. http://www.thecrimson.com/article/2010/11/1/gaga-students-course-professor/

Hollands, Courtney. 2012. Tufts Shows Its Poker Face. *Boston Daily*, January 20, 2012. http://blogs.bostonmagazine.com/boston_daily/2012/01/20/tufts-shows-its-poker-face/

Johnson, Jenna. 2010. OMG: U of South Carolina Adds Lady Gaga Sociology Course. *WashingtonPost.com*, October 28, 2010. http://voices.washingtonpost.com/campus-overload/2010/10/omg_u_of_south_carolina_adds_l.html

Khan, Ejaz. 2012. Top 10 Bizarre University Courses. *Wonders List*, November 9, 2012. http://www.wonderslist.com/2012/11/09/top-10-bizarre-university-courses/

Knich, Diane. 2010. USC Prof is All about Terrorism ... and Lady Gaga. *The State*, October 29, 2010, p. B3.

Low, Amanda. 2013. Newly Famous Professor Teaches Brilliant Class On Lady Gaga and Fame. *Mommyish*, May 26, 2013. http://www.mommyish.com/2013/05/26/newly-famous-professor-teaches-brilliant-class-on-lady-gaga-and-fame/

NBC. 2011. What's That Name?: Celebrity Edition With Justin Timberlake and Lady Gaga. Video. *NBC.com*. http://www.nbc.com/saturday-night-live/video/whats-that-name/n13153

New Freedommkfl Channel. Univercity Teach Course on Illuminati Puppet Lady Gaga. *YouTube video*, uploaded November 4, 2010. https://www.youtube.com/watch?v=dKd9sKr5YOM

Nobel, Carmen. 2011. HBS Cases: Lady Gaga. *Harvard Business School*, September 26, 2011. http://hbswk.hbs.edu/item/6812.html

Oo, Pauline. 2011. Gaga over Gaga. *SCAN Magazine*, February 12, 2011. http://paulineoo.writersresidence.com/samples/gaga-over-gaga

Quinn, Ryan. 2011. Students Vouch for Gaga Class. *The Daily Gamecock*, February 1, 2011. http://scholarcommons.sc.edu/gamecock_2011_feb/18/

RateMyProfessors. 2011. Mathieu Deflem. Rating of December 13, 2011. http://www.ratemyprofessors.com/ShowRatings.jsp?tid=654719

Rosenwald, Michael. 2012. At U-Md., a Class About Lady Gaga. *The Washington Post*, March 9, 2012. http://www.washingtonpost.com/blogs/rosenwald-md/post/at-u-md-a-class-about-lady-gaga/2012/03/09/gIQADw1R1R_blog.html

Scatterplot. 2010. Starstruck. *Blog post*, October 29, 2010. https://scatter.wordpress.com/2010/10/29/starstruck/

———. 2011. Trends in Anonymous Blogging. *Blog post*, June 11, 2011. https://scatter.wordpress.com/2011/06/11/trends-in-anonymous-blogging/#comment-12332

The Seattle Times. 1997. Madonna the Phenomenon Becomes a College Course. *The Seattle Times*, April 8, 1997. http://community.seattletimes.nwsource.com/archive/?date=19970408&slug=2532816

Seelye, Katharine Q. 2010. Beyond ABCs of Lady Gaga to the Sociology of Fame. *The New York Times*, October 29, 2010. http://www.nytimes.com/2010/10/29/us/29gaga.html

Seidel, Chelsey. 2010. Pop Culture Shouldn't Mix with College. *The Daily Gamecock*, November 3, 2010. http://scholarcommons.sc.edu/gamecock_2010_nov/

Springer. 2013. From Professor to Global Sensation: World Goes 'Gaga' for Sociology Course. Press release, May 22, 2013. http://www.springer.com/about+springer/media/springer+select?SGWID=0-11001-6-1420556-0

Strecker, Erin. 2015. Beyonce! Bruce Springsteen! Miley Cyrus! Check Out Some of the Coolest College Courses. *Billboard*, July 24, 2015. http://www.billboard.com/articles/news/6229300/college-courses-artists-beyonce-madonna-miley-cyrus

Torch. 2010. Sociology of Gaga. *Ferris State Torch*, November 17, 2010. http://www.fsutorch.com/2010/11/17/opinions/sociology-of-gaga/

Torres, Amalia. 2014. Lady Gaga, Miley Cyrus y Beyoncé Entran a las Salas de Clases. *El Mercurio* Chile, November 16, 2014. http://impresa.elmercurio.com/Pages/NewsDetail.aspx?dt=2014-11-16&dtB=16-11-2014%200:00:00&PaginaId=10&bodyid=1

Total Drek. Blog. http://totaldrek.blogspot.com
Tyson, Charlie. 2010. Gaga for Gaga: English Course Takes Inspiration from Lady Gaga. *Cavalier Daily*, September 8, 2010. http://www.cavalierdaily.com/article/2010/09/gaga-for-gaga/
UofSC. Twitter Post. October 28, 2010 (8:15 PM). https://twitter.com/UofSC/status/29037645946
USC News. 2010. Sociology Professor Will Teach Lady Gaga Course. *USC News*, October 22, 2010. http://www.sc.edu/news/newsarticle.php?nid=1347#.UKvd745ZHKc

Index

A
ABBA, 204
Absolut Vodka, 61
Academy Awards. *See* Oscars
AC/DC, 196
activism, 3, 8, 24, 60, 63, 110, 126, 136, 140, 145–61, 174, 182, 213
activism in music, 110, 126, 146–50, 152, 154, 157, 159–61
Adele, 39, 53, 130, 177, 204, 213
Adorno, Theodor W., 14, 15, 96, 122, 146, 147
aesthetics
  and culture, 13, 75, 145, 146, 148, 154, 159, 160, 190, 191, 193
Aguilera, Christina, 32, 175, 182
Akon, 37, 56
Aldrich, Doug, 197
Alexander, Jeffrey C., 19, 20, 135
American Horror Story, 200, 203
American Society of Composers, Authors and Publishers (ASCAP), 79
Andrews, Julie, 202

anti-fans, 124, 140. *See also* fans
art, 9, 13, 17, 25, 32, 33, 35, 40, 41, 43, 60, 62–5, 67, 74, 76, 81, 106, 131, 134, 140, 158, 160, 173, 177, 182, 189–205, 213, 226, 227
  and culture, 16
Artist Nation, 57
ARTPOP (album), 4, 36, 39, 53, 54, 57, 59, 60, 77, 100–2, 105, 107, 115, 127, 134, 158, 171, 173, 194–7, 199, 205
artRAVE: The ARTPOP Ball Tour, 39, 54, 57, 60, 61, 132–4, 178, 194–7, 199, 205
Assange, Julian, 214
Ate My Heart, Inc., 76
Atom Factory, 56
audience. *See* fame, audience of

B
Backplane, 115
Backstreet Boys, 32

Note: Page numbers with "n" denote endnotes.

Barbie, 174
Barneys New York, 59, 151
The Beatles, 32, 193
Beliebers, 136
Bennett, Tony, 4, 39, 52, 53, 55, 57, 59, 60, 100, 105, 107, 115, 127, 132, 134, 172, 197–200, 202, 203
Besencon, Laurent, 35, 36, 81, 99
Best Buy, 59, 102, 199
Beyoncé, 101, 177
Biden, Joe, 152, 214
Bieber, Justin, 52, 109, 110, 112, 136, 213
bisexuality, 157, 176, 177, 182, 214
Bissett, Cyntia. *See* Germanotta, Cynthia
The Bitter End, 33
Black, Donald, 74–6, 84–6
Bonnaroo Festival, 201
Boorstin, Daniel J., 20
Born This Way (album), 4, 35, 38, 52–4, 56, 59, 61, 78, 80, 81, 100, 101, 103, 105, 107, 109, 114, 126, 128, 130, 132, 133, 150–3, 155, 156, 159, 173, 177, 178, 195–7, 199, 201, 224, 227, 228
The Born This Way Ball tour, 128, 133, 151, 196, 227
Born This Way Foundation, 151, 153, 156, 159
Botticelli, Sandro, 194
Bourdieu, Pierre, 13
Bowie, David, 45, 60, 193, 198, 202, 203
Boyle, Susan, 213
branding, 64, 181
brand partnerships, 59, 60
Brantley, Lanar, 196
Broadcast Music, Inc. (BMI), 79, 86, 89n4
Brobjer, Andreas, 196

bullying, 151, 152, 157
Byford, Biff, 200

C
Calderone, Jo, 77, 173
Campari, 61
Campbell, Bobby, 36, 56–8, 65, 76, 160, 205
Carl, Lüc, 36, 42, 44, 171, 176, 194, 195
Carter, Troy, 36, 56–8, 65, 66, 101–3, 111–13, 115, 131
Catholic League, 156
celebrity. *See also* fame
  concept of, 19, 22, 24, 40, 41
  fame, 17–25, 40, 41, 45, 73, 97, 135, 211, 217, 227–9
celebrity culture, 1, 3, 5, 17, 19, 21, 22, 26, 40, 41, 123, 159, 211, 217, 226, 228. *See also* celebrity, fame
celebrity studies, 5, 21, 22, 73, 212, 226
censorship, 133, 140
Cheek To Cheek (album), 39, 53, 55, 59, 100, 105, 132, 172, 197, 203
Chopra, Deepak, 151
Christian Parents Forum, 223
classical music, 16, 31, 197–8, 202, 205. *See also* music
Clemmons, Clarence, 197
Clinton, Bill, 149
Clinton, Hillary, 153
Coalition Media Group, 56
Cobain, Kurt, 19
cocaine, 35
Columbus Day Parade, 34
Constantine, Nico, 195, 196
constructionism,, 6, 11, 14–17, 20, 21, 24–6, 40, 96, 122, 123, 134, 137, 145, 147, 154, 177, 179, 190, 191, 204, 211, 212

Convent of the Sacred Heart, 31
Cooper, Alice, 174, 199–2
Cooper, Anderson, 43, 175, 226
copyright law, 79
Corona, Victor, 4, 174, 180
Coulter, Ann, 223
culture. *See also* popular culture, concept of; popular culture, sociology of
   concept of, 12, 17, 19–21, 178
   constructionist perspective of, 6, 11, 14–17, 20, 21, 24, 25, 96, 123, 134, 147, 177, 179, 191, 211
   non-reductionist perspective of, 11, 15, 20, 23, 122, 159
   popular culture, 1, 6, 11–26, 49, 50, 73, 84, 96, 114, 122–4, 145–8, 154, 160, 169, 193, 211
   as praxis, 179
   reductionist perspective of, 18, 19, 97, 146
   sociology of, 11, 13, 15, 19
culture industry, 14, 15, 122, 146
Cuomo, Andrew, 153
The Cutting Room, 34, 35, 192
Cyrus, Miley, 204

D
DADT. *See* Don't Ask Don't Tell (DADT)
The Darkness, 196
Davisson, Amber, 4
Deadheads, 136
Def Jam, 35, 81, 195
Def Leppard, 196
DeGeneres, Ellen, 104, 105, 148
Del Rey, Lana, 177
Demetsenare, Caitlin, 83, 84
Destiny's Child, 34
Devlin, Kareem, 196
Dio, 197
Directioners, 136

disco, 150, 191
disco stick, 171, 204
DJ White Shadow, 56
Donohue, Bill, 156
Don't Ask Don't Tell (DADT), 149, 155
Doritos, 151
Douglass, Frederick, 15
Dr. Dre, 59, 61
Durkheim, Emile, 13, 73, 74, 87

E
Eau de Gaga, 60
EDM, 197
Elberse, Anita, 4, 101, 102
Eminem, 110
ethics
   and culture, 13, 75, 145–61, 191
Excite Worldwide, LLC, 78

F
Facebook, 8, 109–11, 113, 172, 222
fame. *See also* celebrity
   audience of, 136
   and celebrity, 1–3, 5, 6, 11, 17–25, 40, 45, 73, 97, 135, 217, 230
   as commodity, 19
   concept of, 19, 21, 22
   constructionist perspective of, 6, 11, 14–17, 20, 21, 24, 25, 96, 123, 134, 211
   Lady Gaga on fame, 1, 6, 9, 11, 45, 50, 55, 67, 99, 107, 115, 136, 139, 140, 158, 211–13, 217, 218, 221, 228–30
   as pathology, 25
   reductionist perspective of, 11, 15, 18–20, 23, 97, 122
   relational concept of, 19, 21, 22, 24
   sociology of, 2, 6, 10–26, 43, 217–30

FAME (fragrance), 60
The *Fame* (album), 31, 33, 35–7, 40, 42, 53, 56, 59, 61, 80, 88, 100, 104, 108, 128, 131, 150, 173, 195
The Fame Ball Tour, 54, 55, 61, 132, 194
The Fame Monster (album), 38, 44, 45, 53, 80, 100–2, 127, 128, 132, 173, 178, 195, 196, 199
Famous Music Publishing, 65
fan identity, 124, 136
fan interactions, symmetry of, 135, 136, 214
fans, 3, 7, 8, 15, 30, 34, 39, 42, 57, 61, 63, 77, 83, 101, 102, 105, 108–11, 113, 121, 122, 124–31, 133–40, 145, 151, 152, 156, 157, 159, 172–4, 176, 198, 200–5, 214, 224, 229. *See also* anti-fans; Lady Gaga, fans of; Little Monsters; non-fans
fan subculture, 136
Fat White Family, 201
femininity. *See* Lady Gaga, femininity
feminism. *See* Lady Gaga, feminism of
Ferris, Kerry O., 17–20, 40, 96, 134
Florida Family Association, 155
Francescatti, Rebecca, 79, 80, 84
Francis, Paul, 200
Frankfurt School, 14, 96
Freese, Jeremy, 225, 226
Frith, Simon, 15, 50, 51, 98, 191, 201
Furtado, Nelly, 177
Fusari, Rob, 34–7, 56, 76, 80–2, 84, 85, 88, 108, 177, 192, 195

G
Gagapedia, 30, 67n1, 67n3, 116n2, 128, 129
Gaines, Calvin, 80
Gamson, Joshua, 20, 97, 154

gay community, 102, 125, 126, 138, 148, 155–7
gay culture, 138. *See also* LGBT rights
Gay Lesbian and Straight Education Network, 150
Gaynor, Brian, 80
Gays Against Gaga, 155
gender. *See* Lady Gaga, and gender
general public, 10, 113, 133, 134, 200–3, 205, 215
Germanotta, Cynthia, 30, 31, 151, 156
Germanotta, Joanne, 31
Germanotta, Joe, 30–2, 35, 56, 76, 81, 193
Germanotta, Natali, 30, 31
Germanotta, Stefani, 9, 30–6, 65, 76, 78, 79, 81, 82, 88, 89n4, 107–8, 116n3, 177, 192, 194. *See also* Lady Gaga
Goffman, Erving, 40
Goforth, Cole, 152
Golden Globe Award, 203
Goode, William, 18
Good Morning America, 104, 105
Google, 60, 115, 150, 218, 221, 222
Grammy Awards, 175, 198, 201, 202, 226
GuestWiFi, 30, 76
Guggenheim, 60

H
Habermas, Jürgen, 13, 23, 97
Halberstam, Jack J., 4, 179
Haley, Bill, 193
Halford, Rob, 200
Harry, Debbie, 201
Haus of Gaga, 37, 44, 56, 66, 77, 108, 194
heavy metal, 36, 64, 150, 191, 192, 194–7, 200–2. *See also* rock
Herbert, Vincent, 36, 56, 58, 81, 108

Hilton, Nicky, 31
Hilton, Paris, 5, 31
Hilton, Perez, 130
Hitchcock, Alfred, 127
Horkheimer, Max, 14, 96, 122, 146
House of Gaga Publishing, 56, 76, 79, 86, 89n3
Houston, Whitney, 228
Huba, Jackie, 4, 50, 64, 139
The Hunting Ground (documentary), 152

I
iHeart Radio Music Festival, 152
indie rock, 9, 34, 190, 192, 205. *See also* rock
Infectious Grooves, 197
Instagram, 42, 109, 110, 113, 158
Intel, 60, 151
internet, 7, 8, 18, 20, 29, 30, 35, 38, 50, 51, 55, 57, 60, 95–116, 124–6, 137, 151, 154, 175, 176, 181, 192, 217, 218, 220, 222–3
Interscope, 36, 37, 56, 62, 102, 107, 108, 131
Iovine, Jimmy, 36, 56, 58, 102
iPhone, 99, 100
Iron Maiden, 192, 199–201
Islamic Defenders Front, 133
iTunes, 59, 62, 77, 87, 99, 102, 103, 111

J
Jagger, Mick, 32
jazz, 4, 9, 15, 16, 39, 53, 55, 57, 64, 105, 127, 132, 134, 178, 190, 197–200, 202–5, 205n1, 215. *See also* music
Jenner, Kylie, 5
John, Elton, 153, 201, 214
Jolley, Rashida, 197

Judas Priest, 200
justice, 84, 85
and culture, 13, 146, 154

K
Kafafian, Tommy, 34, 88, 195, 196
Kang, Judy, 197
Kardashian, Kim, 5, 228
KatyCats, 136
Kelly, R., 100, 172
Kennedy, Caroline, 312
Khayat, Nadir. *See* RedOne (Nadir Khayat)
Kierszenbaum, Martin, 37, 56
Kimmel, Jimmy, 104
King, Larry, 104, 127, 153
Kinney, Taylor, 39, 171, 176
Kiss (US rock band), 200, 201
Kiss Army, 136
Klapp, Orrin, 18
The Knitting Factory, 33
knowledge, 13, 40, 53, 65, 204
and culture, 16, 75
Kortyka, Steve, 200
Kurzman, Charles, 18, 24

L
Lady Gaga
and activism, 3, 8, 24, 60, 63, 110, 126, 136, 143, 145–61, 174, 182, 213
artistry of, 3, 55, 56, 63, 153, 189, 193, 213
audience of, 3, 6–8, 10, 11, 17, 24, 25, 39, 42, 43, 51, 52, 54, 57, 62–4, 66, 95, 99, 102, 104, 109, 111, 113, 115, 116, 121–40, 154, 159, 160, 172, 198, 200, 202, 203, 205, 212, 213, 215
and brand sponsorships, 7, 59–62, 66

Lady Gaga (*cont.*)
  and bullying, 151–3, 157
  and business, 3, 4, 7, 30, 31, 45, 49–67, 73, 76, 153, 160, 178, 228
  commercial success, 8, 34, 38, 52, 125
  and company tie-ins, 59–62, 66
  and contract disputes, 81–3, 87
  and copyright law, 79
  demography of, 125–31
  early life (Germanotta, Stefani), 30–4
  economics of, 3, 8, 49, 50, 63–6, 84, 133, 160, 212
  on fame and the fame, 45
  fans of, 122, 133, 172, 202, 205
  and fashion, 37, 42, 43, 56, 62, 63, 78, 81, 109–11, 124, 129, 133, 173, 229
  femininity, 138, 169, 180–2
  feminism of, 4, 170, 178–82
  and gay culture, 138
  and gender, 3, 9, 24, 127, 134, 152, 169, 170, 175, 177–8, 180–3, 191, 205, 213, 228
  geography of, 131–4
  geometry of, 74–6, 83–7
  influence of, 159
  and the internet, 7, 8, 18, 20, 29, 30, 35, 38, 50, 51, 55, 57, 60, 95–116, 124–6, 137, 151, 154, 175, 176, 181, 192, 217, 218, 220, 222–3
  and jazz, 4, 9, 15, 16, 39, 53, 55, 57, 64, 105, 127, 132, 134, 178, 190, 197–200, 202–5, 205n1, 215
  lawsuits involving, 8, 74, 76, 85, 87
  and LGBT rights, 149, 151, 157, 159, 160
  and Little Monsters, 8, 31, 77, 121–40, 145, 160, 174, 202
  live tours by, 4, 31, 37–9, 52, 54–7, 61, 101, 104, 115, 126–8, 130–4, 150, 151, 153, 172, 175, 178, 180, 194–7, 199, 201, 205, 227
  and marketing strategies, 50, 137
  and media, 3, 4, 6, 17, 24, 38, 39, 43, 51, 57–60, 62, 63, 65, 77, 81, 85, 87, 88, 95–116, 121–6, 128, 131, 138, 139, 169, 177, 182, 212, 213, 215, 217–23, 225, 227–9
  and monstrosity, 127, 174, 180, 198, 199
  as Mother Monster, 128, 140
  music of, 4, 113
  and news media, 38, 77, 106–7, 213, 218–22
  and pop music, 1, 8, 9, 11, 25, 51, 52, 75, 97, 107, 108, 124–6, 132, 134, 136, 147, 173, 177–9, 181, 190, 191, 193, 197, 202, 204, 205, 218, 228
  as product, 62–4
  and public sphere, 111–15, 170
  and radio, 38, 57, 95–116, 124, 125, 138, 172, 194, 213, 220, 221
  on rape, 152, 158
  recordings by, 80, 99–102
  and religion, 9, 13, 145–8, 153, 154, 157–9
  and RICO charges, 83
  as rock star, 174, 178, 183, 195, 199–202, 204
  sexiness of, 170, 173, 174
  and sexism, 9, 170, 177–7, 182
  sex of, 169–83
  sexuality of, 170, 181
  sexual orientation of, 9, 149, 154, 170, 172, 176–7, 182
  and the Sociology of Fame (course), 2, 6, 10–26, 43, 217–30

styles of, 24, 189–205
and television, 1, 17, 33, 38, 42, 43, 55, 57, 59, 95, 98, 99, 102–6, 112, 113, 115, 116n2, 124, 172, 175, 197, 199, 200, 213, 219–22, 226–8
and trademark law, 77–9
transition to Lady Gaga, 35, 177, 190, 192, 193
wealth of, 52–5
Lady Gaga Street Team, 137
Lady Starlight, 36, 192, 196, 201
Lagerfeld, Karl, 214
Lang, Mutt, 196
law, behavior of, 74–6, 87. *See also* Black, Donald
Lawrence, Don, 32
Lazer/Wulf, 201
Led Zeppelin, 32, 34, 196
Leno, Jay, 104
Leone, Bob, 34, 88
LGBT rights, 149, 151, 157, 159, 160. *See also* gay community
Little Monsters, 8, 31, 77, 121–40, 145, 160, 174, 202. *See also* monster claw
littlemonsters.com, 109, 111, 113, 115, 136
Live Nation, 57, 61, 76, 83
Livingston, Jay, 226
Lollapalooza, 36, 99, 116n1, 192
London, Brian, 196
Lorde, 177, 205
Lower East Side (New York), 33, 35, 37, 41, 42, 192–4, 196, 200

M
Mackin Pulsifer, 33
Madison Square Garden, 33, 105, 195
Madonna, 4, 42, 52, 156, 182
Manifesto of Little Monsters, 31, 127–9

Manson, Marilyn, 199, 201
Margolis, Cindy, 20
marijuana, 195
marketing, 3, 4, 7, 14, 50, 51, 63–6, 103, 137, 155, 228
Marshall, David, 97
Martin, Peter, 16, 17
mass media, 96, 97. *See also* media
Matthew Effect, 23
May, Brian, 197
Ma, Yo-Yo, 49
McCartney, Paul, 200
McCurdy, George, 196
meat dress, 63, 149, 174
media. *See also* internet; print media; radio; television
and fame, 96–9
and music, 96–9
Megadeth, 199
Mercury, Freddie, 35
Mermaid Music, LLC, 56, 76, 81, 83
Metallica, 192
Microsoft, 60
Miller, Toby, 14
Mills, C. Wright
on fame, 19, 21, 22, 96, 97, 122, 123
Minaj, Nicki, 177
Miracle Whip, 61
The Monster Ball Tour, 61, 101, 126, 131, 132, 150, 153, 172, 180, 194, 196
monster claw, 128, 129, 202. *See also* Little Monsters
Mötley Crüe, 150, 195, 196, 199
MTV, 63, 101, 109, 112, 132, 150, 221
music. *See also* classical music
empiricist theory of, 16
jazz, 4, 9, 15, 16, 39, 53–5, 57, 105, 127, 132, 134, 178, 190, 197–200, 202–5, 215

music (cont.)
  pop music, 1, 8, 9, 11, 25, 51, 52, 75, 97, 98, 107, 108, 124–6, 132, 134, 136, 147, 173, 177–9, 181, 191, 193, 197, 202, 204, 218, 228
  and popular music, 1, 2, 4, 6, 8, 11, 12, 14–19, 26, 50, 51, 55, 58, 62, 64, 65, 79, 87, 95, 97–9, 104, 107, 111, 112, 114, 121–4, 126, 131, 134, 136, 138, 140, 146, 147, 159–61, 169–72, 174, 177, 178, 181–3, 190, 191, 211–13, 221, 223
  rationalist perspective of, 16, 17
  rock music, 6, 8, 63, 190–2, 196, 202, 205
  social-rationalist perspective of, 16, 177
  sociology of, 14–16, 123, 146, 147
musical theater, 33, 132, 199, 202
music culture, 49, 211
  and music industry, 50–2, 95
music industry, 1, 6, 26, 34, 44, 45, 50–2, 55, 56, 58, 62, 64, 65, 85, 86, 95, 98, 99, 101, 112, 114, 148, 178, 179, 212, 214. *See also* music culture
MySpace, 8, 35, 36, 108, 109

N
National Equality March, 148
New Kids on the Block, 19, 97, 131, 228
Newman, Brian, 172, 200
New York City, 30–5, 37, 41, 44, 55, 59, 81–3, 102, 105, 131, 151, 153, 171, 173, 192–4, 196, 199, 201. *See also* Lower East Side (New York); Upper West Side (New York)

New York University (NYU), 33, 192
non-fans, 124, 140. *See also* fans

O
Obama, Barack, 110, 149, 153
O'Donis, Colby, 37
Office Depot, 151, 155
One Direction, 136
O'Neill, Jennifer, 81, 82, 84
Orlan, 80, 81, 84
Osbourne, Kelly, 130
Oscars, 5, 105, 134, 152, 158, 202, 203

P
Page, Jimmy, 196
Paglia, Camille, 181, 182, 204
Pandora, 111
Parsons, Brockett, 196
Parsons, Talcott, 12, 23
Pentagram (US heavy metal band), 192
Perrin, Andrew, 225
Perry, Katy, 110, 136, 156, 177, 204
Ping, 111
Pink Floyd, 32, 193
Polaroid, 60, 61
politics in music. *See* activism
Pop, Iggy, 201
pop music, 1, 8, 9, 11, 25, 51, 52, 75, 97, 107, 108, 124–6, 132, 134, 136, 147, 173, 177–9, 181, 190, 191, 193, 197, 202, 204, 205, 218, 228. *See also* rock music
popular culture. *See also* culture
  concept of, 1, 2
  sociology of, 1, 6, 11–26, 73
popular music. *See* music
praxeology, 13
print media, 98, 106. *See also* media

Prizeo, 151
pure sociology, 74, 75. *See also* Black, Donald
PureVolume, 35, 108, 116n3
Pussycat Dolls, 37, 131
pyro bra, 180
Pythian Temple, 30, 193

Q

Queen (UK rock band), 35, 197, 201

R

Racketeer Influenced and Corrupt Organizations (RICO), 83
radio, 38, 44, 57, 95–116, 124, 125, 138, 172, 194, 213, 220, 221, 227. *See also* media, and fame; media, and music
Randy Shilts Visibility Award, 155
Rationalism. *See* social rationalism
RedOne (Nadir Khayat), 36, 37, 39, 56
Reid, Antonio, 35
Reid, Harry, 149
religion. *See* activism; Lady Gaga, and religion
Richardson, Terry, 100, 172
Rihanna, 110, 177
Riley, Taja, 80
Riley, Teddy, 80, 85
Rilke, Rainer Maria, 31, 43
Rivington Rebels, 195
rock, 6, 8, 9, 15, 16, 19, 32–6, 63, 136, 147, 161, 174, 177, 178, 183, 189–205, 205n1
rock music, 6, 8, 9, 63, 190–2, 196, 200–2, 204, 205. *See also* pop music
Rodemeyer, Jamey, 152
Rodgers, Nile, 202

The Rolling Stones, 32, 201

S

Sabbath, Black, 192
San Loco, 36
Sarubin, Joshua, 35
Saturday Night Live, 1, 104, 105, 227
Saxon (UK heavy metal band), 200
Schmidt, Eric, 115
Schneider, Joseph, 18
Sebelius, Kathleen, 151
Servicemembers Legal Defense Network, 155
sex. *See* Lady Gaga, sex of
sexiness. *See* Lady Gaga, sexiness
sexuality. *See* Lady Gaga, sexuality
Shepard, Matthew, 149
Simmel, Georg, 15
Simmons, Gene, 200–1
Skype, 61
Slipknot, 199
Smith, Alex, 200
social control and law, 75, 86–8
social geometry, 74–6, 84, 87. *See also* Black, Donald
social rationalism, 17. *See also* sociology of music
Society of European Stage Authors and Composers (SESAC), 79
sociology of culture, 11, 13, 15, 19. *See also* culture
sociology of fame, 2, 6, 10–26, 43, 217–30. *See also* fame
sociology of music, 14–16, 123, 146, 147. *See also* music
SoundCloud, 111
space, concept of, 75
Spears, Britney, 37, 173, 182
Spencer, Herbert, 15
The Spice Girls, 19
spotify, 57, 111

Springsteen, Bruce, 32, 193, 197, 201
Starbucks, 59
Starland, Wendy, 34, 81, 82, 85, 88
Stern, Howard, 57, 158
Stewart, Tim, 196, 197
Sting, 200, 201
St. Jerome's, 36, 195
Stramaglia, Massimiliano, 4
Street, John, 147
The Strokes, 34, 192
Subculture. *See* fan subculture
Sullivan, Brendan Jay, 29, 42
super Bowl, 5, 105, 134, 198, 203, 223
Swifties, 136
Swift, Taylor, 101, 110, 132, 136, 177, 180, 204, 213
SXSW (festival), 194

T
Team Love Child, 35, 81
technology, 30, 57, 61
  and media, 60, 98, 124 (*see also* media, and fame; media, and music)
  television (TV), 1, 17, 33, 38, 42, 43, 55, 57, 59, 95, 98, 99, 102–6, 112, 113, 115, 116n2, 124, 172, 175, 197, 199, 200, 213, 219–22, 226–8. *See also* media, and fame; media, and music
360 deal, 58, 62
Tillo, Ricky, 196
Timberlake, Justin, 227
time, concept of, 1, 11
Tonight Show, 104
Too Faced Cosmetics, 78
trademark, 8, 76–9, 84–7
transmission Gagavision, 108, 109
Trevor Project Award, 155
Trump, Donald, 2

tumblr, 109, 111, 155
Turner, Graeme, 4, 19, 20, 123
twitter, 8, 37, 101, 109, 110, 113, 129–31, 137, 149, 150, 152, 172, 175, 200, 201, 220, 222, 226

U
U2, 32
Ultraviolet Live, 33
University of South Carolina, 5, 217, 219, 220
Upper West Side (New York), 30, 36, 193

V
Vanderbilt, Gloria, 31
Van Halen, 194
Van Krieken, Robert, 20
Veblen, Thorsten, 13
Vevo, 59, 109, 110
Video Music Awards (VMAs), 44, 63, 101, 132, 149, 153, 173, 199
Virgin Mobile, 61, 150, 153
VMAs. *See* Video Music Awards (VMAs)
Vulpis, Joe, 34

W
Wal-Mart, 102
Walters, Barbara, 176
Wango Tango Festival, 127
Warhol, Andy, 22, 172, 193, 194
Warhol, Candy, 194
Weber, Max, 13, 15, 18, 19, 23, 24, 73, 87
Westboro Baptist Church, 156
West, Kanye, 132
Whitesnake, 197
Wikipedia, 29, 30, 63, 67n1

Winehouse, Amy, 36, 39
Winfrey, Oprah, 52, 104, 105, 151
Woman of the Year Award, 155, 178, 203

Y
Yale Center for Emotional Intelligence, 151

YouTube, 34, 41, 43, 52, 57, 60, 103, 109, 110, 113, 149, 152, 158, 223, 227

Z
Zappa, Frank, 50
Zombie, Rob, 199
Zuckerberg, Mark, 111

The manufacturer's authorised representative in the EU is Springer Nature Customer Service Centre GmbH, Europaplatz 3, 69115 Heidelberg, Germany. If you have any concerns regarding our products, please contact ProductSafety@springernature.com

Printed and bound by CPI Group (UK) Ltd, Croydon, CR0 4YY

23/03/2026

02076673-0003